Date Due

CONFEDERATION COLLEGE
CHALLIS RESOURCE CENTRE

THE Congress DICTIONARY

THE WAYS AND MEANINGS OF CAPITOL HILL

PAUL DICKSON
PAUL CLANCY

With a special foreword by
the Honorable Thomas P. "Tip" O'Neill, Jr.

With research assistance
from Charles D. Poe

JOHN WILEY & SONS, INC.

New York • Chichester • Brisbane • Toronto • Singapore

To Nancy
and Barbara

Text design by Lee Goldstein

Library of Congress Cataloging-in-Publication Data:

Dickson, Paul.
    The Congress dictionary : the ways and meanings of Capitol Hill
  Paul Dickson and Paul Clancy : with a special foreword by Thomas P.
  "Tip" O'Neill.
        p.   cm.
    Includes bibliographical references.
    ISBN 0-471-58064-3
    1. United States.   Congress–Dictionaries.   I. Clancy, Paul R.,
  1939– .   II. Title.
  JK1067.D5   1993   93-6859
  328.73′003–dc20

Printed in the United States of America

10 9 8 7 6 5 4 3 2 1

CONTENTS

In America an immense number of new words are needed to embody the new political facts, the compact of the Declaration of Independence, and of the Constitution— the Union of the States—the new States— the Congress—the modes of election—the stump speech—the ways of electioneering— addressing the people—stating all that is to be said in modes that fit the life and experience of the Indianian, the Michiganian, the Vermonter, the men of Maine.

WALT WHITMAN

FOREWORD

By Thomas P. "Tip" O'Neill, Jr.

When Paul Clancy and Paul Dickson asked me to reflect on the language of Congress, the first thing that came to mind was my old pal Silvio Conte who died recently. I thought, poor Sil, four bells did ring for him. You may know that when the bells ring four times throughout the offices and committee rooms on Capitol Hill, it's the signal for final adjournment. But for those of us who spent a good part of our lives in Congress, it has another, more solemn, meaning.

The vocabulary of Congress and of politics is a rich stew of history. Growing up in a Boston neighborhood where politics was a way of life, we heard it constantly. In fact, we became part of that history. Stump speeches, political clubs, smoke-filled rooms, getting out the vote. That was part of us. We're the ones who made the speeches, formed the clubs, and filled the rooms with smoke. The old days and the old vernacular—that's in our blood.

When I got my start in politics 60 years ago, patronage was what local politics was all about. If you handed out buttons for snow removal crews or day passes for road workers, they remembered where they came from. They worked the polls and the phones for you. They helped get out the vote. I learned patronage politics at the feet of my father, Thomas P. O'Neill, Sr., who went from bricklayer to the powerful position of sewer commissioner. The basis of his power was the public service jobs he controlled. "Governor," they called him. He was a ward boss, part of a political machine that looked after people. In those days, *patronage* was a term of honor.

When I was coming up in politics it was rough and tough. Strictly hardball. I helped lead the takeover of the Massachusetts House of Representatives, a fact that frightened the Brahmins and Yankees so much that they fought desperately to keep me from being elected speaker. They literally tried to steal the election by buying votes. But it backfired and I became one of the toughest speakers anybody remembered. With only a four-vote majority, I had to use iron discipline to keep our members in line. You could lose your patronage; you could lose your committee assignments if you voted the wrong way. Discipline and loyalty, that's what you had to have. A member couldn't even take off to sing at a wake without clearing it with me.

But the vocabulary of Congress was entirely different. It was the language of compromise and getting along. It had to be. Instead of one leader and a few committee chairmen having all the power, everybody had power. You had to find ways of getting people together. I always got more out of putting my arm around a fellow if I disagreed with him, and saying, "Hey, let's you and I work this out." I even let members kick me in the teeth publicly when they felt it would help them in their districts—and we were still friends.

With the minority, fairness became my rule. What the hell, we control the House, we control it. But in fairness you can't let the other fellow just hang out on a limb. You let him know. No objections? Okay. No problem. Always give him his due. Always give him his day in court. Always respect the fact that he is your opposition. You get a lot more with honey than with vinegar.

Now the era of compromise is gone, probably for a long time. It's not just party but partisanship. Confrontation, finger-pointing, going for the jugular. It saddens me that some people are so hell-bent on seizing the advantage that they'd deliberately wreck the institution. There are no issues anymore, just questions of character. There's no confidentiality, just leaks and scoops. And gridlock, don't forget that. Today's political bosses are the people who hand out PAC money—and there's too much of it, as far as I'm concerned. If this is the new language of Congress, I prefer the old.

But in some ways it's still the same old lingo, the same old talk. Public service. Working for your constituents. Finding ways to compromise. To me politics will always be local. And people, no matter how much money you spend winning their support, like to be asked. And they like to be thanked.

So if this book helps put these expressions in perspective, if it helps people understand the ins and outs, if it sharpens their appreciation of the fantastic game of politics, it will render a great service.

Washington, D.C.
June 1993

ACKNOWLEDGMENTS

The authors gratefully thank all who helped with contributions and suggestions, but especially David Hess of the Knight-Ridder Washington Bureau and House Historian Ray Smock for their extraordinarily careful reading of the manuscript and trenchant suggestions. The book's quality and consistency were bolstered by them. Also one more tip of the hat to Charles D. Poe for his inexhaustible research work, which stretched over several years.

We also thank the many members of both houses and their staffs who helped. Special thanks to congressional aides Jeff Biggs, Dan Buck, Lisa Caputo, Mike Casey, Nancy Coffee, Jack Cole, Dennis Fitzgibbons, Sheri Powar, Steve Richardson, Sam Stratman, Bill Tate, David Wildes; Walter Olezak of Congressional Research Service; Scott Lilly of the Democratic Study Group; David Lashar of the House Wednesday Group.

Lobbyist Tom Korologos; media consultant Dan Walter; former aide Stewart Gamage; Lou Peck and Bud Newman of *Congress-Daily; San Francisco Examiner* columnist Chris Matthews; Rick Bloom of *National Journal;* David Tighe of American Political Network; David Mason of the Heritage Foundation; Senate historians Dick Baker and Don Ritchie and assistant historian Liz Strannigan; photo archivist John Hamilton; and assistant House historian Cynthia Miller; Senate Commission on Art registrar John O'Dell; Assistant House Parliamentarian Charles Johnson.

For early and very helpful readings of the manuscript, Frank Eleazar, Dan Rapoport, and Elizabeth Webber. Special thanks to Randy Roberts, the Western Historic Manuscript Collection, the University of Missouri, Columbia, for extraordinary help in digging material out of the Peter Tamony Collection.

INTRODUCTION

Words are the coin of the realm in this place. Millions of words have echoed through this chamber and found their way to the printed page. Give to the word merchants who labor here continuing sensitivity to the influence of the spoken word.

Help them to appreciate the power of words to inspire, to discourage, to console, to convict, to persuade, to alienate, to honor, to disparage, to encourage, to disappoint, to comfort, to embarrass, to edify, to offend, to strengthen, to weaken, to motivate, to immobilize, to give hope, to frustrate, to purify, to pollute, to build, to destroy.
— *Invocation by Senate Chaplain Richard C. Halverson,
opening a session, 1984*

Most of what is said in Congress sounds like a foreign language and requires an interpreter....Congress becomes so entangled in vocabulary that people often have to work past midnight to figure out what they're doing.
— *Susan Trausch,* Washington Post, *March 16, 1986*

Looking ahead, the leadership wishes you a felicific respite from your lucubrations here. May you, after a reposeful holiday, return to these difficile tasks with renewed verve and reviviscent strength.
— *Robert C. Byrd, as Whip, wishing the House
a Happy Easter*

What language do they speak around here?
— A Congressional Intern Handbook, *by Sue Grabowski*

Washington, D.C., is a city of odd slangs, dialects, and jargons (bureaucratese, Pentagonese, legalese, diplomatese, among others). At this latitude and longitude, "Fort Fumble" is the Pentagon, the "sound of the city" is a reference to paper shuffling, "reprogram-ming" is moving money from one place to another, and "get-ting riffed" (short for "reduction in force") is the same thing as losing your job. The city is peopled with insiders, Beltway ban-dits, GS-11's, influence peddlers, superlawyers, LA's, death-squad Democrats, and supply-siders.

One also has to keep one's bearings. The "other end of Penn-sylvania Avenue" means something different depending on where one stands—or sits—and if you are in the Pentagon, "across the river" is a reference to the White House or Congress, but if you are on north side, the same term alludes to the Pentagon.

Of all of these discernible jargons, the most fascinating may be that time-honored tongue spoken on Capitol Hill. Some of the words, names, and phrases peculiar to Congress are as old as, or older than, the Republic, whereas others are as recent as the 103rd Congress and its first encounters with the Clinton White House in 1993. What they all have in common is that they are actually used in the day-to-day working of the national legislature.

For a bill to become law it must survive a linguistic meteor shower. It may be subject to filibusters, pigeonholes, gridlock, vetoes, killer amendments, poison pills, or other deadly sub-stances. On the other hand, it may be recalled from a recalcitrant committee, Christmas-treed, fast-tracked, given a modified closed rule, and placed on a train that is leaving the station.

Members of Congress go instantly from outsider to insider, climb the leadership ladder, serve as gatekeepers, designated hit-ters, or bomb-throwers. They become boll weevils, gypsy moths, or (in a throwback to the British Parliament) backbenchers. They may stay in office long enough to progress from young Turk to old bull or may be involuntarily retired by their constituents. The terms are ever changing. A frustrated Bill Clinton, for in-stance, coined still another opprobrium for those who would not rubber-stamp the president's legislative agenda by labeling them the "guardians of gridlock."

In each case, the legislators and the laws they make are creatures—and creators—of the language of Congress. It is the language of rules, traditions, and political reality. Those hoping to understand "the process," as insiders have described the way things work on Capitol Hill, must have a guide to that language.

Without a parliamentarian or a seasoned lobbyist whispering in one's ear, having a dictionary of meanings and origins is the next best thing.

The following collection of terms is presented in the hope that the language of Congress will become less of a mystery to the rest of us. Be forewarned: not all of it is "proper" or correct English. It can be as slangy as the language heard in any high-school locker room. As one reporter—with an eye to the Hill—put it more than 30 years ago, "This is the only town in Christendom where corrupting the English language is a community project."

Besides the arcane slang and jargon, we have also defined and discussed some of the most basic and traditional terms of American political and legislative life, including building-block words like *bribery* and *candidate*. We have attempted to explain the most complicated procedures in plain English—and have tried to make them entertaining along the way.

The purpose of this book is to take those words, names, and phrases and define many of them beyond a mere dictionary definition, giving a full explanation for all that lies behind the term, bringing it into the realm of an encyclopedic entry.

To the extent possible, the authors have attempted to build histories for some of the more important terms with subsections on *Etymology* and/or a citation as to when the term was *First Used*. Terms that have an application off the Hill are tagged as *Beyond the Floor*, and there are some notes slugged *Usage*. When the reader might find it necessary or helpful to read the definitions of other words in the descriptions, the pertinent words are set in **boldface** type.

As is lexicographically—if not politically—correct, terms are listed in "as is" condition, as they exist and as we found them. A construction like Madam Chairman may not please everyone; but it is the time-honored form of address for a women who heads a committee or subcommittee.

AA Administrative assistant. Title with the most consistent profile from office to office: an AA is almost always a member's top aide and is typically in charge of personnel, political, and financial operations. Very few people on the Hill call aides by their full title; instead they tend to refer to Congressman Smith's AA or the Senator's **LA** (legislative assistant). In his book *Running in Place: Inside the Senate,* James A. Miller says, "AA's generally have logged strong records of association with their bosses—colleagues from private law practice, campaigning, or simply long-time friends. Closeness and trust are paramount between the AA and the member, an AA makes decisions for a Senator hundreds of times a day."

aardvark politics A term that emerged in 1992 to describe a political movement with no prior history and no future, specifically the presidential campaign of Ross Perot.

The phenomenon was described in the September 30, 1992, issue of *USA Today* by former Presidential candidate Eugene McCarthy, who explained, "The aardvark, like the Perot compaign, is a kind of existential experience, not continuing anything from the past or moving or changing to become something in the future."

above the fold Term used by politicians and journalists to describe a news story that is important enough to appear above the fold, on the top half of the page of a standard non-tabloid newspaper.

Abscam FBI code name for its 1980–81 investigation of congressional ethics. Agents posing as Arab businessmen enticed members of Congress to help with U.S. investments, gambling licenses, and other favors in exchange for cash. Seven members of Congress were convicted and forced to resign. The term derives from Abdul Enterprises, the FBI's dummy corporation.

abusers Associated with the **House Bank** scandal, the word was used on April 1, 1992, by the House Ethics Committee to describe the 22 current and past House members whose monthly **overdrafts** exceeded their net monthly salaries.

academic pork Funds earmarked for politically influential universities. The Congressional Research Service reported that $700 million had been appropriated for favored institutions in 1992—"an escalating and corrosive spiral of unconstrained growth in academic pork," said Rep. George Brown (D-Calif.). *See also* **pork.**

access What lobbyists and journalists believe they gain by cultivating members and their staffs over time: the ability to sit down with them and talk. It is claimed that campaign contributions do not buy votes, but they do buy access.

acronym A pronounceable formation created by combining the initial letters or syllables of a string of words. Acronyms are heard often in Congress and tend to be most common in hearings before the various committees dealing with space and the military, where one is likely to hear of MAD (mutual assured destruction, a concept of nuclear planning) and ADCOMSUBORDCOMPHIB-SPAC (the Navy's Administrative Command, Amphibious Forces, Pacific Fleet Subordinate Command). *See also* **pacronym** *and box,* "Acronyms and Initialisms on the Hill."

across the board Describing a budget modification in which a predetermined percentage is added to or subtracted from the budget of an agency; for instance, an across-the-board cut of 3 percent in military funding. Under the **Gramm-Rudman-Hollings Act,** any expenditure that exceeded specific budget targets would result in across-the-board cuts in all programs. *See also* **meat ax; sequester.**

ACRONYMS AND INITIALISMS ON THE HILL

There have been thousands—and probably tens of thousands—of letter-words generated by the business of Congress. Some are more interesting than others:

RAT SOB The late Ohio Republican Robert A. Taft (1889–1953) insisted that the Senate mail room occasionally used this as a shorthand address for him at the Senate Office Building.

HASC, HAC, SASC, SAC Military acronyms for House Armed Services Committee, House Appropriations Committee, Senate Armed Services Committee, Senate Appropriations Committee.

SCCSIAMRNASNPWPPPPPP The Select Committee to Conduct a Study and Investigation of All Matters Relating to the Need for Adequate Supplies of Newsprint, Printing and Wrapping Paper, Paper Products, Paper, Pulp and Plywood—and, at 20 letters, perhaps a record initialism. SCCSIAMRNASNPWPPPPPP came into and went out of existence just after World War II.

act A **bill** or **joint resolution** that has been passed by both houses of Congress and signed into law by the president. Also, a bill is redesignated as an act after passage by either House or Senate, even though it may not ultimately become law.

ad hoc Latin for "to this." In Congress, the term may refer to a committee that is created to perform a specific task and then disband. Also, an approach to dealing with issues as they arise, rather than with foresight.

ADI In political advertising, initialism for the area of dominant influence of a media outlet.

adjourn To end a **legislative day** or session; or within a session, to close shop for a brief period with a "time certain" to return. For procedural reasons, however, the Senate frequently decides to **recess** rather than adjourn, allowing it to stretch one legislative day over several calendar days.

adjournment crush Period of one or two weeks before adjournment, when major bills are debated long into the night and controversial ones are dropped because of the crush of time.

adjourn sine die Adjournment at the end of a term; literally "without a day" being set for reconvening. It is used when a session officially ends. (The last two words in this phrase are pronounced "sign-y dye.")

administration bill Any bill that is part of the White House's legislative agenda.

administrative assistant *See* **AA.**

adoption The approval of a proposal, usually of an amendment, before final passage.

advice and consent The Senate's constitutional responsibility to confirm or reject proposed treaties and nominees, including ambassadors, cabinet members, top officials, federal judges, and Supreme Court justices. In some instances, the role is mechanical,

A scene from *Advise and Consent,* Otto Preminger's 1962 film about smear tactics on Capitol Hill. Henry Fonda, who plays a secretary of state nominee accused of being a Communist, defends himself in a Senate hearing. *See* **advice and consent.**

such as conferring thousands of military commissions and promotions with a single vote.

Etymology: The term is British and has been in use in England for more than 1,200 years.

advocacy gap The disproportionate influence that business lobbyists, in contrast to consumer and environmental lobbyists, often have over government legislative, regulatory, and enforcement decisions. The term came into use in the late 1970s, when it was claimed that the ratio was approximately 80:1.

affair Fund-raising event. Congressional affairs range from bull roasts to fancy dinners, and the cost of admission may range from $10 to thousands of dollars.

against the mail A perilous way of voting: against the seeming wishes of constituents as expressed in letters.

ahead of the curve In the position of anticipating problems before they surface. This is where astute players and politicians would like to be. Hedrick Smith, in his book *The Power Game,* called this "one of Washington's most telltale phrases." Reagan Budget Director David Stockman sought to be "ahead of the power curve," according to Smith.

aide One of thousands of assistants—almost always anonymous—who work for members of Congress. Top aides include **AAs** (administrative assistants), **LAs** (legislative assistants), and **press secretaries,** and some earn over $100,000 annually.

AIPAC American–Israeli Public Affairs Committee. One of the most powerful lobbies in Washington, it boasts a $12-million budget, 55,000 members, and a paid staff of 100. It is known as "the lobby." When President George Bush complained late in his term, "I'm up against some powerful political forces" in seeking to delay $10 billion in loan guarantees to Israel, he didn't overestimate by much when he said there were "a thousand lobbyists working the other side."

Air Congress Nickname for the 89th Military Airlift Wing at Andrews Air Force base, which provides some free travel to members of Congress and their families. An audit of the Wing by the General Accounting Office showed that between May 1990 and April 1991 some 337 trips, constituting 16 percent of the Wing's activities for the period, were flown for Congress.

Sen. Howell T. Heflin (D-Ala.) listens to an aide during the Iran-Contra hearings in the summer of 1987. *See* **aide.**

aisle A passageway between desks, but also a division between parties in the House and Senate. Traditionally, when facing forward, Democrats sit on the left side of the center aisle in both houses, Republicans on the right. "My friend across the aisle" may not be a friend at all, but simply an adversary of the competing party.

AKAGA Acronym puckishly constructed to describe President George Bush's notion of "a kinder and gentler America."

Alice in Wonderland Descriptive of political notions that are fanciful, almost hallucinatory, like the imagined world of the Lewis Carroll masterpiece. Sen. Paul Sarbanes (D-Md.) used this term during an August 10, 1992, press conference to describe a Republican analysis of Democratic presidential candidate Bill Clinton's economic plan. Two days later the *Washington Post* said the same thing of Housing Secretary Jack Kemp's plan to expand economic growth by lowering marginal tax rates.

allegator (Pronounced "alligator") Derogatory reference to one who makes allegations. During the 1991 confirmation hearings for Supreme Court nominee Clarence Thomas, Sen. Orrin Hatch (R-Utah) said, "The allegator, or the alledger, I guess I'd better say. Let me strike the word 'allegator.' I don't want that misconstrued." The late Sen. Sam Ervin (D-N.C., 1896–1985), chairman of the Senate Watergate Committee, often used the term with more humorous intent.

All-Male Club *See* **Men's Club.**

allowances

1 Amount of money provided to congressional offices for certain expenses, such as hiring clerks.

2 Amounts included in the budget to cover possible additional expenses, such as pay raises.

amen corner Pocket of supporters at a political function; political cheering section. The term comes from the name of the section in rural churches where congregants lead responsive amens. In some Protestant churches this area was to the immediate right of the pulpit, where those who agreed with the preacher expressed their approval. In an April 24, 1884, debate over whether the secretary of agriculture should be given floor privileges, Sen. John J. Ingalls (R-Kans.) recalled that a recent member, "when commiserated upon the fact that he was compelled to go to what is commonly known as the amen corner, frankly said that any seat in the Senate is better than none."

amendment A proposed or actual change to a **bill,** an **act,** or the Constitution. Bills can be amended by either house at various stages of the lawmaking process. Amendments may be offered in committee or **on the floor.** Senators may propose **riders** that are totally unrelated to the bill under discussion, but their House counterparts do not have this right. Some amendments seek to add text to a bill, others seek to delete some or all of a bill's provisions, and still others seek to substitute language. An amendment "in the nature of a *substitute*" is one that would replace an entire bill; one that merely modifies a few terms is a *perfecting amendment.* Amendments to amendments (second degree) are permitted, but not amendments to amendments to amendments. *See also* **clinker** *and* **constitutional amendments.**

Anita Hill bump Voters' reaction to the hearings that confirmed Supreme Court Justice Clarence Thomas and ultimately disregarded the testimony against him by professor Anita Hill. The defeat of Sen. Alan Dixon (D) of Illinois by Carol Moseley Braun in 1992 was seen as an instance of this **bump.**

annex

1 Room or rooms belonging to a member but separated from the main office suite. Annexes house staff and equipment.

2 Buildings used for the overflow from the well-known official public buildings of the **Hill.** They tend to be less attractive buildings converted from another purpose, such as the old Congressional Hotel, which is now a House annex.

appeal In both the Senate and the House, a member may challenge the ruling of the presiding officer. In the House, the speaker's rulings are considered final, but a senator may take his or her case to the body as a whole. Reversals are rare, since the presiding officer is a member of the majority party.

appear To be physically present at governmental functions, especially in an official capacity, or as a witness. One does not *take part* in hearings; rather, one *appears* before a committee.

appearance The impression a political figure makes on the public. A politician must avoid not only impropriety but the appearance of impropriety, especially in accepting gifts from those with an interest in legislation.

appointment *Political appointment. See* **patronage** *and* **plum.**

apportionment The allocation of the fixed number of House seats to the states based on population. Reapportionment occurs after the decennial census. In 1911, following the 1910 census, Congress froze the number of districts at 435 in the belief that a larger number would be unwieldy. At the time the average district size was 235,223. After the 1980 census, there was a clear shift of representation away from the Snowbelt to the Sunbelt. New York, for instance, lost 4 seats and Florida gained 4. In 1990 the trend continued, with New York losing 3 and Florida again adding 4. California jumped from 45 to 52.

Because all states must have at least one representative, wide disparities in district populations are possible, from 803,655 in Montana to 455,975 in Wyoming. The ideal, based on census data, would be 572,466.

appropriation The funding of government agencies and programs; the granting of the money—but not always all of it—contained in the **authorization.** Appropriation bills originate in the House. Because they hold the "power of the purse," appropriation committees have much power.

Archie Bunker District A conservative, predominantly white, and usually ethnic blue-collar district whose constituents are not unlike the main character in the long-running "All in the Family" television series.

architect The primary shaper of a bill or the driving force behind it. The architect is not necessarily the **author,** but the intellectual force that drives an idea, often over a period of years.

architect of the Capitol The official who is charged with the care of the U.S. Capitol building, its artworks and grounds, as well as the House and Senate office buildings and the buildings of the Library of Congress and the Supreme Court. The architect also manages ceremonies held in the capitol or on Capitol grounds. *See box,* "Their Capitol Ideas."

THEIR CAPITOL IDEAS

   WILLIAM THORNTON (1759–1828). There was no official title, "Architect of the Capitol," but Thornton was an architect and his design for the Capitol was formally approved by president George Washington on July 25, 1793, and praised for its "grandeur, simplicity and convenience." He was awarded $500 and a city lot for his design.

   BENJAMIN HENRY LATROBE (1764–1820). Appointed by President Thomas Jefferson in 1803 and reappointed by President James Madison in 1815, Latrobe redesigned much of the north and south wings, then oversaw the Capitol's restoration after the British burned it in 1814. His interiors included Statuary Hall, the Old Senate Chamber and the Old Supreme Court Chamber.

   CHARLES BULLFINCH (1763–1844). Appointed by President James Monroe in 1818, he continued Latrobe's restoration of the north and south wings and designed the original low wooden dome. Bullfinch also planned the Capitol grounds and the original earthen west terrace.

   THOMAS USTICK WALTER (1804–1887). Appointed by President Millard Fillmore in 1851, Walter designed the Capitol's north and south extensions, where House and Senate now meet, as well as the familiar cast-iron dome. Construction of the dome was begun in 1855 and completed in 1863, the year that the Statue of Freedom was placed on top.

   EDWARD CLARK (1822–1902). Appointed by President Andrew Johnson in 1865, Clark was Thomas Walter's student and chief assistant. Among his many achievements, he completed the extension project in 1868 and oversaw the construction of the Library of Congress. He also introduced electricity, steam heat, and elevators to the Capitol.

   ELLIOT WOODS (1865–1923). Appointed by President Theodore Roosevelt in 1902, Woods supervised the construction of the first House and Senate office buildings and the installation of the first subway.

   DAVID LYNN (1873–1961). Appointed by President Calvin Coolidge in 1923, Lynn was responsible for the addition of the Longworth House Office Building, the Supreme Court Building, the Adams Building Annex of the Library of Congress, and the Botanic Garden Conservatory.

   J. GEORGE STEWART (1890–1970). Appointed by President Dwight D. Eisenhower in 1954, Stewart extended the east central front of the Capitol, completed the new (Dirksen) Senate Office Building, and oversaw the construction of the Rayburn House Office Building and its connecting subway.

   GEORGE MALCOM WHITE (1920–   ). Appointed by President Richard Nixon in 1971, White is responsible for the construction of the James Madison Building of the Library of Congress and the Hart Senate Office Building. He also oversaw the restoration of the Old Supreme Court, the Old Senate Chamber, and the west central front of the Capitol. In 1993, he oversaw the removal, restoration, and replacement of the Statue of Freedom on the Capitol dome.

Are they in?/Are they out? Questions asked to determine if Congress has reconvened (is in session) or adjourned (is out of session).

arm-twisting An extreme method of compelling another to comply, used only rarely in modern politics. "Anything that could be called arm-twisting is not my style," House Speaker Thomas S. Foley (D-Wash.) told us in an interview. "People like to talk about arm-twisting, but courtesy and respect for other people's views is as much a part of political life around here as it is in any other aspect of human endeavor, and rudeness or domineering arrogance is not going to be successful anywhere."

Army-McCarthy hearings *See* **McCarthyism.**

arrest Members of the House or Senate who are absent without leave during **quorum calls,** even while in committee, may be "arrested" by the **sergeant-at-arms** and brought to their respective chambers. Members so absent may also be fined or docked part of their pay. *See* **bed check/bed-check vote**; *also box,* "Feet First."

articles Instead of an indictment, the House considers articles of impeachment, a list of particular charges, when accusing presidents, judges, or other high public officials of serious misconduct. *See* **impeach.**

as Maine goes . . . So goes the nation, according to a maxim of presidential elections. Less true now than in its original coinage, it nevertheless has many offspring. "As the baby boom generation goes, so goes the nation," wrote George F. Will in his book *The New Season: A Spectator's Guide to the 1988 Election.* Or, recalling George McGovern's trouncing as the 1972 Democratic nominee, Everett Carll Ladd, Jr., in his book *Where Have All the Voters Gone?,* offered, "As goes Massachusetts, so goes the District of Columbia."

ETYMOLOGY: The assertion dates back to 1840, when it began as a presidential campaign slogan of William Henry Harrison, a Whig, who defeated the incumbent, Martin Van Buren.

As the late John Ciardi explained in his last book on the mother tongue, *Good Words to You,* "At that time because of the wintry blasts of November, Maine's election was held in September. Its returns were in, therefore, about six weeks before those of the rest

of the country, and Harrison supporters could not resist making a slogan of their clear victory." As the Whigs became Republicans and came to dominate the state, they continued to use the slogan—now as a portent of victory—even after Election Day in Maine was moved to the same day as in the rest of the nation.

assaults Legislators, who now carefully cloak their debates in civility, were once armed and dangerous. Members have pulled

"The assault in the U.S. Senate chamber on Senator Sumner."

This infamous incident was said to have signaled the beginning of the Civil War in Washington. This engraving first appeared in *Frank Leslie's Illustrated Newspaper* of June 7, 1856. *See* **assaults.**

guns on each other on the floor, and, although no shots have been exchanged between members in the chambers, duels outside were rather common. In 1826 Henry Clay, the secretary of state and future senator from Kentucky, responded to insults uttered by the hotheaded Sen. John Randolph of Virginia with a demand for satisfaction. On April 8, in the Virginia countryside, the two men fired at each other twice, both of Clay's bullets passing through Randolph's flowing cloak. Randolph, who regretted his harsh words, hit a stump behind Clay the first time, then shot into the air and announced, "I do not fire at you, Mr. Clay." That was enough to satisfy Clay and the duel ended. But Sen. David Broderick of California was not as fortunate as Clay. He insulted California Supreme Court Justice David Terry and on September 16, 1859, paid for it with a fatal shot to the chest.

There have been assaults with hickory sticks, canes, and fists. The vitriolic Charles Sumner of Massachusetts called fellow Sen. A. P. Butler of South Carolina "one of the maddest zealots" who had chosen as his mistress "the harlot Slavery." This enraged Butler's nephew, South Carolina Rep. Preston Brooks. On May 22, 1856, Brooks entered the Senate chamber with a cane and beat Sumner to the ground.

The worst fistfight was probably the one between South Carolina senators John McLaurin and "Pitchfork Ben" Tillman on February 28, 1902, after Tillman accused McLaurin of letting "improper influences" affect his vote on a treaty with the Philippines. Enraged, McLaurin branded Tillman's charge "a willful, malicious,

---

A LOADED REVOLVER

In the midst of a heated debate over slavery on April 17, 1850, Thomas Hart Benton of Missouri and Henry Foote of Mississippi finally had enough of each other's insults and advanced toward each other in the Old Senate Chamber. Foote, who had been wounded three times in duels, drew a loaded pistol from his coat. Benton, who himself had killed a man in a duel, squared off and advanced toward Foote. According to James H. Hutson, in his 1989 book *To Make All Laws: The Congress of the United States,* Benton shouted, "Let him fire! Stand out of the way! I have no pistols! I disdain to carry arms! Stand out of the way and let the assassin fire!"

Pandemonium broke loose but Foote was disarmed before a shot could be fired, and both senators, still seething, were returned to their seats.

and deliberate lie." As Sen. Robert Dole of Kansas recounts the battle in his book *Historical Almanac of the United States Senate:* "Upon hearing this, the fifty-four-year-old Tillman jumped forward and struck the forty-one-year-old McLaurin above the eye. McLaurin returned a punch to his adversary's nose. Both men traded blows until separated by a doorkeeper and several senators." *See box,* "A Loaded Revolver."

assistant majority leader/assistant minority leader Alternative terms for majority whip/minority whip. Most prefer the shorter term, but Sen. Alan Simpson (R-Wyo.), the assistant minority leader, prefers the longer. In 1991, after Sen. Robert Dole (R-Kans.), the minority leader, helped Majority Leader George Mitchell (D-Me.) with a bill, the National Journal remarked, "No wonder some call Dole the 'assistant majority leader.' " *See also* **whip.**

AstroTurf campaign The term that emerged in early 1993 to describe artificial **grass-roots** lobbying campaigns. For instance, whereas spontaneous letters and calls on a new tax bill—even if fueled by talk-show outrage—would constitute a grass-roots campaign or movement, an AstroTurf campaign is one that has been orchestrated and may yield such things as a hundred or more "personal letters" in which the penmanship may differ but the wording is identical.

ETYMOLOGY: The term refers to the trade name of the synthetic grasslike turf installed in the Houston Astrodome in 1965. As a trade name applied to politics, it now joins **Teflon** and **Velcro.**

Atari Democrats Those who foresee a bright future in high technology and electronics. The term was coined by Elizabeth Drew of the *New Yorker* and alluded to the electronic game and computer company. It lost much of its appeal in 1983 when Atari cut its U.S. work force and moved those jobs to Taiwan, but television analysts still seem fond of it.

attack ads Political advertisements with a specific purpose: to lower an opponent's standing with the voters. Candidates know that this approach means taking the low road, but many are convinced that it works. As political analyst Montague Kern said

On Cable News Network on March 19, 1990, "Negative advertising is perceived by campaigns to move the numbers and it does." When candidates attack, they are said to "go negative."

Campaign consultants shy away from "the N-word" and use the more benign-sounding "comparative advertising." *See box,* "On the Attack."

attack dog A member of Congress who, in a partisan cause, readily grills witnesses or nominees in a hostile or confrontational manner. During the 1991 confirmation hearings for Supreme Court nominee Clarence Thomas, the term was applied to those who attacked the credibility of University of Oklahoma law professor Anita Hill, who had accused Thomas of sexually harassing her. Soon after the hearing ended, on December 18, 1991, the *Washington Post* reported that New York Gov. Mario Cuomo, a Democrat, had branded Sen. Alfonse D'Amato (R-N.Y.) an "attack dog" and refused to apologize. *Compare* **lapdog.**

attack fax News release critical of one's opponents faxed to journalists during a political campaign.

at the desk   Describing the status of a bill or resolution that has been passed by the House and is being held at the Senate clerk's desk instead of being referred to a committee. It is an intricate parliamentary maneuver usually employed by the leadership, but any senator may use it. After a bill is read by title a first and second time, it is required to lie at the desk for one day before referral. If a senator objects after each reading to further consideration of the bill, it automatically goes on the Senate calendar for consideration and may be taken up for immediate consideration. The tactic has been used to keep civil rights legislation from hostile committees. *See also* **held at the desk.**

author   The one who drafts, introduces, and steers a bill through to passage. The title is usually conferred on the chairman of the committee or subcommittee that reports the bill. *See also* **chief sponsor.** Also, a verb: to author, almost always followed by "bill" or "legislation."

authorization   The act of establishing a program and setting its general level of funding. The process of authorization must be followed by that of **appropriation** before a program can go into effect. There are often great disparities between what is authorized and what is appropriated.

Autopen   The trade name of a machine that signs a legislator's signature. It keeps legislators—or staff members—from getting writer's cramp. It also assures that mail can come into an office and be sorted, answered, signed, sealed, and delivered without the officeholder or anyone other than a clerk seeing it.

awareness   Pollster jargon for the public's realization of a candidate's existence, including favorable, unfavorable, and neutral impressions. Media consultants said that in 1992 George Bush had a 99 percent public awareness—with 1 percent having no idea who he was. *See* **name recognition.**

aye   An affirmative vote, even though a **roll-call** vote is referred to as "the **yeas and nays**." When actually spoken, the responses are "ayes" and "noes."

babies Members who are the offspring of particular political forces. The best known were the **Watergate babies,** the 75 Democrats and 17 Republicans who came to office by way of the 1974 elections following the **Watergate** scandal. This reform-minded "Class of '74" dented the seniority system by overthrowing a senior committee chairman and granting more power to subcommittees. Other well-known "babies" include "Proposition 13 babies," who rode to office on the popularity of citizen referendums like California's "Prop 13," which opposed increases in property taxes; and "patronage babies," a tag applied to congressional employees who got their first jobs through the generosity of a political patron. *See also* **class of —** *and* **notch babies.**

backbencher Member with low seniority, usually in the House of Representatives. This is a British House of Commons term and refers to newcomers, who are seated at the back of Parliament. It has no literal meaning, however, since the House, unlike the Senate, has no assigned seating.

In its British context, the term implies more. In their *Parliamentary Dictionary*, L. A. Abraham and S. C. Hawtry say of the backbencher:

> Although a supporter of the party to which he belongs, he is generally regarded as freer to differ from its policy than his colleagues on the front benches. The term therefore conveys a suggestion of what Gladstone called "the greater freedom and less responsibility" belonging to the rank and file of the parliamentary armies.

back burner The figurative position on which legislation with low priority is placed. The back burner in Congress, where more than 90 percent of bills are ignored, is huge. *See also* **front burner.**

backdoor spending Spending provided for outside the normal channels of appropriations. **Entitlements,** which are payments guaranteed to all qualified persons, comprise the major portion of these payments. Other avenues for this spending are *borrowing authority* and *contracting authority*—allowing the agency in question to contract for goods and services that Congress will have to deal with when the bills come due.

Backdoor financing goes back to 1932, during the Hoover administration, when Congress created the Reconstruction Finance Corporation and allowed it to borrow money from the Treasury from funds raised by the sale of U.S. bonds.

ETYMOLOGY: It appears that the door alluded to in backdoor spending is the door to the U.S. Treasury. At times the full metaphor is stated. In 1969, for instance, when a backdoor scheme for foreign aid was killed in the Senate, President Eisenhower asked for $700 million to come through the front door of the Treasury.

background An arrangement with the media in which an official agrees to provide information on condition that he or she not be quoted directly and that the information not be attributed to an individual by name or recognizable title. Since congressional aides rarely speak on the record—their bosses always get the credit—stories citing "congressional sources" are nearly always provided "on background." Members of Congress frequently ask to "go on background" while covering sensitive issues, then return to **on the record** when they don't mind being quoted. *See also* **deep background** *and* **off the record.**

backgrounder Interview or briefing session in which a member of Congress or other official gives information "on background." From time to time, backgrounders become an issue in Washington. Perhaps the most famous was an incident in December 1971 when Henry Kissinger, then President Nixon's foreign policy advisor, gave a backgrounder in which he stated that the president might cancel a Moscow visit unless the USSR exerted more pressure on the India–Pakistan War. The *Washington Post* and *New York Times* both identified Kissinger as the source, as they felt that it would be deceptive to their readers if he were not identified on this highly important matter.

back room Where deals are made: not a specific place, but a concept of arriving at agreements off stage, out of the public eye.

back-room boys Those who, in days gone by, wielded power behind the scenes. The term embraces both elected officials and their unelected cronies.

back flip A change in position, often sudden. A vote switch. *See also* **flip flop.**

backlash Unintended opposite reaction by the electorate to a candidate's attack on an opponent, especially one that is blatantly racial.

ETYMOLOGY: The term was first used widely in the 1964 presidential election, when white voters were feared to be showing negative reaction—a backlash—to black social gains.

backloading Delaying tax cuts—and therefore revenue losses—until the future. Former Office of Management and Budget Director David stockman used this term in describing the debate over when to put the 1981 Reagan tax cuts into effect. Congress, he said in his book, *The Triumph of Politics*, phased in revenue losses, thereby backloading them "into the foggy future two or three elections down the road."

back-scratching Supporting—or not opposing—another legislator's proposal in order to obtain similar treatment for one's own, as in "I'll scratch your back if you scratch mine." There may be similar, tacit agreements between reporters and legislators.

bag, in the A condition of being certain, the outcome known before a decision is made. But this can be a dangerous assumption, especially at election time. The term also refers to a member of Congress whose vote can be counted upon. Before the charges of sexual harassment were lodged against Supreme Court nominee Clarence Thomas, the White House assumed that "it [Senate confirmation] was in the bag," the *Washington Post* reported on October 9, 1991.

Baker v. Carr The case that resulted in the Supreme Court's landmark "one person, one vote" decision in 1962, which set the stage for legislative **reapportionment**. In that opinion, Justice Felix Frankfurter wrote, "In a democratic society like ours, relief must come through an aroused popular conscience that sears the conscience of the people's representatives."

balanced budget A budget in which income equals or exceeds spending. Most states require balanced budgets, but the federal government does not, leading frequently to cries for a balanced-budget constitutional amendment.

balkanization The process of breaking up into smaller, sometimes hostile, units, as the modern-day Balkans have done—and continue to do. In a congressional context, the term is used to describe either the breakup of a majority coalition or the proliferation of competing and overlapping subcommittees. It has also been applied to what Congress did to the Pentagon after World War II, when three separate uniformed services, the Army, Navy, and Air Force, were split into four with the creation of an autonomous Marine Corps. When there is a threat to free trade among the 50 states, the specter of balkanization is raised.

bank *See* **House Bank.**

barn burner One who plunges forward no matter the cost, like the legendary Dutch farmer who burned down his barn to destroy the rats inside. The term is also applied to a speech in the same vein, either highly partisan or ideological. "Hubert's weakness was the two-hour barn burner," Sen. Barry Goldwater (R-Ariz.), in his autobiography, said of one-time Senate colleague Hubert Humphrey (D-Minn.).

barnstorming Making whirlwind campaign appearances and speeches around the country, like the pilots who gave touring exhibitions in the early days of aviation, when barns were used as auditoriums for these performances.

ETYMOLOGY: The term comes from the American theater. The original meaning, first found in 1883, applies to theatrical road shows that staged their rural performances in barns. The term was later adopted by itinerant baseball teams, preachers, and flying circuses.

barons Generally, committee chairmen who, through seniority, have gained and held power. Formerly, conservative Southern Democrats who ruled in a feudal manner and could not be dislodged from their posts.

barrel, over a In politics, to be so beholden to special interests as to be at their mercy.

baseline In budget parlance, how bad things will look in the future if existing policy remains unchanged.

bashing The practice of casting aspersions upon one group or another, including Congress. Thus, Washington-bashing, Japan-bashing, oil company–bashing. After being mugged near Dupont Circle in June 1990, Rep. Gerry Studds (D-Mass.) said, "This gives a new meaning to 'Congress-bashing.' "

Mark Twain, a devoted Congress-basher, wrote: "It could probably be shown by facts and figures that there is no distinctly native American criminal class except Congress."

Other examples of the -bashing formation include government-bashing, gay-bashing, press-bashing, and—among politicans on the campaign trail—tele-bashing.

Bay Window Brigade Irreverent name for those aging members of the House and the Senate who are also members of the Army Reserve. In previous years, their help in getting more appropriations for the services resulted in Reserve promotions for the obliging members. Since at least the 1870s, bay window has been American slang for a protuberant belly.

Mark Twain, center, one of the most adroit of Congress bashers. This photograph from the late 1860s shows Twain, then a reporter, with fellow newsmen. During his years in Washington he also served as secretary to a U.S. senator. *See* **bashing.**

beauty contest A nonbinding primary election; a vote that does nothing more than measure popularity.

bed check/bed-check vote The legislative tactic of calling for a vote to determine how many members are on the Hill or, if late at night, reachable in their beds. In the Senate, it generally means any late-night attempt to compel the attendance of absentees, by **arrest** if necessary.

A bed-check vote in the House is a vote on approving the daily journal: It serves to identify who is in attendance; it also serves, if a minority is so inclined, to waste time.

See **sergeant-at-arms**; *also box*, "Feet First," p. 279.

bedfellow Literally, a person sharing one's bed, from the Middle English *bed falawe*. In politics, one found in proximity to or in cooperation with another. Thus, Charles Dudley Warren wrote in the book *My Summer in a Garden* (1871), "Politics makes strange bedfellows."

The Readers Digest Treasury of Humor for 1975 quoted the following from the *Los Angeles Times:* "The reason politics makes strange bedfellows is because they all like the same bunk."

Beige Book Name for the Federal Reserve's periodic report on the economic conditions in its 12 economic districts based in Boston, New York, Philadelphia, Cleveland, Richmond, Atlanta, Chicago, St. Louis, Minneapolis, Kansas City, Dallas, and San Francisco. So called because of the color of its cover.

> **BELLS, LIGHTS, AND BUZZERS**
>
> **Senate Bells**
> - **One—yeas and nays**
> - **Two—quorum call**
> - **Three—call of absentees**
> - **Four—adjournment or recess**
> - **Five—7 ½ minutes remaining to vote**
> - **Six—if lights on, temporary recess; if off, morning business concluded**
>
> **House Bells**
> - **One (short)—teller vote**
> - **One (long)—a quorum of 100 present in Committee of the Whole**
> - **Two—recorded vote**
> - **Three—quorum call**
> - **Four—adjournment**
> - **Five—electronically recorded vote**
> - **Six—recess**

bells Each house has its own coded system of electric signals—not really bells—and flashing lights around the faces of its clocks, which tell members what is going on and call them for votes and quorums. Even the House and Senate handball courts are equipped with buzzers. Capitol Hill restaurants once sounded buzzers or dinner bells as a courtesy to their important guests. *See box,* "Bells, Lights, and Buzzers."

bells and whistles Puff and hyperbole of the type that is sometimes employed by an agency to "sell" a program on the Hill. A common characteristic of a bells and whistles program is that it offers "something for everyone."

Beltway The name for the interstate highway that rings the city of Washington as it runs through the inner suburbs of Virginia and Maryland. In Washington parlance, however, the term refers rather to a state of mind found within the area outlined by the highway—an idea may make perfect sense **inside the Beltway** but not **outside the Beltway.**

ETYMOLOGY: The term was coined in 1951 to describe what to that point had been known as a "circumferential highway." With the advent of the Washington Beltway, the term was capitalized as a reference to this particular road.

Beltway bandit A consultant working out of the many think tanks and consulting firms that compete avidly for government business in the Washington, D.C., area, many of them located along the Capital Beltway. The term as used is more jocular than hostile, and some of the ilk will actually use it to identify themselves.

FIRST USED: William Safire, who devoted most of his March 4, 1984, column to this term, reported that the earliest use he could find was in a *Washington Post* story of January 25, 1978, by Jerry Knight: "Some 'Beltway bandit' ought to be hired to put one team of computer experts to work designing crime-proof defenses."

Best Congress Money Can Buy, The Title created by the late journalist-philanthropist Philip Stern for his 1988 book on special interests and campaign financing. At Stern's funeral on June 3, 1992, noted economist and former Ambassador to India John Kenneth Galbraith delivered a eulogy to Stern, during which he expressed the opinion that it was the best title ever given to a book and that it would be around for a long, long time as a description and indictment of Congress.

ETYMOLOGY: A Fourth of July speech that Mark Twain wrote in 1875 to deliver in London but never gave contains this sentence: "I think I can say with pride that we have some legislatures that bring higher prices than any in the world." This is the closest to the "finest Congress money can buy" phrase often attributed to Twain but never found in his writings.

bicameralism The principle of a two-house legislature; the organizing principle behind the U.S. Congress and integral to the concept of **checks and balances** in government.

bidding war Contest for support between proponents and opponents of legislation, with **sweeteners** added to gain votes from different factions.

Big Casino The grand prize in politics: the presidency. In 1974, Ronald Reagan referred to the presidential election as "the big casino," according to William Safire in *Safire's Political Dictionary*. But Robert Ruark gave the term a more lethal connotation in his novel *The Honey Badger* (1964): "This is, Alec thought, the Big Casino. The Real Riffle. The Last Flutter . . . . It is a state of existence called Ain't."

big enchilada The top dog, the one who holds the real power. During the Senate **Watergate** hearings in 1973, the term was applied to former Attorney General John Mitchell, who controlled President Richard Nixon's re-election campaign.

ETYMOLOGY: Term coined by Nixon White House aide and amateur chef John Ehrlichman in reference to Attorney General John Mitchell, on one of the Watergate tapes, according to Sylvia Cole and Abraham H. Lass in their *Dictionary of 20th Century Allusions*. It would appear to be a stand-in for "big cheese," while "whole enchilada" was that era's Tex-Mex metaphor for "the big picture."

Big Four In relation to transportation bills, and the billions of dollars in **pork barrel** projects that go with them, the term refers to the top-ranking Democrats and Republicans on the House Public Works and Transportation Committee and its Surface Transportation Subcommittee. In Pentagonese, the term refers to the top-ranking members of the House and Senate Armed Services committees and the defense subcommittees of House and Senate Appropriations.

big tent *See* **Republican big tent.**

Big Three, the Business, labor, and agriculture, traditionally the most powerful lobbies on Capitol Hill.

big-ticket item High-priced item in an appropriation bill, often military hardware like the B-2 Stealth bombers, with price tags of $860 million apiece.

bill A proposed law. Bills introduced in the House are given the letter designation **HR** followed by a number, while Senate bills are designated with the letter **S.** The average length of bills grew from 4 pages in 1970 to 20 in 1992, with some commanding hundreds of pages. Over 90 percent of all bills fail to be enacted.

Some lawmakers know little of the contents of bills. Former Sen. Barry Goldwater (R-Ariz.), in his autobiography, *Goldwater*, said, "The average congressman introduces three dozen or more bills a year. Members don't even pretend to know what's in them

Screen legend Jimmy Stewart registers astonishment at a bill in Frank Capra's 1939 cinema masterpiece *Mr. Smith Goes to Washington.* In this film Stewart, as the naive congressman of the title role, finds reels of corruption in the U. S. Senate. *See* **bill.**

or what's happening on some of the committees they serve." At a **markup** of a complex telecommunications bill in July 1992, Rep. Barney Frank (D-Mass.) joked, "I'd rather vote on it than take a test." *See box,* "Bills, as in William."

Billion-Dollar Congress Term applied to the Congress of 1889-90, which was the first Congress to appropriate that much to run the government. The term was again applied to Congress in 1976—this time in reference to the cost of running Congress itself. The 1993 tab for Congress, excluding external operations like the General Accounting Office, was $1.2 billion.

a billion here, a billion there... Words invoked facetiously as money is spent and the deficit gets deeper. The phrase is shorthand for an oft-stated line made famous by Senator Everett Dirksen (R-Ill.): "A billion here, a billion there, and pretty soon you're talking about real money."

Biographical Directory of the United States Congress Reference book that lists and discusses the careers of the more than 11,000 Americans who have served in Congress from 1789 to 1989. The 2,104-page directory, published in 1989 by the Joint Committee on Printing of the U.S. Congress in the Observance of the Bicentenial, cost $82.

bipartisanship The practice of two political parties working together toward a common solution.

Bircher Member of the right-wing John Birch Society or someone who shares the extreme, virulently anti-Communist views of that group. With the default of Communism the term has lost much of its punch, but there was a time when it was a powerful label that was sometimes used as a slur. "The term 'Bircher' has become one of the day's most hateful and most misused political epithets," says an editorial in the *San Francisco Chronicle* for March 4, 1963. "Political leaders who know better are employing it deliberately to smear opponents. Others fling the term around so carelessly that the mud of Birchism splatters conservatives of all hues."

BILLS, AS IN WILLIAM

This short item appeared in the April 28, 1991, *Washington Post* Sunday magazine under the heading *That was then, this is now.*

From the December 10, 1885, "Notes and Gossip" column in the *Washington Critic,* a respected newspaper of the time:

"There are forty-three Congressmen named William, which in the sage opinion of the Philadelphia News accounts for the number of bills."

Oh, sure, we laughed too—until we learned that 14,618 bills were introduced in the 49th Congress, which was in session at the time. And that only 9,257 bills were introduced in the last Congress, when only 35 congressmen were called William or—more affectionately—Bill.

Think about this until the next election.

birds and bunnies *See* **tree-huggers.**

bitter-ender One who sticks with beliefs, however archaic or untenable, until the bitter end.

ETYMOLOGY: The political term was appropriated from the nautical one for the end of a cable or rope that is wound around the bitt, or deck post on a boat.

Black Book List of favors done for—and owed to—others. Although some reports indicate he kept one as majority leader, Sen. Robert Byrd (D-W. Va.) denies it existed.

black budget Part of the Pentagon and CIA budgets where costs are hidden for security reasons. Writes Tim Weiner in his book *Blank Check: The Pentagon's Black Budget* (1990), "The secret weapons, secret wars and secret policies it pays for are shielded from public debate." For years the B-2 Stealth bomber was secretly funded in this manner.

Black Caucus The formal organization of blacks in Congress. Membership grew from 9 when it was created in 1969 to 43 in 1993.

black program An agency or project whose costs and very existence are so cleverly embedded in the federal budget that neither the public nor members of Congress can track it. A question posed by a reader in the February 24, 1991, issue of *Parade* magazine underscores the confusion this term can engender: "In terms of congressional appropriations, any difference between 'a black program' and a 'program for blacks'?"

Black Republican During the Civil War, the term referred to hard-core abolitionists. It resurfaced in former House Speaker Joseph Martin's memoirs. Martin, a Republican from Massachusetts who served brief terms in the 1940s and 1950s, quotes Franklin Roosevelt ordering an assistant to call the head of the Bureau of Public Roads and "tell him I am sending down a Black Republican, and I want him to give him a road."

blacks in Congress In the 204 years of congressional history, 89 black Americans have served in Congress: 85 in the House and 4 in the Senate. The first was Republican Hiram R. Revels, who was seated in the Senate on February 25, 1870, after Mississippi was readmitted to the Union. He served until March 3, 1871. Joseph H. Rainey, a Republican from South Carolina, was the first black member of the House. He served from December 12, 1870, to March 3, 1879. The 1992 elections brought 17 new black members, the largest gain in history.

bloc Lawmakers who are linked by a common interest that may go beyond party—e.g., the farm bloc—and tend to vote as a unit when it comes to their common interest. Among candidates in Southern elections, "bloc vote" was code for the black vote; the term was used when accusing opponents of courting votes among blacks.

"The first colored senator and representatives, in the 41st and 42nd Congress of the United States."

This 1872 Currier and Ives portrait shows, seated, left to right, Sen. Hiram R. Revels of Mississippi, Rep. Benjamin S. Turner of Alabama, Rep. Josiah T. Walls of Florida, Rep. Joseph H. Rainy of South Carolina, and Rep. R. Brown Elliot of South Carolina; standing, Rep. Robert C. De Large of South Carolina and Rep. Jefferson H. Long of Georgia. *See* **blacks in Congress.**

block A move by a senator to hold up, sometimes interminably, a nomination by a president of the opposite party. All that is necessary is to inform Senate leaders and the nomination is frozen.

blocking In congressional **redistricting**, including enough traditionally Democratic ethnic minorities in a district (35–45 percent) to maximize Democratic support.

blood on the floor A description of the atmosphere in the House or Senate after a major fight, particularly of a partisan nature, where rhetorical wounds have been inflicted.

blue slip The House alone has the authority to initiate revenue legislation, a prerogative the Senate sometimes forgets. When the House Ways and Means Committee detects such an infringement, the House unfailingly passes a resolution saying the Senate has improperly invaded its territory and sends the bill back with the resolution, printed on blue paper, attached. The House is said to have blue-slipped the Senate.

blue smoke and mirrors Verbal sleight-of-hand used to sell a dubious program to Congress or a candidate to the public. Independent presidential candidate John Anderson quipped in 1980 that Ronald Reagan's economic policies would need "blue smoke and mirrors" to work. Journalists Jack Germond and Jules Witcover used the phrase as the title for their 1981 book on the 1980 presidential election.

ETYMOLOGY: The phrase goes back at least to journalist Jimmy Breslin's 1975 book, *How the Good Guys Finally Won,* a recounting of the events leading up to Nixon's resignation. Breslin described then Majority Leader Tip O'Neill's masterful illusions of power as "beautiful blue smoke rolling over the surface of highly polished mirrors." *See also* **smoke and mirrors.**

Board of Education Chummy term for the onetime informal gatherings of speakers of the House and their trusted allies. Begun by Republican Speaker Nicholas Longworth of Ohio and Democratic Leader John Nance Garner of Texas in the 1920s, the meetings mixed whiskey, strategy, and gossip. Democratic Speaker Sam

Rayburn of Texas continued the sessions, in a cozy first-floor room beneath the Speaker's Lobby, with members of the Democratic leadership. Rayburn referred to his meeting place simply as "downstairs." Republican Leader Charles Halleck of Indiana organized an opposition counterpart, "The Clinic."

body Both the House and Senate are legislative bodies. Members may refer to "this body" when talking about their own institution and **the other body** when talking about their counterparts.

body slam A devastating political comment. Vice-presidential candidate Lloyd Bentsen's statement, "Senator, you're no Jack Kennedy," during his 1988 debate with then Sen. Dan Quayle (R-Ind.), still holds the body-slam prize. The term is borrowed from wrestling.

bogeys Spending targets given to the Armed Services by the secretary of defense. The term is derived from military slang, dating back to the Second World War, for enemy aircraft.

boll weevil Nickname for conservative Southern Democrats in their role as pests who keep the pressure on the Democratic majority. The term, referring to insects that infest and damage cotton plants, alludes to the peskiness of the bug and the fact that, as one Southerner put it, "People have been trying to eradicate the boll weevil for a long, long time." Later these Democrats gave themselves the collective title of the Conservative Democratic Forum. In 1981, when the Conservative Democratic Forum bucked party leaders to support President Reagan's economic proposals, the term *boll weevil* was very much in the news. More than one boll-weevil Democrat has become a Republican, but the most publicized example was Phil Gramm of Texas, who made the switch in 1983.

The term is still in use, but it lost some of its significance in 1989 when conservative Georgian Sam Nunn led the unified Democratic charge in the Senate against the confirmation of John Tower as secretary of defense.

ETYMOLOGY: The term dates back to the Eisenhower years, when a group of conservative Democrats under the leadership of Howard

Smith of Virginia—and later of Omar Burleson of Texas—took the name of the destructive insect for themselves. William Safire reached this conclusion in his syndicated "On Language" column for August 30, 1981. Safire had been told by Burleson about the term, "We were men of like minds."

See **gypsy moth** for another group that deliberately took the name of a pest.

bolting Withdrawing from one's party or group.

bombast Pompous language that, like the soft padding material from which its name derives, has little substance.

bomb-thrower A legislator who will not compromise; an unyielding force.

bomfog Acronym for "Brotherhood of Man, fatherhood of God," New York Gov. Nelson Rockefeller's pompous and oft-used phrase during his campaign against Barry Goldwater in the 1964 New Hampshire Republican primary. The acronym, coined by cynical reporters and seemingly combining "bombast" and "fog," became a synonym, especially among such reporters, for high-sounding speeches. *See also* **MEGO.**

boodler Early generic nickname for **lobbyist.**

Book *See* **Beige Book, Black Book, Green Book, Pig Book, Plum Book, Prune Book,** *and* **Scare Book.**

boondoggle A project or program that wastes the taxpayers' money.

Etymology: The term was coined in 1925 by Robert H. Link, a Rochester, New York, scoutmaster to describe a plaited lanyard made by Boy Scouts as a special handicraft. In 1929 the term was given broader distribution within the scoutng world when a boondoggle was presented to the Prince of Wales in 1929 at the World Jamboree of Scouts. According to the editors of *Webster's Word Histories,* who have done considerable research on this term, the term make the leap from lanyards to public affairs when it appeared in a *New York Times* headline of April 4, 1935. The *Times*, which spelled the term as two words, was alluding to an investigation into a relief program and a witness who testified that he had taught "boon doggles" to relief recipients. He identified these boondoggles as crafts—making leather belts, or fashioning a sleeping bag from a piece of canvas. *Webster's Word Histories* descirbes what happened next: "The *Times* story was picked up in many other newpapers, and boondoggle and boondoggling were quickly adapted by opponents of the New Deal as terms for moneywasting, unproductive projects." *See also* **-doggle.**

Bork To block the confirmation of a Supreme Court nominee. This eponymous verb refers to Robert Bork, who was nominated to the Supreme Court in 1987 by Republican President Ronald Reagan but rejected by the Senate by a vote of 58–42, after critics attacked his narrow and conservative interpretations of constitutional protections. In 1991, on the eve of the Senate confirmation hearings for Clarence Thomas's nomination to the Supreme Court, the term was very much in use. "We're going to Bork him," was a widely quoted line on Judge Thomas from Flo Kennedy, a feminist lawyer.

borrowing authority *See* **backdoor spending.**

bottle up To hold a bill in committee, not letting it reach the floor. A measure in such a state is said to be "bottled up."

bottom line An estimate of the basic meaning, or sometimes the budget impact, of an action.

bought A condition in which one's vote has allegedly been purchased through contributions or favors. According to Christopher Matthews in his 1988 book *Hardball,* then Rep. John Breaux (D-La.), when asked if his vote could be bought by a Reagan administration favor, replied, "No, but it can be rented." Another cynical view: Nineteenth-century Pennsylvania Republican political boss and Senator Simon Cameron defined an honest politician as "one who when bought, stays bought."

bounce Sudden rise in a candidate's standing in the polls—a literal bounce in the line tracking popularity. Also known as a **bump.**

Bourbon One who clings tenaciously to the old order of things political and social. Most often, Southern Democrats who perpetuated old, often racist policies during the civil-rights battles of the 1960s. Originally, a member of a French ruling family.

boys Clubby, now largely dated term for like-minded group members: tobacco boys, oil-state boys, speaker's boys, steel-town ethnic boys.

boys' night out A weekly dinner attended by a clique of House members who live alone in Washington. The group has been dominated by California Democrats, including onetime Budget Committee Chairman Leon Panetta, and it is not all boys: Rep. Nancy Pelosi (D-Cal.) frequently goes along. One of their favorite haunts is Giorgio's Italian restaurant.

Bradley effect The phenomenon of candidates, especially blacks, receiving fewer votes among whites than polls indicated. As Los Angeles Mayor Tom Bradley, a Democrat, discovered in running for governor of California in 1982, some whites are reluctant to admit to pollsters that they would vote against a black candidate, even when they intend to.

brain dead Said of one who is not thinking; acting stupidly. This term derives from the medical/legal term describing a patient with a pulse and heartbeat but no brain function. Congress members were sure Bill Clinton didn't mean them when, during his 1992 run for president, he referred to Washington as "brain dead." "It's clear he's directing his criticism to the administration and the president," said Senate Majority Leader George Mitchell (D-Me.).

branch An arm of government, the legislative being one, the executive another, and the judicial the third. Lobbyists and the federal bureaucracy have been called the fourth.

When Congress has failed to challenge the president, it has been called the "broken branch," or, as Sen. Joseph Clark (D-Pa., 1957–69) was fond of calling it, "the sapless branch."

breach The act of overspending within appropriations categories under the 1990 budget agreement. The agreement would cure the breach by **sequestering** other funds within that category.

bread-and-butter liberal One who believes in the basics of jobs, housing, education, and health care.

break ranks To vote or take a position contrary to the leadership of one's party.

bribery Offering gifts in exchange for legislative favors. Accepting bribes is a federal crime. Members or staff members who accept "substantial" gifts may be fined up to three times the value of the gift, sent to prison for 15 years, and disqualified from holding federal office. Members are advised to send back the crystal vases and television sets, but to keep the fruit and cookies.

brief To explain an issue to a senator, representative, or staff member.

briefing A session called by a congressman, government official, or interest group to explain a bill or program. Some congressional committees hold separate briefings for lobbyists and the press.

bringing home the bacon Obtaining federal projects or dollars for one's state or district. *See also* **pork** and **pork barrel.**

broker

1 One who acts as intermediary in negotiating a deal. A *brokered convention* is one in which no one wins a majority of delegates, and brokers, or *kingmakers*, become powerful forces in selecting a nominee.

2 To arrive at a deal through a broker; one speaks, for instance, of a bill that has been brokered.

brown bagger A senator or representative from a state close enough to Washington, D.C., to enable him or her to commute from home every day.

Bubba factor The potential impact of rural Southern Conservatives on an election. Bubba is an affectionate characteronym for a Southern male with a taste for pickup trucks, beer, and stock car races.

The emergence of Bill Clinton as a candidate and then as president created several variations on the theme of Bubba, including "Bubba Ticket" for the Bill Clinton–Al Gore Southern male ticket in 1992.

ETYMOLOGY: Bubba is a male nickname that appears to come from a childish Southern rendering of the word "brother."

buck slip Letter used by congressional **caseworkers** to pass along a constituent's problem to a government agency. The computer-generated letter asks the agency for a response, which the congressional office then passes back to the constituent.

budget The immense document the president sends to Congress each January estimating in detail the cost of running the govern-

The 1982 hearings on the budget featuring (left to right) Murray Weidenbaum, chairman of the Council of Economic Advisors, Secretary of the Treasury Donald Regan, and Budget Director David Stockman. *See* **budget.**

ment for the upcoming fiscal year and asking for specific **appro-priations.** The president's proposal forms the basis for hearings on the budget and is usually changed only slightly.

Before 1974, spending decisions often were made without regard to future costs or the overall budget. Partly because of President Richard Nixon's refusal to spend certain appropriated funds for programs he did not approve of, Congress in 1974 passed the Budget and Impoundment Control Act. It created the House and Senate budget committees and a separate Congressional Budget Office. The budget committees introduce their own budget resolutions, which, when approved, become guidelines for spending that are not always followed.

Budget Agreement A complex and politically costly accord between Congress and the White House to reduce deficit spending over a five-year period. The 1990 agreement set ceilings for major funding categories that could be breached only by raising taxes. It contained some tax increases, a departure from President George Bush's "read-my-lips, no-new-taxes" promise, made while he was a candidate for the office in 1988. Bush later called the agreement a "mistake."

budget authority Authority granted by Congress to the executive branch to spend, borrow, or enter into contracts. *See also* **backdoor spending.**

budget hawks The growing ranks of members who are militant about spending cuts. The term derives from the Vietnam War–era label for pro-military politicians. In the same vein, a few "superhawks" were spotted during the budget wars of the 1993-94 Congress.

budget resolution Concurrent resolution, not a law, setting out the congressional spending priorities for the next five fiscal years.

bulldog A politician known for his or her stubborn, unrelenting grip or stance.

bulls and lions The chairmen of the House's most powerful committees, such as Dan Rostenkowski (D-Ill.) of Ways and Means,

Jack Brooks (D-Tex.) of Judiciary, and John Dingell (D-Mich.) of Energy and Commerce. *See also* **old bull.**

bully pulpit Theodore Roosevelt's description of the Senate before the Civil War, when famous speakers articulated great issues of the day.

bump

1 To oust, sometimes unceremoniously, another member from a committee leadership position by virtue of one's seniority. In April 1992, Strom Thurmond of South Carolina announced he would take over as ranking Republican on the Senate Armed Services Committee, replacing Virginia's John Warner.

ETYMOLOGY: The expression, dating back at least to the 1820s, comes from boat racing: when a boat bumps or nudges ahead of another in line on the water. Its sharp-elbowed modern equivalent is the act of depriving a ticketed airline passenger of a seat in an overbooked flight. In politics you don't get a compensating free ticket.

2 Rise in a candidate's standing in the polls. For instance, a presidential candidate can expect a post-convention bump in the polls. In the summer of 1992 the *Washington Post* insisted that Democratic nominee Bill Clinton had gotten a "double-bump"—the first being the "love-fest" Democratic convention in New York and the second being the withdrawal of Ross Perot from the campaign.

Same as **bounce;** *see also* **Anita Hill bump.**

bums Collective name for public officials when opinion is running against them. From the expression **"throw the bums out."** This goes back at least to 1937, when the expression "dem Bums" was affectionately applied to the Brooklyn Dodgers baseball team.

bundles for —— Name for a sometimes successful publicity stunt, staged when members of Congress claim they can't live on their salary: Protestors collect cheap food and clothing and pile it up outside members' offices. Thus embarrassed, legislators have lost their zeal for pay raises.

ETYMOLOGY: The name comes from the successful "Bundles for Britain" campaign during and immediately following World War II. It supplied war-ravaged England with food and clothing.

bundling The practice of a political action committee (**PAC**) giving an elected representative a bundle of checks as opposed to one large one. Bundling is a scheme for getting around campaign reform rules that limit gifts by PACs to $5,000 and those by individuals to $1,000. To bundle, the PAC puts its own check into a pile of individual checks from its members and delivers the bundle. In 1986, the *Wall Street Journal* reported that some $6.5 million in bundled money had been pumped into 10 key Senate races that year. This technique is legal, but it becomes illegal if pressure is applied to an individual employee of one of the PACs to become part of the bundle.

bunk

1 Meaningless oratory designed to impress one's constituency.

2 Politics viewed with a cynical eye.

ETYMOLOGY: This word was coined in Congress and derived from a place in the mountains of North Carolina. During the nineteenth century, Felix Walker, a Republican representative from the Tarheel State, made a habit of rising to say something for his home county of Buncombe regardless of what issue was under discussion. His "few words for Buncombe" became synonymous with provincial Babel and regional rhetoric. Wilfred Funk notes in his book *Word Origins and Their Romantic Stories* that the *Niles' Weekly Register*, published in Philadelphia from 1811 to 1849, used the term regularly and that "talking to (or for) Bunkum" was well known in 1828. Over time the term was clipped to "bunk."

Several slang dictionaries have claimed that the senator's name was Buncombe, but this is totally incorrect.

The word **debunk** is a derivative of bunk and first came into play in the 1920s.

bunker mode A state of legislative combat in which the minority, especially in the House, delays the majority, forcing votes on procedures that are usually automatic, such as approving the *Journal*, suspensions (*see* **suspension days**), and even **adjournment.** It is resorted to as a **delaying tactic** when all else fails.

Burton To redistrict in such a way as to strongly favor one's own party; to **gerrymander** in the modern sense. The verb was created from the name of the late Rep. Phillip Burton (D-Calif.) who, on the heels of the 1980 census, in the words of the *New York Times,* "drew, depending on your point of view, one of the most outrageous or brilliant political maps ever." What Burton accomplished was to create a district in San Francisco in which Democrats were secure and Republicans would be routinely slaughtered.

Burtonmander To gerrymander in the manner of the late Phillip Burton (D-Calif.) who is widely regarded as, to quote the *Washington Post* in 1991, the modern "Master of Gerrymander." The term is a blend of **Burton** and **gerrymander.**

bury To defeat a measure by a wide margin or put it so far down on a committee's agenda that it is unlikely to reemerge.

business as usual Expression of disgust about how things, especially politics, seem never to change, despite campaign vows to the contrary.

ETYMOLOGY: The phrase was given a political/diplomatic cast when, in the opening days of World War I, a young Winston Churchill stood in the Guildhall of London and declared, "The maxim of the British people is 'business as usual.'" As William Safire explains in his book *I Stand Corrected*, "This was a defiant maxim, telling the world that not even war could interrupt the steadfast work of the British people."

buzzword A voguish word that enjoys widespread but brief popularity, usually associated with a political or social issue.

Byrdlike In the manner of Democratic Sen. Robert Byrd of West Virginia, the Senate's most meticulous vote-counter, who went door to door, member to member, and kept a list of those in favor and those against.

Byrd rule An obscure rule written by the powerful Sen. Robert Byrd (D-W.Va.), chairman of the Appropriations Committee, in the 1980s to prevent "extraneous" matters from being attached to budget reconciliation bills. The tactic is useful because these bills are immune to **filibusters** and other **delaying tactics.** Byrd raised the rule in 1993 to keep President Clinton's health care package from being considered as part of his deficit-reduction plan.

by request Said of legislation submitted as a favor to the president or someone else. Submitting a bill by request, however, does not mean that it is being endorsed by the requestee.

cage Storage room, in the sometimes peculiar parlance of Capitol Hill.

calendar An agenda or list of the bills, resolutions, and amendments that are coming up for consideration. To a certain degree this term is a misnomer because it is not a calendar in the normal sense of the word but rather a list.

The Senate has a single calendar for bills. The House has five: the Union Calendar, for appropriations, authorizations, and revenue bills; the Discharge Calendar, for discharge petitions; the Consent Calendar, for noncontroversial bills; the House Calendar, for nonfiscal public bills, such as claims against the government or immigration waivers; and the Private Calendar, for private bills. On both the Senate and House calendars, bills are recorded in numerical order.

The Senate has two calendars. The Calendar of Business, or legislative calendar, contains bills reported from committees and ready to be taken up; the **Executive Calendar** is the one to which nominations and treaties are referred for confirmation or ratification.

Calendar Wednesday A seldom-used procedure that allows House committees to bypass the all-powerful Rules Committee. On Wednesdays, the speaker may, at his discretion, call the roll of committees, whereupon chairmen bring to the floor bills that have been approved in committee but blocked by Rules. But the bills must be taken up on the floor by Thursday at noon, and opponents may kill them with **delaying tactics**.

Calendar Wednesday came about in response to the autocratic rule of Speaker Joseph G. Cannon (R-Ill.), who kept bills he did not like off the floor. It was used successfully in 1950 to bring a fair employment bill to the House floor.

call of the chair A condition of **recess** subject to the will or "call" of the leadership: a recess called by the Chair.

call of the House Alphabetical **roll call** of members of the House of Representatives to determine the presence of a quorum. This procedure, adopted in 1896, is now carried out by electronic device.

campaign finance The funding of elections, which is a matter of much debate and concern as costs continue to soar and candidates are forced to find contributions to pay the bills. A study by the group Common Cause found that incumbent senators spent nearly $4.5 million each against challengers in 1990. A Federal Election Commission report in August 1992 said that as of June 30, House and Senate candidates had spent $96 million more than they had during the same 18-month period two years before—a 50-percent increase, from $191 million to $287 million.

campaign reform The goal of changing the way congressional races are funded so that political action committees (**PAC**s) have less influence and challengers have a better chance. Most campaign reform proposals, whether limiting the amount of contributions, providing for public matching funds, or limiting the amount candidates may spend, have been defeated or vetoed. With support from the White House in 1993, the chances for a compromise bill were improved.

candidate One seeking to be elected or reelected to office.

ETYMOLOGY: From the Latin *candidatus*, which originally meant "a person dressed in white." As Wilfred Funk said in *Word Origins and Their Romantic Stories* (1978), "When a Roman politician went campaigning he took care that his toga was immaculately

"The way we become senator nowadays."

This cartoon appeared in the January 20, 1890, issue of *Puck,* a satirical New York weekly. *See* **campaign finance.**

Robert Redford creates a sound bite in the title role of the 1972 Michael Richie film about elective politics, *The Candidate.* *See* **candidate.**

white so that he could make the best impression possible." Funk also notes that the root word *candidatus* can be seen in the word *incandescent,* which means "white and glowing," and in *candid,* which means "frank and honest."

caning   *See* **assaults.**

Cannonism   The autocratic rule of Speaker Joseph G. Cannon, who, by his power of recognizing members, appointing committees, and sitting as chairman of the Rules Committee, could make or break legislation or careers. The Illinois Republican, for whom the Cannon House Office Building is named, served as speaker from November 1903 to March 1911. "Behold, Mr. Cannon, the Beelzebub of Congress," he once told a gathering. "Gaze on this noble, manly form. Me, Beelzebub! Me, the Czar!" Whether this outburst, surely with a waved cigar, was in jest or not has never been clear. Cannon's dictatorship was ended in 1910 in a bipartisan revolt. *See* **czar** *and* **insurgents.**

Rep. Joseph G. Cannon (R-Ill.),
Speaker of the House 1903-1911,
chompin' on a stogie.
See **Cannonism.**

Capitol The houses of Congress, and their office buildings, as a physical entity. The Capitol covers about four acres, with a height, to the base of the **Statue of Freedom**, of 287 feet. The building contains 540 rooms and 850 doorways. It holds the chambers of the House (in the south wing) and the Senate (in the north wing). In the center of the second floor under the **dome** is the **Rotunda**, a circular ceremonial space that also serves as a gallery of paintings. The Capitol and its grounds lie at the point where the four quadrants of the city of Washington converge. In his report to President George Washington of June 28, 1791, Major Pierre Charles L'Enfant, the Frenchman engaged to plan the new Federal City, described the placement of the Capitol: "After much menutial search for an eligible situation, prompted, I may say, from a fear of being prejudiced in favor of a first opinion, I could discover no one so advantageously to greet the congressional building as is that on the West End of Jenkins Heights, which stands as a pedestal waiting for a monument."

Almost all of the nation's political leaders have a direct association with this site, but some more than others. President George Washington laid the cornerstone of the Capitol on September 18, 1793. Attempts made in the twentieth century to locate that cornerstone have failed, and its whereabouts remain a mystery.

John Quincy Adams was inaugurated president in the Old Chamber (now **Statuary Hall**) on March 4, 1825, and later, as a member of the House of Representatives, he was fatally stricken by what appears to have been a stroke in the same room on February 23, 1848. He lay in the Speaker's Office (now the Lindy Boggs Ladies' Reading Room) for three days and died there. Many famous figures have lain in state in the Rotunda, including Pierre Charles L'Enfant (1825), Abraham Lincoln (1865), John F. Kennedy (1963), and the bodies of the Unknown after the World Wars and the Vietnam War.

Capitol Flag Office Tucked away in the basement of the House, this office is responsible for continually raising American flags on an 18-foot pole and flying them for at least 30 seconds each so that a constituent can obtain a flag that officially flew over the Capitol. As many as 300 flags are flown on a normal day. The single-day record, according to the *New York Times,* occurred on

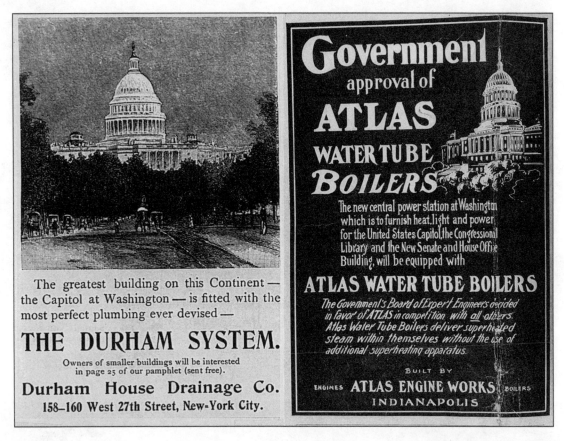

The greatest building on this Continent — the Capitol at Washington — is fitted with the most perfect plumbing ever devised —

THE DURHAM SYSTEM.

Owners of smaller buildings will be interested in page 25 of our pamphlet (sent free).

Durham House Drainage Co.
158–160 West 27th Street, New-York City.

Government approval of **ATLAS** WATER TUBE **BOILERS**

The new central power station at Washington which is to furnish heat, light and power for the United States Capitol, the Congressional Library and the New Senate and House Office Building, will be equipped with

ATLAS WATER TUBE BOILERS

The Government's Board of Expert Engineers decided in favor of ATLAS in competition with all others. Atlas Water Tube Boilers deliver superheated steam within themselves without the use of additional superheating apparatus.

BUILT BY
ENGINES **ATLAS ENGINE WORKS** BOILERS
INDIANAPOLIS

Images of the Capitol in ads from an earlier time, when any association with the national legislature was an implied endorsement of the product. *See* **Capitol.**

the occasion of the Bicentennial, July 4, 1976, when 10,471 flags were flown. To accomplish this, 18 temporary flagpoles had to be erected.

Capitol Hill The 88-foot rise of land—properly Jenkins Hill—on which the Capitol Building is situated and from which the U.S. Congress surveys the rest of its domain, which has been roughly defined as "the rest of the world."

Capitol Police The uniformed force of police officers, under the direction of the **sergeant-at-arms**, that guards doors and entryways on Capitol Hill, investigates threats against members, carries out undercover drug investigations, protects against bugging

The view from Pennsylvania Avenue in 1860, looking toward Capitol Hill and the unfinished dome. Pennsylvania Avenue at the foot of the Hill was once a prime area for lodging, commerce, and pleasures of the flesh. *See* **Capitol Hill.**

Capitol Hill today, an uncluttered and neatly manicured campus for Congress. *See* **Capitol Hill.**

and wiretapping, and performs other duties. In 1992, the force numbered 1,124 and its budget was $64 million.

capture theory A common and long lived hypothesis about federal agencies and some congressional committees: that they become tools of the interests they are supposed to regulate.

caretaker *See* **seatwarmer.**

carpetbagger Contemptuous term for an outsider, generally a politician or promoter, whose attempts to win favor are resented.
ETYMOLOGY: Before the Civil War, the term described anyone traveling light and was usually applied to itinerant adventurers, embezzlers, and bankers. After the Civil War, the term was applied to poor Northern whites who headed South to take advantage of the social, racial, and economic turmoil There. These adventurers carried all of their worldly goods with them—often in carpetbags—to satisfy property residence requirements in the South. Their influence was such that some historians have called the period following the Civil War the Carpetbag Era in American politics. Over time the term has come to mean anyone who comes from the outside to exert control.

casework The business of dealing with the problems of constituents. It is a constant in the workings of a congressional office and commands a major portion of lower-level office staff time. Casework is commonly handled in either the Washington or home office and involves problems associated with Social Security, Medicare, the Veterans Administration, and the Department of Agriculture.

The ability to handle casework successfully is seen as a great advantage for the incumbent, who is able to show constituents diligence and determination on their behalf.

caseworker Staff member whose prime responsibility is constituent problems.

cash on hand The as-yet-unspent funds in a politician's campaign **war chest.** During campaigns, candidates try to show as much cash on hand as possible in their reports to the Federal Election Commission to deter potential opponents and to avoid media stories saying they are having financial troubles. *See box,* "Loaded: The House's Top Twenty Unspent War Chests, June 1992."

LOADED: THE HOUSE'S TOP TWENTY UNSPENT WAR CHESTS, JUNE 1992

Member	Cash on Hand
Charles E. Schumer (D-N.Y.)	$2,133,183
Steven J. Solarz (D-N.Y.)	2,071,215
David Dreier (R-Calif.)	1,883,463
Dan Rostenkowski (D-Ill.)	1,456,682
Robert G. Torricelli (D-N.J.)	1,356,977
Richard A. Gephardt (D-Mo.)	1,088,705
James H. Quillen (R-Tenn.)	1,070,141
Matthew J. Rinaldo (R-N.J.)	1,015,406
Michael A. Andrews (D-Tex.)	1,006,291
John J. LaFalce (D-N.Y.)	893,411
John D. Dingell (D-Mich.)	883,123
Henry A. Waxman (D-Calif.)	851,920
Norman F. Lent (R-N.Y.)	822,283
Carlos J. Moorhead (R-Calif.)	734,432
Patricia Schroeder (D-Colo.)	723,200
Sander M. Levin (D-Mich.)	717,804
Robert T. Matsui (D-Calif.)	704,097
Bill Archer (R-Tex.)	681,310
Thomas S. Foley (D-Wash.)	646,069
Joe Moakley (D-Mass.)	642,630

Source: Federal Election Commission.

---

casualty list List published periodically in the newspaper ***Roll Call*** that tallies the members who have died, retired, or been defeated during the year. Carried since 1956, it has become a means of getting a fix on congressional turnover. The name was adopted by the House Press Gallery in 1992 to keep track of the record number of members not returning. The 1992 list: 65 retired, 2 died, 19 defeated in primaries, 24 defeated in general election. *See also* **incumbent**.

cats and dogs and... One of the many names given to the amendments that Congress is likely to attach to its bills. The *Wall Street Journal* of August 7, 1992, said nothing leaves Congress without a lot of "cats and dogs and tin cans" attached to it.

caucus

1 A closed-door meeting of party members in either house to elect leaders, establish party policy, and set the legislative agenda.

2 Any informal, temporary gathering of lawmakers working on a course of legislative action, usually relating to one issue or interest. For instance, the late 1970s saw the emergence of a group that Senator Daniel P. Moynihan (D-N.Y.) called the Northeastern Caucus, whose purpose was to save New York and other nearby cities from bankruptcy. Although they do not seek visibility outside Congress, such in-house caucuses have been formed to support steel, gasahol, tourism, seaports, and textiles. The Sun Belt Caucus, on the other hand, is made up of lawmakers from 17 southern and southwestern states who, among other things, have taken the position that the 1990 census shortchanged their section of the country. *See box,* "Informal Caucuses."

3 Members who meet regularly to monitor and advance the aims of a specific interest group. Three prominent, current examples that have been in place for more than a decade are the Congressional Black Caucus, the Congressional Hispanic Caucus, and the Congressional Caucus for Women's Issues. These groups are, if not permanent, at least likely to stay around for many years to come.

USAGE: The official name for this type of caucus is a **Legislative Service Organization.**

4 To hold or meet in a caucus. Members caucus, often rancorously, over a particular issue to decide their party's position.

ETYMOLOGY: This term is an Americanism that first arose in the context of Boston politics and political clubs called caucuses. It first appears in print in John Adams's diary for 1763 in the context of a "caucus club," and there are many other early references of this sort.

INFORMAL CAUCUSES

Congress has many informal caucuses, most of them with small staffs and limited office space. For example, there are House caucuses on the following topics:

- Baltic States and Ukraine
- Irish Affairs
- arms control and foreign policy
- the arts
- automobiles
- blacks
- the Mexican border
- science and technology
- women
- Hispanics
- the future
- Soviet Jews
- human rights
- rural matters
- space
- steel
- the Sunbelt
- territories
- textiles
- Vietnam veterans
- environment and energy
- exports
- health care
- military reform
- travel and tourism

The *Oxford English Dictionary* notes that the word's origin is obscure. Three theories exist:

1. One explanation is that the word comes from the Algonquin word *caucauasu* and refers to a tribal council. Several dictionaries, including the *Century Dictionary, Webster's Ninth New Collegiate Dictionary,* and *Webster's New International,* subscribe to this theory. Other dictionaries and individual lexicographers, however, have questioned it. In his *Second Browser's Dictionary*, however, the late John Ciardi terms the American Indian root "to be indisputable," alluding to John Smith of Virginia, who recorded ca. 1625 the Indian word *caw-cawessough* meaning "advisor."

2. An alternative theory appears in *The Slang Dictionary* (London: Chatto and Windus, 1903): "This is an American term, and a corruption of *caulker's meeting* being derived from an association of the shipping interests at Boston, previous to the War of Independence, who were very active in getting up opposition to England." This claim has led to some metaphoric jumps in *The Slang Dictionary*, such as "A caucus is [therefore] a secret meeting to prevent leaks in the ship of state," which seem fanciful.

3. Writing in the quarterly journal *American Speech* in 1943, etymologist LeRoy G. Barrett tells of finding a note in the papers of John Pickering explaining that caucus "consists of the initials of six men.... The words are in a vertical column with the initial letters spaced a little way from the second letters":

    C oulson
    A dams
    U rann Joyce, Jr.
    C oulson
    U rann
    S ymmes

Below the list, Pickering made this note as to its source: "From B. Russell, who had it from Sam'l Adams and Paul Revere. Samuel Adams was a member of a Caucus Club in 1765 and there is mention of three caucuses—North, Middle and South—to which Adams belonged."

cave in To bow or change position under pressure.

cave of the winds Journalist Warren Weaver, Jr.'s pet term for the U.S. Senate. It appeared in his book, *Both Your Houses,* which was published in 1972, before the Senate changed its **filibuster** rules from two-thirds required to defeat a filibuster to three-fifths. This cuts down the wind slightly.

On January 27, 1993, Sen. Harry Reid (D-Nev.) quoted from a letter by songwriter Woody Guthrie about his days working for the Works Progress Administration during the Depression: "I ain't got enough wind to be in office."

CBO *See* **Congressional Budget Office.**

censure The act of disciplining a fellow member through a vote of disapproval or condemnation. This may be by **reprimand, severe reprimand,** censure, condemnation, or **expulsion.** The Constitution specifies that each house may "punish its Members for disorderly Behavior, and, with the Concurrence of two thirds, expel a Member."

centerpiece One or more pieces of legislation that are counted among the key accomplishments of a given Congress. "Legislation providing insurance for the elderly against catastrophic illness, which was hailed as a centerpiece of the achievements of the 100th Congress," said a September 1989 *Washington Post* article, "has turned out to be one of the 101st Congress's biggest headaches."

chairman The elected head of a committee or subcommittee, always a member of the party in power, who presides over meetings, administers oaths to witnesses, hires and directs staff, and sets salaries. The chairman obtains the job through **seniority**, although in recent years some have been deposed after losing favor with members of their party in the committee.

In Congress, chairmanships are the real sources of power and prestige, conferring on the holder of the office the ability to pass or thwart legislation. One is not only called "Congressman," "Congresswoman," or "Senator" but "Mr. Chairman" or "Madam

Dan Rostenkowski addresses the press in his role as chairman of the House Ways and Means Committee. This photograph was taken in September 1986 after final agreement was reached on a benchmark tax reform package. Rostenkowski wears a sign saying "Gone Fishin'," signaling the end of a long and arduous process. *See* **chairman.**

Chairman." For some, a Hill Democrat told the *Washington Post* in June 1992, a chairmanship "is almost life itself."

USAGE: A female committee head is, as of this writing (1993), still referred to as "Madam Chairman." The neutral "chairperson" is seldom if ever used.

chairman's mark Informal designation of those bills proposed by committee chairmen before being considered by that committee. The "mark" amounts to a goal or target set by the chairman. It has been applied both to budget bills and to deficit reduction packages in the House.

chamber The room in which each house of Congress meets; thus the House Chamber and the Senate Chamber.

chaplain Spiritual counselor. Both the House and Senate have full-time chaplains who are responsible for seeing that each session begins with a prayer. The Supreme Court in 1983 ruled that prayers in Congress do not violate the Constitution.

The Senate Chamber as it appeared after World War II, when it was still configured for two senators each from 48 states. *See* **chamber.**

Van Wyck Brooks, in his *New England: Indian Summer, 1865–1915* (1940), said that someone once asked Edward Everett Hale, the minister and writer who served as Senate chaplain (1903–09), if he prayed for the senators. "No, I look at the senators and pray for the country," he replied.

The late Peter Marshall, who served from 1947 to 1949 and was the Senate's most popular chaplain of modern times, used to open Senate sessions with prayers such as this: "We confess, our Father, that we know we need Thee, yet our swelled heads and our stubborn wills keep us trying to do without Thee. Forgive us for making so many mountains out of molehills and for exaggerating our own importance and the problems that confront us."

cheap shot An unnecessarily but deliberately rough comment about a political opponent, especially an opponent who is not present to reply.

ETYMOLOGY: This is a recent term that first appeared in print in 1971, according to the 10th Edition of the *Merriam-Webster Collegiate Dictionary*. Early uses of the term applied to contact sports like prizefighting and football, where the meaning was obvious and literal.

checkoff Method of some political action committees (**PACs**) to build their **war chests** by payroll deductions, or "checkoffs," authorized by employees.

checks and balances The theory of government according to which one **branch** balances another. In some cases, Congress keeps the executive in check by overseeing its actions and approving its budget. The courts keep the legislative branch in check by ruling on the constitutionality of its laws—and the legislative exercises control over the courts by passing new laws, passing on nominees, and offering constitutional amendments.

ETYMOLOGY: In an American context, the term dates back to the Federalists, who prescribed it as the necessary limitation required to protect the varied elements of society. It is defined in *The Federalist, No. 51* as a system "...so contriving the interior structure of the government as that its several constituent parts may, by their mutual relations, be the means of keeping each other in their proper places." The term migrated to the United States from Britain; according to William Safire in *Safire's Political Dictionary*, it may have been the creation of seventeenth-century philosopher James Harrington.

chief counsel Head of a committee or subcommittee staff, usually a lawyer.

chief sponsor The principal **author** of a bill, often the chairman of the committee that held hearings, drafted the bill, and reported it to the floor.

chilling effect Impact of words or actions that serve to suppress and/or depress those they are aimed at. The term is applicable to many situations (the effect of censorship on the arts, for example) but most commonly used in the context of congressional **redistricting** when a new district weakens one party to such an extent that it has a hard time finding a candidate to run.

chit A favor owed by one member of Congress to another. To call in one's chits, or to cash them, is to balance the ledger.

Chowder and Marching Society An informal group of conservative Republican House members in which onetime House Minority Leader Gerald Ford (R-Mich.) played a prominent role and continued as a member into his presidency. It still exists and apparently meets for lunch on Wednesdays, although an aide to Rep. Bill Paxon (R-N.Y.), its most recent chairman, said its affairs are secret. *Chowder party* is an obsolete term for a political mass meeting.

ETYMOLOGY: In *Good Words to You*, the late poet and etymologist John Ciardi hunted in vain for a group that actually carried the exact name—as in, the Aloysius X. McGillicuddy Chowder and Marching Society—but added in semi-despair that

> city politicians often organized such outings in which constituents "marched" for McGillicuddy, ate his "chowder," and drank his beer (for which the city would pay later). It is probably by association with these politically sponsored outings that the name came into being in whimsical usage to label any quaintly busy social group that seeks to be insistently festive.

Christmas express The surge of congressional **junkets** just after Congress adjourns and just before Christmas.

Christmas tree bill A bill adorned with extra, often unrelated pieces of legislation especially, targeted tax breaks and hometown projects. In the *Wall Street Journal,* reporter Alan Otten explains: "On Capitol Hill, the practice of tagging a host of special-interest amendments to a popular bill is known as 'Christmas-treeing' that bill."

Chrysanthemum Club Label for those opposed to penalizing Japan for unfair trade practices.

civility Politeness. It is a common tenet of legislatures that civil discourse and behavior, even if only formalities, are necessary for the conduct of business. But Congress goes through periods, as it did in the waning days of the Bush administration, when civility goes out the window. Rep. David Obey (D-Wis.) said in August 1992, "The name of the game for the true zealots is to deny the place its ability to function with civility." *See* **comity.**

Claghorn A pompous, garrulous political figure named for the bombastic Senator Claghorn of comedian Fred Allen's radio show of the 1940s.

clambake Any special event held to rally a politician's faithful supporters, featuring food, speeches, and other entertainments. This usage is based on the general sense of the term, meaning a seashore feast at which clams and other seafood is steamed or baked.

Class of —— Term used to identify a group of legislators who come to Congress in a given year. The most famous was the Class of '74, consisting of 103 politicians who swept into Congress in the wake of President Richard Nixon's resignation. These members were also known as the **Watergate babies.** Classes have also been called **clubs.** The House Class of '92 had 110 new members.

clean bill A new version of a House bill, complete with a new number, prepared after a committee has reworked the original. It allows the bill to move on its own rather than having each revision voted on individually. Called an **original bill** in the Senate.

cleanup hitter A member of Congress who can be counted on to bring home a bill's main points in a closing speech. The term is primarily heard in the House, where Democratic and Republican leaders look to rising stars for their speech-making abilities.

ETYMOLOGY: The term derives from baseball slang for a power hitter who drives in runs. *See also* **designated hitter.**

clerk of the House Chief administrative officer of the House whose Senate counterpart is the **secretary of the Senate.** The clerk calls the roll and certifies the passage of bills.

clinker An **amendment** or **rider** to a bill that is so out of place that it stands out like a wrong musical note. In November 1973, President Nixon complained about "a couple of clinkers" in the Alaska pipeline bill with which business groups were unhappy. *See also* **joker.**

ETYMOLOGY: The term derives from the Dutch *klinker,* a vitrified brick that clinks when struck.

cloakroom

1 One of the narrow, L-shaped rooms, with well-worn leather chairs, at the back of both chambers of Congress, originally meant simply as a place to hang coats. Now these rooms serve as gathering places and communication centers. Staffs of Democratic and Republican cloakrooms make regularly updated recordings of current and anticipated floor activities and help find members who are needed for votes. Much lore is attached to cloakroom deals, but former Sen. Edmund Muskie (D-Me.) held that "*Nothing* happens in the cloakroom. *Nothing.* The cloakroom is where you go to rest your ass."

2 Any place where deals are made and votes traded. When Lyndon Johnson, who had little use for debate, was Senate majority leader, he gave this advice: "You have to work things out in the cloakroom and when you've got them worked out you can debate a little before you vote."

close How members, aides, or lobbyists describe deals that are virtually sewed up.

closed doors Much of the work of Congress takes place in negotiations closed to the press and public, with only unresolved differences going to the House and Senate for votes. Politicians are sensitive to criticism that they act "behind closed doors," but they claim the alternative would be chaos.

Defending the weeks of private sessions in the majority leader's office over the 1990 Clean Air Bill, Sen. John Chafee (R-R.I.) said that at one point he counted 57 people in the room: "It was the closest thing to the Black Hole of Calcutta we have seen around this place."

closed hearing Hearing from which the press and public are barred and, as many Hill reporters have ironically noted, from which it sometimes takes hours for the principal news to be leaked.

closed rule A ground rule for debate set by the House Rules Committee forbidding amendments. It is as rare as an **open rule,** which allows unlimited amendments to be considered. Most House bills are considered under **modified rules,** where specified amendments may be considered. The Senate has no such debate-limiting rules.

closed shop Former Speaker Thomas P. O'Neill (D-Mass.) used this term to describe President Richard Nixon's penchant for installing loyal aides in every department to observe and report back on top-level actions. He was "a leery and nervous president who ran a closed shop," O'Neill said in his autobiography, *Man of the House.*

close ranks To come together on an issue or nomination along party or caucus lines.

closet liberal/closet conservative One who quietly leans in one of those two directions, and might be lured across the line if the right issue came along.

close to the chest Where some politicians like to play their cards.

closure *See* **cloture.**

cloture Process by which debate can be limited in the Senate without unanimous consent. When invoked by roll call vote—three-fifths of those present and voting—it limits each senator to one hour of debate. Perhaps because it sounds more like a medical than a political term, it is seldom used outside of Congress and government textbooks. *The Associated Press Style Book and Libel Manual* advises using *closing debate* or *ending debate* instead.

clout Influence, usually powerful, derived from one's political or social connections. It may be applied to legislators, staffers, or lobbyists. One who has clout is capable of delivering a heavy blow, either for or against.

club, the Powerful congressional insiders, but most often the Senate, with its privileged, exclusive membership. During the 1991 confirmation hearings for Supreme Court Justice Clarence Thomas, the Senate and, more accurately, the Judiciary Committee, was branded an "all-male club." *See also* **Men's Club.**

coattail The ability of a presidential candidate to help win seats in Congress for members of his or her party. A candidate who can pull others along is said to have *long coattails*. Immediately following George Bush's election in 1988, *USA Today* carried the headline "LACK OF COATTAILS REMINISCENT OF '60." On July 31, 1992, columnist George Will called Bush's poor prospects for November 1992, an **undertow.** The July 22, 1992, *Los Angeles Times* noted that Democratic presidential and vice-presidential nominees Bill Clinton and Albert Gore would likely cling to the "skirt-tails" of California's popular Democratic Senate candidates Barbara Boxer and Dianne Feinstein.

ETYMOLOGY: *Success with Words: A Guide to the American Language,* published by the *Reader's Digest,* says that this construct is "probably from Victorian romping games in which a man played the horse and a child held on to or rode on his coattails."

coauthor Another original **signatory** to a bill. A bill often has several, including leaders on the issue from both parties. This gives the measure a greater chance of passing.

codel State Department jargon for a visiting congressional delegation, usually consisting of several members, their spouses, and one staffer each. Codel is a blend word of "congressional" and "delegation."

code of conduct Rules about gifts, contributions, travel, and **conflicts of interest** by which congressional members are expected to abide.

codify To take a policy and turn it into law: to make it part of the code of law.

coffee klatch An informal meeting arranged by a political candidate's manager, during which the public can meet the candidate and ask questions.

ETYMOLOGY: The term is a literal translation of the German *kaffee klatsch,* meaning a gathering during which neighbors drink coffee and chat.

coffer A chest or strongbox in which money or valuables are kept. In politics, a campaign **war chest.**

COLA Acronym for cost of living adjustment; often used in debates and hearings on Social Security disbursements and Civil Service and congressional pay and pensions.

cold turkey In the context of Congress, this slang term for the abrupt kicking of a habit (drugs, cigarettes, alcohol) is applied to the sudden termination of a program. For instance, during the summer of 1989, House Armed Services Committee Chairman Les Aspin (D-Wisc.) called for a cold turkey freeze on the funds for the Stealth bomber.

colleague Term of address used by a member of the House or Senate to refer to another member.

College of Cardinals

1 Name given to one of Congress's most powerful inner circles, the 13 House appropriations subcommittee chairmen and ranking minority members. Unlike their namesakes in Rome, however, these collegians have no particular group function, either as electors or as counselors. Their average length of service in the House in 1992 was 28 years.

2 A group of senior officials in the Central Intelligence Agency.

ETYMOLOGY: The term refers to the cardinals of the Roman Catholic Church, who serve as a privy council to the Pope and elect his successor.

colloquy By tradition, the term for a conversation in the House and Senate. Unlike real conversations that are actually spoken, colloquies can be scripted in advance (or for that matter afterward, any time up to midnight) and placed in the **Congressional Record.** Until July 31, 1985, these "conversations" appeared as part of the day's debate. Now, special symbols or typefaces indicate speeches not actually made.

comity Civilized behavior and common courtesy extended by members of the two houses to their colleagues and the White House and vice versa. It is said to be on the decline. *See* **civility.**

President-elect Bill Clinton on a December 8, 1992, courtesy visit to the Capitol. *See* **comity.**

commemorative bill A piece of legislation commemorating something. More than one-third of the bills passed by Congress each year are to celebrate a day, week, or month. Child Care Awareness Week, National Barbershop Quartet Month, National Dairy Goat Awareness Week, and National Duckling Month are but a few. The all-time high was reached in the 99th Congress (1985–86) when 275 commemoratives—41 percent of all public laws—were approved. The newspaper *Roll Call* has called the practice a "harmless vice," but Rep. Dave McCurdy (D-Okla.) said it reinforces the "public perception that Congress wastes too much time on trivia." *See also* **weeks and days.**

commitment A pledge of support. Once made in Congress, commitments are said to be broken only at great cost.

Committee of the Whole The entire membership of a legislative body, usually the full House, temporarily turned into a committee to speed up a procedure. The formal name is the Committee of the Whole House on the State of the Union.

Committee on Committees Formerly the Democratic members of the Ways and Means Committee, who approved the membership of all other committees. In 1975 this power was shifted to the **Democratic Steering and Policy Committee,** chaired by the speaker, with approval by the Democratic Caucus.

Committee on Rules The body that sets rules and time of debate on each House bill.

committee report Written report accompanying each bill, giving its merits and demerits.

committees These are the all-important working groups of Congress, each with jurisdiction over areas of the government and public life. With the power to move or bury legislation, there is no doubt that, as future president Woodrow Wilson—then studying for a Ph.D. at Johns Hopkins University—put it in 1885: "Congress in session is Congress on public exhibition, whilst Congress in its committee rooms is Congress at work."

In 1992, there were in the House 22 standing committees, 147 subcommittees, 5 select or special committees; in the Senate, 16 standing committees, 87 subcommittees, 4 select or special committees; and 12 joint committees and subcommittees. Congressional committees had 3,945 employees, with appropriations of

COMMITTEE ASSIGNMENTS

IN THE SENATE The job of determining committee assignments in the Senate falls to each party, whose committee on committees weighs the requested assignments of new senators. By Senate rules, each senator shall serve on two "A," or major, committees and may serve on one or more of the relatively minor "B" or "C" committees. The following lists show some but by no means all of the committees at the various levels.

"A" Committees
- Agriculture, Nutrition, and Forestry
- Appropriations
- Armed Services
- Banking, Housing, and Urban Affairs
- Commerce, Science, and Transportation
- Energy and Natural Resources
- Environment and Public Works
- Finance
- Foreign Relations
- Governmental Affairs
- Judiciary
- Labor and Human Resources

"B" Committees
- Budget
- Rules and Administration
- Small Business
- Veterans Affairs
- Select Committees on Aging and Intelligence
- Joint Economic Committee

"C" Committees
- Ethics
- Indian Affairs
- Joint Taxation
- Library
- Printing

IN THE HOUSE The House, through its rules, gives more power to the party in power, which since 1955 has been the Democratic party. House members are limited to one exclusive committee or one major and one nonmajor committee, or to two nonmajor committees. Generally, members bid for three subcommittee assignments on their major committees and two on their minor committees. Recommendations are made to the Democratic Caucus by the Democratic Steering and policy Committee, which uses "exclusive," "major," and "nonmajor" categories. Republicans refer to them as "red," "white," and "blue" committees.

Exclusive Committees
- Appropriations
- Rules
- Ways and Means

Major Committees
- Agriculture
- Armed Services
- Banking, Finance, and Urban Affairs
- Education and Labor
- Foreign Affairs
- Energy and Commerce
- Judiciary
- Public Works and Transportation

Nonmajor Committees
- Budget
- District of Columbia
- Government Operations
- House Administration
- Interior and Insular Affairs
- Merchant Marine and Fisheries
- Post Office and Civil Service
- Science, Space, and Technology
- Small Business
- Veterans Affairs

Standards of Official Conduct and select, special, and joint committees do not fall into these categories.

$221 million. Top staff salaries were $119,000 in the House and $126,000 in the Senate. Under pressure to cut its budget, the House in 1993 appeared ready to cut some staff and eliminate some select committees. The Senate voted to cut committee budgets by 7.6 percent. *See box,* "Committee Assignments."

committee system Method by which both houses of Congress deal with appropriations, authorizations, and the other details of legislation. Because the system is indispensable to the orderly operation of Congress, but not expressly authorized in the Constitution, it has been called an element of the "unwritten Constitution."

companion bill A bill that is identical or very similar to one introduced in the other house.

competitive district Congressional district in which the margin of victory is less than 60 percent, which is a declining phenomenon. In 1990, 89 percent of congressional incumbents received at least 60 percent of the vote.

compromise To reach an agreement by mutual concession. Most major legislation is the product of compromise between factions, usually agreed to before House or Senate consideration. Congress, with equal representation from small and large states in the Senate and proportional representation in the House, is itself the product of the **Great Compromise.** This compromise, worked out by the framers of the Constitution, gave small states equal representation in one of the two houses, the Senate.

compromise committee *See* **conference committee.**

concurrent resolution A measure that must be approved by both houses but does not require the president's signature and does not have the force of law. Such resolutions tend to concern themselves with the rules of the two houses and to convey sentiments, such as congratulations, or express the "sense of Congress" on policy matters. A similar resolution passed by one house and also lacking the force of law is known as a **simple resolution.** A resolution passed by both houses with the force of law is a **joint resolution.**

"A little disagreement in conference committee—'We can't tolerate dictation.'"

This view of a conference committee in action depicts one member's unwillingness to be dictated to. *See* **conference committee.**

condemnation *See* **censure.**

conferee Member of a **conference committee,** usually a person of some seniority on the committee from which the legislation being considered originated.

conference Term favored by Republicans in the House and by many in the Senate for the word **caucus.**

conference committee Panel of members from both houses, usually key members of the committees that handled the bill under consideration, given the job of working out a compromise between the usually different versions of a bill passed by the House and Senate. Sometimes called a *compromise committee,* this body is not supposed to consider material not mentioned in the bills. But bills have been known to be substantially revised while in conference. Most conferences that were formerly secret are now open. With a complicated bill, there may be more than 200 legislators involved. The result is that most of the negotiating is done by the bill's managers and their staffs.

Conferences are either "free" or "simple" (Thomas Jefferson's terms): In *free conference*, conferees are free to accept the language of the other body; in a *simple conference*, they have simple instructions not to give in on certain matters. The Senate usually prefers free conferences and has instructed its managers to withdraw from a conference if their counterparts are instructed to be inflexible.

confession Informal meetings in the House chamber that former Speaker Thomas P. O'Neill, Jr. (D-Mass.), held with representatives seeking favors or attention.

confirmation The evaluation by the Senate of presidential nominees to goverment posts. Although the word implies approval, the opposite is possible. The process involves confirmation hearings by a committee and a vote by the full Senate. *See also* **advice and consent.**

Clarence Thomas in the witness chair during the September 1991 hearings to confirm his appointment to the Supreme Court. Because of the testimony against Thomas by law professor Anita Hill, this particular confirmation created intense interest and controversy. *See* **confirmation.**

conflict of interest As the House *Ethics Manual* simply states, this is "a situation in which an official's conduct of his office conflicts with his private economic affairs."

Being totally innocent of conflict is next to impossible. As Sen. Jacob Javits (R-N.Y.) once told the Senate, "If we tried to disqualify ourselves because of any relationships we have to any of these matters we vote on, we probably would sit here mute and voteless most of the time." Sen. Robert Kerr (D-Okla.) said, "If everyone abstained on the grounds of personal interest, I doubt if you could get a quorum in the U.S. Senate on any subject." *See also* **code of conduct** and **impropriety.**

Congress

1 The House and Senate taken together; the U.S. Congress.

Usage: This interesting note appeared in the 1929 Merriam-Webster periodical *Word Study:* "President [Woodrow] Wilson, who was particularly careful in his English, always referred to 'the Congress.' The particular Congress we always have in mind is that which assembles at Washington in obedience to the directions of our Constitution, but the word is an old one and there have been many congresses in human history. In Latin, from which the word comes, it signifies 'a stepping or coming together.' " *See box,* "Congress Is..."

Etymology: From the Latin *congressus,* meaning "to come together." The word first appeared in written English in 1528.

2 A period of two legislative years corresponding with the term of a member of the House of Representatives. Such periods are given a number—for instance, the 100th Congress was in existence from the beginning of 1987 to the end of October 1988. The 101st Congress was elected in November 1988 and was seated in January 1989. Congresses tend to become typified for their level of activity. For instance, the 100th was seen as one that passed a number of bills but avoided key issues (air pollution, banking reform, the budget deficit).

Congress from Hell House Speaker Thomas Foley (D-Wash.) used this term to characterize the 102nd Congress (1991–92) and

---

CONGRESS IS...

...a body of men who meet to repeal laws.
—*Ambrose Bierce*

...an institution designed only to react, not to plan or lead.
—*Jimmy Breslin*

...so strange. A man gets up to speak and says nothing. Nobody listens—and then everybody disagrees.
—*Russian visitor Boris Marshalov*

...the great commanding theatre of this nation, and the threshold to whatever department or office a man is qualified to enter.
—*Thomas Jefferson*

SENATOR HOAR JUSTICE HARLAN SENATOR BERRY CHAPLAIN MILBURN OF THE SENATE SENATOR SHOUP SENATOR BROOKE

THE STEPS OF THE CAPITOL, AT THE
OPENING OF THE FIFTY-SEVENTH CONGRESS

its turmoil over bank overdrafts, unpaid restaurant bills, and legislative gridlock.

Congressional Budget Office The CBO, created by the Budget and Impoundment Control Act of 1974, analyzes budget proposals and provides economic forecasts.

congressional charter An officially granted blessing offered by the U.S. Congress to such organizations as the Boy Scouts of America, the United Spanish War Veterans, and the American Chemical Society. In 1992 the charter provision was killed as a congressional benediction, occasioning this comment from Rep. Barney Frank (D-Mass.), chairman of the House Judiciary subcommittee on administrative law and governmental relations: "We have done our best to get Congress out of the trivia business."

Although the business of the charters was meaningless and the petitioning for them was a nuisance, they had an insidious side in that the chartering seemed to suggest that Congress knew something about the groups and had some supervision over them. When they were abolished, Rep. Frank pointed out that a group asking for the preservation of the memory of Albert DeSalvo, the Boston Strangler, could have been given such a charter as there was no way for Congress to check such things out.

This 1923 Franklin Booth poster illustrates what was once the importance of a Congressional charter. *See* **congressional charter.**

congressional campaign committee Partisan unit working to promote the re-election of sitting party members and the election of new ones. The first congressional campaign committee was created by Radical Republicans who did not trust the national committee of the party. The Democratic committee came into being in 1880. Today each party has a campaign committe in each House.

Each Congress has its own identity and key figures. Depicted by *Collier's Weekly* is the opening of the 57th Congress in 1903. In the front row at the left, Sen. George Hoar walks with Justice John Marshall Harlan. Behind and to the right of them is the one-legged Sen. James Berry, and to the right of him are the Rev. and Mrs. W. H. Milburn. Milburn was the chaplain of the Senate. *See* **Congress.**

Congressional Club A powerful fund-raising apparatus, not really a club, set up by Sen. Jesse Helms (R-N.C.) to help elect conservatives.

congressional district Area from which a member of the House is elected. District lines are redrawn by the state legislatures whenever the number of representatives changes through the process of **reapportionment.** There are 435 congressional districts, with each state guaranteed at least one. The ideal population based on the 1990 census would be 572,466, but there are wide disparities. *See also* **apportionment** *and* **redistricting.**

congressional exemption *See* **exemption.**

congressional government Woodrow Wilson's term for the Congress-dominated government that obtained before 1901, the year Theodore Roosevelt began asserting executive power. Power constantly shifts back and forth between Congress and the executive. *Compare* **imperial presidency.**

congressional immunity Arrangement by which witnesses giving testimony to a congressional committee give up the **Fifth Amendment** protection against self-incrimination on the promise that the testimony will not be used later to prosecute them.

congressional investigation Staff investigation, followed by hearings, to obtain information rather than to consider legislation or nominations.

Congressional Journal The official record of the proceedings of the House and Senate. The *Journal* is not a verbatim record but a record of actions taken. The House insists on its right to control what goes in the *Journal,* "even to the extent of omitting things actually done," according to the House *Rule Book.* But in practice, the House does not allow members to kill a bill by amending the *Journal.*

congressional liaison Lobbyist sent to Capitol Hill by the White House and executive agencies.

congressional mailings coordinator Position created by the U.S. Postal Service in 1990, according to the official *Postal Bulletin,* to "resolve any congressional mailing problems." The appointment of 170 of these coordinators was seen as one more example of how massive the congressional postal business has become.

Congressional Medal of Honor Since 1910, America's medal of honor for acts of military bravery. It is the highest military honor that can be conferred upon an American.

congressional pay Congressional salaries have risen slowly through the years, often hampered by fears of public outrage over self-awarded increases. Pay is now tied to the federal cost-of-living index. In 1993, members agreed to forego their 1994 cost-of-living increase and freeze their pay at $133,600 for one year. *See box,* "Salaries of House and Senate Members."

congressional privilege Constitutional provision that prevents members of either house from being arrested for any reason except for treason, a felony, or a breach of the peace. This has been interpreted to mean all indictable crimes. In addition, the Constitution's "Speech or Debate Clause" protects members from being prosecuted over the contents of speeches made on the floor.

Congressional Record The daily record of debate, votes, and remarks of both chambers. It is a periodical published by the Government Printing Office for each day Congress is in session. Current circulation is about 21,500, with the bulk of the copies going to libraries, lobbyists, and law firms. The *Record* of the 101st Congress, ending in 1990, consisted of 35,523 pages at a production cost of $17 million.

As a record of the day's business, it is subject to occasional criticism, as members can become part of the spoken record without actually speaking. A celebrated case in point was the *Record* of October 18, 1972, containing a speech by Hale Boggs (D-La.) that praised the legislation enacted in that session. Boggs was dead on October 18; his airplane had crashed in Alaska two days earlier. The *Record* now makes a distinction between what is spoken and

SALARIES OF HOUSE AND SENATE MEMBERS

Year	Salary	Year	Salary
1789–95	$6 per diem	1969–75	$42,500
1795–96	$6 per diem (House)	1975–77	$44,600
	$7 per diem (Senate)	1977–79	$57,500
1796–1815	$6 per diem	1979–82	$60,662.50
1815–17	$1,500	Dec. 1982–83	$69,800 (House)
1817–55	$8 per diem	July 1983	$69,800 (Senate)
1855–65	$3,000	1984	$72,600
1865–71	$5,000	1985–86	$75,100
1871–73	$7,500	January 1987	$77,400
1873–1907	$5,000	March 1987–89	$89,500
1907–25	$7,500	1990	$96,500 (House)
1925–32	$10,000		$98,400 (Senate)
1932–33	$9,000	January 1991	$125,100 (House)
1933–35	$8,500		$101,900 (Senate)
1935–47	$10,000	August 1991	$125,100 (Senate)
1947–55	$12,500	January 1992	$129,500
1955–65	$22,500	January 1993	$133,600
1965–69	$30,000		

The vice president, the speaker of the house, the Senate president pro tempore, and the majority and minority leaders of both chambers receive additional pay. As of 1993, their salaries are:

Office	Salary
Vice president	$171,500
Speaker of the house	171,500
Senate president pro tempore	148,400
Majority and minority leaders	148,400

*Per year, unless stated otherwise.
Source: Congressional Research Service.

what is not spoken. In the section that covers the Senate, insertions and **ghost speeches** are indicated by small, round bullets. For the House, they are printed in sans serif type.

The *Record* is also known for leaving out noteworthy events. It was the only publication in the United States reporting on the events of Congress that missed the story of fanatics shooting up the House on March 1, 1954, and seriously wounding five of its members.

Congressional Research Service The research arm of the **Library of Congress.** The CRS works exclusively for Congress, conducting research, analyzing legislation, and providing information at the request of committees and members.

congressman A member of Congress, now especially a male member of the House of Representatives. According to Merriam-Webster's *Collegiate Dictionary*, 10th Edition, the word first appeared in English in 1780. In the early 1970s, an attempt was launched to gain acceptance for such terms as congressperson and congresspeople, but although they appear in major dictionaries, they are seldom if ever used in the traditional context of Capitol Hill business. Even more unlikely to achieve acceptance is "congresscritter," the term created and used by Tom Clancy in his 1991 novel *The Sum of All Fears*.

congressman at large Representatives from such states as Alaska, Delaware, Montana, North Dakota, South Dakota, and Wyoming, where the sparse population yields only one district for the whole state.

congresswoman Now the preferred term for a female member of the House of Representatives. The term dates from 1917, when first applied to Jeannette Rankin, the first woman elected to Congress. *See* **Women in Congress.**

conservative One who believes in limiting government solutions and leaving the answers to the marketplace. The philosophy has many stripes, including traditionalists opposed to change, neo-conservatives opposed to liberal social programs, and the radical right favoring radical change. The Republican Party has been the conservatives' battleground, with the middle and the right struggling for control. Some in Congress have sought conservative alternatives to tackling social problems. *See* **new paradigm.**

conservative coalition An informal voting alliance of Republicans and Southern Democrats, frequently constituting a majority or, at least during the Reagan and Bush eras, enough votes to uphold vetoes.

Conservative Democratic Forum The proper name given to themselves by the **boll weevils.**

THE HIGH-TARIFF STATESMAN, AS HE FELT WHEN HE DELIVERED HIS GREAT SPEECH AT WASHINGTON, AND—

AS HE LOOKED WHEN HE TRIED TO EXPLAIN IT TO THE BOYS AT HOME

Drawn by E. W. Kemble

TRYING TO SQUARE HIMSELF

[inset] *"The high-tariff statesman, as he felt when he delivered his great speech at Washington, and —[center] as he looked when he tried to explain it to the boys at home."*

In this cartoon, E. W. Kemble shows how the congressman in favor of high tariffs must ultimately face up to his constituents. *See* **constituent.**

consider To take up a bill or amendment in Congress.

constituency An elected official's district or state; **constituents** collectively. Speaker of the House Sam Rayburn (D-Tex.) insisted that House members had two constituencies: their voters back home and the other members of the House.

constituency development An effort by a corporation or special interest to influence groups of potential voters within a state or congressional district by targeting contributions to them.

constituent Person residing in a member's district or state. Members commit considerable staff time to giving this person a favorable impression of his or her accomplishments. Staff case-workers focus on constituents' problems with the government. Newsletters, voter surveys, and press secretaries tell the constituent of the member's successes.

There are differing schools of thought on the matter of constituents. The witty, caustic journalist H. L. Mencken said, "There are some politicians who, if their constituents were cannibals, would promise them missionaries for dinner."

But more than one congressman has grown weary of pandering to the voters. According to John F. Kennedy in *Profiles in Courage,* Rep. John Steven McGroarty (D-Calif., 1935–39) once wrote a constituent: "One of the countless drawbacks of being in Congress is that I am compelled to receive impertinent letters from a jackass like you in which you say I promised to have the Sierra Madre mountains reforested and I have been in Congress two months and haven't done it. Will you please take two running jumps and go to hell."

Constitution The fundamental laws and principles of the U.S. government comprising 7 articles and 26 amendments. It has been the supreme law of the nation since its adoption in March 1789.

constitutional amendments Since the founding of the republic, thousands of amendments to the Constitution have been proposed, but just 27 have been approved. It is a difficult and sometimes lengthy process, as the 1992 ratified amendment to prevent Congress from voting itself a pay raise showed.

An amendment must receive a two-thirds majority vote in both houses and then must be ratified by three-fourths (38) of the states. Thirty-three amendments have been submitted for ratification. One of the most noted failures was the Equal Rights Amendment **(ERA)**. Approved by Congress in 1972, it fell three states short of the required number and officially died on June 30, 1982. State legislatures or—as in the case of prohibition repeal—state conventions vote on ratification.

Also available as a means of amending the Constitution, but never tried, is the constitutional convention, which Congress must convene if requested to do so by the legislatures of two-thirds (34) of the states. Scholars say conventions would be dangerous because they cannot be restricted as to subject matter.

contact sport What politics is said to be, especially in New York, with its aggressive media and contentious political groups.

contempt of Congress Charge leveled against those who obstruct the business of Congress. For instance, a witness who refuses to answer the questions of a congressional committee may be charged with contempt of Congress and, if convicted, sent to prison. The House, unlike the Senate, may also detain a recalcitrant witness in the custody of the **sergeant-at-arms.**

continuing body The Senate. Unlike the House, where all members stand for election every two years, the Senate has six-year staggered terms, with one-third being up for election on even-numbered years. The Senate's rules carry over from one session to the next.

continuing resolution Measure taken at the end of a fiscal year in which **appropriations** have not been approved to allow a program—or the government itself—to keep operating without an appropriation. Most resolutions keep the money flowing for a few days or weeks, but recently some resolutions have extended spending authority for the full fiscal year. *CRs*, in Capitol Hill jargon, have been used as vehicles for controversial measures, or as **riders** that could not pass on their own.

contracting authority *See* **backdoor spending.**

control The power of the majority party to dominate the affairs of either body. Democrats have controlled the House since 1955 and the Senate—with the exception of the four years from 1985 to 1989—since 1959.

control room Hotel hospitality suite, set aside for a **junketing** congressional delegation, furnished with alcohol, snacks, and long-distance telephones lines.

conviction politician One who acts on the basis of ideology rather than politics. Columnist George Will described Ronald Reagan as working "for an ideological movement before he began seeking office."

Cordon Rule Senate rule requiring that committee reports print in a contrasting italic type the changes that the bill would make in existing law. The House has a similar requirement: the **Ramseyer Rule.**

core constituency A candidate's most ardent and forgiving supporters. A more humorous slant on their devotion was provided by *USA Today* columnist Joe Urschel, who described them on July 2, 1992, as "people who'll believe anything."

corn for porn The deal in which House and Senate negotiators dropped prohibitions against subsidies by the National Endowment for the Arts for "patently offensive" sexual exhibits in exchange for preserving low grazing fees on federal land. It has nothing to do with corn, but the name was so catchy it stuck.

corridors The hallways of the Capitol or office buildings, but, more importantly, the setting for informal meetings, interviews, and deals.

Corrupt Practices Act Law enacted in 1925, limiting expenditures in House and Senate races. It has been amended many times, under the rubric of **campaign reform.**

cosmetic vote A vote cast for or against a measure for the benefit of one's constituents but not affecting the bill's outcome. A senator, for instance, who noisily voted for a largely **grandstanding** bill to cut credit card interest charges, while assuring banks in his state that the bill would never get out of a House–Senate conference committee, would have cast such a vote.

The Senate private reception area, in which just about everything—floors, walls, window cases, and columns—is made of marble. *See* **corridors.**

cosponsor Person joining in the sponsorship of a bill. Except to indicate a bill's strength or to serve as a signal to constituents, the practice of cosponsoring is relatively meaningless. In the 101st Congress (1989–90), Rep. Cardiss Collins (D-Ill.) cosponsored 1,143 measures—a modern record. *See* **sponsor.**

cost overrun The practice of defense contractors and other government suppliers of charging more for their products or services than originally estimated.

counterfeit congressman Someone posing as a member of Congress. Although seldom heard of today, such imposters were once enough of a problem that guidebooks to the city of Washington warned of them. This passage from the 1869 version of John B. Ellis's *The Sights and Secrets of the National Capital* explains the problem:

> Persons visiting Washington on business are very frequently the dupes of imposters, with which the city abounds. These scoundrels represent themselves as members of Congress, or as belonging to one of the important branches of government, and offer their services to facilitate your business in any way that lies within their power, for which they ask a sum which varies with the nature of the business, or of the service they propose to render. Such men are simply imposters, who are constantly on the watch for strangers, out of whose simplicity and ignorance of public affairs they expect to reap a rich harvest. It is best to decline all offers of assistance in Washington, whether gratuitous or for a stated compensation, unless the party making the offer is known to you as a man of integrity and capable of carrying out his promises.

courtesy visit Brief appointment with a legislator staged by a lobbyist or lawyer for a client. It is a ritual by which an **influence peddler** displays clout.

court stripping Taking away from the federal courts the power to decide certain cases. Efforts by conservatives, never successful, would have shifted to state courts the jurisdiction for such matters as busing to achieve racial desegregation and school prayer.

cover A safe position; for instance, voting for a bill that has no chance of passing. This was applied in 1992 to a balanced budget bill that would provide lawmakers with political cover while opposing a constitutional amendment on the same subject. *Newsweek* explained this term in 1989: "Among the favorite words in everyday Capitol Hill conversation is *cover;* it is a noun meaning a position on an issue that is structured so as to avoid any political cost." Rep. Patricia Schroeder (D-Colo.) gave the term new imagery in October 1992, describing President George Bush's tax-credit alternative to the family leave bill as "asbestos underwear to cover his backside."

cover-up An attempt to conceal or minimize an illegal or un-ethical act. The authors of *The Dictionary of American Slang*, Harold Wentworth and Stuart Berg Flexner, cite its use as a term for concealment as early as 1949 when, in a movie called *Johnny Alegro*, a character says: "The phoning is just a cover-up." Along with **smoking gun**, cover-up is a term that will be everlastingly tied to the **Watergate** conspiracy.

cracking In **redistricting**, the fragmenting of minority communities into many districts, thus diluting minority voting strength. *See also* **packing** and **stacking.**

crib sheet A piece of paper or index card with points to be made during a floor speech.

crony Longtime friend. In politics the term denotes, not flatteringly, any close acquaintance or ally.

cross-filing In California, before 1959, Republicans and Democrats were allowed to run in each other's primaries and were occasionally nominated by both parties. In such a case, there would not be a general election.

cross the aisle To vote with the other party; to figuratively cross to the other side of the chamber where the opposition sits.

crosswalk To shift budgetary amounts from one classification to another.

CRS Initialism for **Congressional Research Service.**

C-SPAN Acronym for the Cable Satellite Public Affairs Network, the cable television network that began gavel-to-gavel House coverage in 1986 and began telecasting U.S. Senate proceedings on June 2, 1986.

It is worth noting that C-SPAN neither originates the signal nor controls the cameras. The special cable network simply picks up the feed provided by the House and Senate television facilities; it adds chamber music during quorum calls and votes to fill periods of inactivity.

cutaway Television term for filming a reporter asking questions and listening to answers after an interview. This practice gives the editors more than one camera angle and thus allows them to more smoothly edit an interview. A daily scene on the Capitol grounds is of television reporters being filmed apparently listening and talking to no one.

CYA Initialism for "cover your ass." The expression for the common practice in government and politics of protecting oneself from criticism and making sure that one's decisions are authorized, in writing, or cannot be traced at all.

czar

1 In Congress, an autocratic, dictatorial leader, usually a speaker of the House or a committee chairman. When Thomas B. Reed (R-Me.) threw out the **disappearing quorum** in 1890 and pushed through other reforms, he was vilified as a "czar" and a "tyrant."

The title was also bestowed on "Uncle Joe" Cannon, the Illinois Republican who reigned as speaker from 1903 to 1911. Former Rep. Fred Schwengel (R-Iowa), more recently director of the U.S. Capitol Historical Society, said Cannon held absolute power over committee assignments. "You signed a letter of resignation from the committee when you joined," he said. "If a guy didn't behave, Uncle Joe put a date on it and you had resigned." *See* **Cannonism.**

2 In the executive branch, czars are not always dictators. "Drug Czar," for instance, is merely shorthand for director of drug enforcement activities.

Etymology: The term for the omnipotent ruler of Russia until the 1917 Revolution was first applied to any despotic politician or industrialist and later found its way into other walks of life. When Judge Kenesaw Mountain Landis became Commissioner of Baseball in the wake of the 1919 "Black Sox Scandal," he was given extraordinary powers. Landis was fond of saying, "Czar is what they call me when they don't call me rogue."

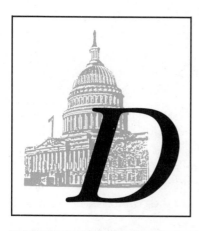

D Conventional abbreviation for Democrat, as in "D-S.C." for a Democratic member from South Carolina.

"Daily Digest" A section at the back of each day's *Congressional Record* that summarizes chamber action and committee meetings in the House and Senate.

damage control After an embarrassing incident or costly vote, aides and political operatives invoke countermeasures, such as press conferences and calls to reporters, to soften the unfavorable publicity. Damage control follows a damage assessment, also conducted by aides.

dance card A daily schedule of meetings produced by a member's staff.

Dance with the one who brung you Pay attention to voters and supporters who put you in office or you won't be there long. This expression is usually used as an admonition to politicians not to forget their political base, the constituents who elected them.

dark The condition of not having any paid advertising during a campaign. Media strategists say that "going dark" because of a shortage of funds is an almost unthinkable mistake, because a candidate cannot then respond to attacks. "That is such a void, any opponent can crush you," said Dan Walter of the Media Team, a Republican media consulting firm.

dark horse Politician not known to be a candidate who, at a deadlocked convention, unexpectedly receives the nomination.

ETYMOLOGY: This term derives from racing slang for a little-known horse that unexpectedly goes to the front. The term made the jump from horse racing to politics later in the nineteenth century, when it was applied to a candidate nominated without advance publicity. According to the 10th edition of the *Merriam-Webster College Dictionary*, it first shows up in the context of horse racing in 1831.

In *A Browser's Dictionary*, John Ciardi makes the fascinating point that the term was coined by British statesman and novelist Benjamin Disraeli in a book, *The Young Duke*, published in 1831. A line in the book refers to "A dark horse which had never been heard of..." sweeping to triumph. Ciardi reported that the term moved to British track usage to American tracks and then to politics.

dark side of the moon A contemptuous characterization of the minority party in the House. The phrase is also used to describe anything that is obscure or covert. In a December 18, 1992, Public Television special, comedian Mark Russell said that the dark side of the moon is "the stuff the CIA unveils to the new president."

day parts Those parts of a day in which media time is bought: for instance, A.M. news, soap opera, early news, prime time, late news. A potential audience, whether it is the elderly, working couples, or stay-at-homes, is reached by targeting parts of the day when they watch television.

dead The status of legislation after being defeated or inviting so much opposition that it has no chance of passage.

dead duck A politician who is sure to be defeated.

deadlock Term used to describe the common static condition in which Congress and the executive branch frequently find themselves. The distrust, bickering, and undercutting of each other's authority grew during the 1980s and led to a characterization of the two branches as being hopelessly deadlocked. A March 1992 report from the National Academy of Public Administration, entitled *Beyond Distrust: Building Bridges Between Congress and the Executive,* warned that unless reason could prevail, deadlock would create long-lasting damage to government.

dead on arrival Describing the condition of White House measures that are sent to Congress despite overwhelming opposition and the likelihood of defeat.

deadwood Useless politicans who, like the dead branches of a decaying tree, should be removed. In fighting words during his 1992 re-election campaign, President George Bush remarked that the deadwood in Congress should be discarded. Rep. Pat Schroeder (D-Colo.) responded with a new metaphor for the White House: "petrified forest."

deal Congress relies on legislative transactions to make things work: deals between lawmakers, deals with interest groups, deals with the executive branch. During the months-long negotiations over the Clean Air Act in 1990, every section of the massive bill was locked in a deal with the White House, and any amendment that did not measure up was called a *deal breaker,* one that would invite a veto.

Opposing an amendment to require cleaner-burning gasoline, Sen. Max Baucus (D-Mont.) said, "This is a deal breaker. It is a deal breaker because, if it passes, it will seriously jeopardize the passage of any clean air legislation this year."

dean

1 Senior member of a state's legislative delegation.

2 Longest-serving member of a legislative body or political group. In his book *American Freedom and the Radical Right,* Edward L. Ericson describes North Carolina Republican Jesse Helms as "dean of the New Right in the Senate."

Dear Colleague Traditional salutation used in letters in which one member asks another for support or cosponsorship of a bill. In Sue Grabowski's *Congressional Intern Handbook* (1986), this term is deftly defined as a "hustle" in the form of a letter.

Dean of the Senate George W. Norris (Ind.-Neb.), seated, is shown on the last day of his 40-year Senate career in 1943. Conferring with him is Sen. Guy M. Gillette (D-Iowa). *See* **dean.**

death-squad Democrats Late 1980s label, coined by their critics, for Democrats who supported right-wing dictators in Latin America.

death watch Description by former Speaker Jim Wright (D-Tex.) of the intense media attention before his June 6, 1989, forced resignation for improprieties in office. He said it "makes one feel like a hunted animal driven to his lair." *See also* **feeding frenzy.**

debate Argumentation and discussion in Congress while examining bills and issues. In the House, the time of debate on any given matter is restricted by the **Rules Committee.** There is a one-hour rule in the House, but during debate over amendments in the **Committee of the Whole,** a five-minute rule applies, with many speakers being allocated only a minute or two. Rules that have become increasingly strict in the House in recent years make spontaneous debate impossible. So-called **modified closed rules** limit amendments to those approved by the

"A stormy sitting."

This drawing from an 1888 *Harper's Weekly* depicts a Senate shorthand reporter, cool-headed in the eye of the storm. *See* **debate.**

TALK, TALK, TALK

In 1963 reporter Arthur Edson of the Associated Press created his own "Congressional Glossary of Terms," which included this entry:

Debate—House version   Don't be misled by this word; in the House, there is no such thing.

With 435 members, time is severely limited. On important issues, where everyone wants to talk, a congressman thinks he has hit the jackpot if he gets as much as five minutes at the House microphone.

So he gets his great opportunity and drones until time runs out and the gavel falls. Orator follows orator, with hardly anyone listening to what is said—except, possibly, the fellow doing the talking.

Possibly no vote is ever changed by House debates. That's why they are usually attended by a smattering of members, chiefly those waiting to get into the act.

The House is the exact reverse of a fancy shop which uses its showcases to tempt the customers to buy. If you want to appreciate the House, you have to march right in to the committees, where the work is done, and investigate the interesting stuff on the shelves yourself.

Edson defined "Senate style" this way: "It is not true that senators talk longer and say less than any other similar body in the world. It only seems that way."

Rules Committee, so there can be no surprises. Speeches, often no longer than one minute, are scripted for television and, because they take up all allotted time, leave no room for give-and-take between opponents. There are no such restrictions in the Senate, where members may speak as long as they wish, as long as they do not **yield** the floor. Furthermore, debate in the House must be **germane**, or relevant to the matter at hand, whereas in the Senate germaneness is required—but rarely enforced—for the first three hours only. The only brakes applied to Senate speech-making during debate are **unanimous consent** agreements. As a result of the differences, the length of legislative debate is predictable in the House and, until agreements are reached or **cloture** invoked, totally unpredictable in the Senate.

In his book *Both Your Houses: The Truth About Congress,* journalist Warren Weaver, Jr., says debate in the Senate consists of a series of unrelated, "end-to-end speeches," to which no one listens. The senators are influenced by their mail, by lobbyists, "their wives, their mistresses, their staff, and their indigestion. But not by debate." *See box,* "Talk, Talk, Talk."

debt, federal The amount of money owed by the American public as a result of federal borrowing. Early in 1993, the debt stood at $4.2 trillion. Interest to be paid in 1993 was projected to be $214 billion.

Declaration of Conscience A 1950 manifesto against Sen. Joseph McCarthy (R-Wisc.) written by Sen. Margaret Chase Smith of Maine and other Republicans deploring the "selfish political

"Congressional row, in the U.S. House of Representatives, midnight of Friday, February 5th, 1858."

In this engraving from *Frank Leslie's Illustrated Newspaper,* Rep. "Bowie Knife" Potter (left) is pulling off the wig of Rep. William B. Barksdale; Potter held the wig over Barksdale's head and proclaimed, "Hurrah boys, I've got his scalp," causing an uproar of laughter. The fight arose over the issue of slavery. *See* **decorum.**

exploitation of fear, bigotry, ignorance, and intolerance" of which "certain elements of the Republican party" were guilty. McCarthy was never mentioned by name in the declaration. The strategy failed and McCarthy was not stopped until four years later. *See* **McCarthyism.**

decorum An elaborate code of proper congressional conduct and appearance, from attire to speech-making. It is improper in the House, for instance, to impugn the motives of a colleague, and disorderly words, after being re-read by the clerk, may be "taken down," or stripped from the record, by ruling of the chair. *See also* **words taken down.**

Smoking is forbidden, and hats (once required while sitting, not while debating) may not be worn. Coats and ties for men and "appropriate attire" for women are required. On July 17, 1979, Speaker Tip O'Neill (D-Mass.) requested that a House member without a tie leave and return properly dressed, and O'Neill would not recognize the member until he did so. Interfering with a speaker is not permitted, although an opponent may ask if the gentleman or gentlelady will yield for a question. *Jefferson's Manual,* the collection of procedural rules by which the House generally abides, also discourages "hissing, coughing, spitting, speaking, or whispering to another." *See box,* "Not in This Committee."

deep background An arrangement with the media in which an official gives information on condition that the reporter may use the material but may not quote directly from it or attribute it to anyone. This practice differs sharply from **background** interviews, which yield information that reporters can use crediting unnamed "congressional sources" or "administration sources." *See also* **backgrounder**, **deep throat**, *and* **on background**.

deep-six To destroy incriminating evidence in a political scandal.

ETYMOLOGY: The noun for burial at sea, in at least six fathoms, became a verb during the 1973 **Watergate** hearings. White House counsel John Dean said he had been instructed by President

Richard Nixon's domestic affairs advisor, John Ehrlichman, to consign to the deep a briefcase that held incriminating documents.

deep throat A generous but protected confidential source. This term derives from the code name given to the informant who helped *Washington Post* reporters Bob Woodward and Carl Bernstein unravel the **Watergate** scandal in the 1970s. The phrase was inspired by a 1972 X-rated movie of the same name. *See also* **deep background.**

deferral Action or inaction that delays the expenditure of funds. Deferrals may not extend beyond the end of the then-current fiscal year.

deficit The excess of budget outlays over receipts. President Bill Clinton pledged to cut the deficit, which was running at about $300 billion in 1993, to $200 billion by 1997. The budget approved by the House in March 1993 was supposed to cut the deficit to $184 billion by 1997.

deficit spending An excess of government spending over revenues. In 1992, in spite of budget-cutting laws and agreements, the deficit was about $290 billion, considerably short of the $400 billion predicted in January—largely because of lower spending on failed savings and loan institutions. Frustrated over their inability to do anything about the deficit, several prominent members of Congress quit. Noting the discontent, Sen. John C. Danforth (R-Mo.) said in a March 29, 1992, letter to the *Washington Post,* "Deep down in our hearts we believe that we have been accomplices to doing something terrible and unforgivable to this wonderful country. Deep down in our hearts we know that we have bankrupted America and that we have given our children a legacy of bankruptcy."

delaying tactics Methods used by a bill's opponents to postpone a sure outcome. Such tactics include engaging in a **filibuster**, demanding **quorum calls**, and forcing time-consuming **roll-call** votes on insubstantial amendments. Explaining why he forced such votes during the 1993 budget debates, Rep. Dan

"Nonsense! If it gets too deep, you can easily pull me out!"

Cartoonist Herbert Johnson depicts the plight of the Milquetoastian taxpayer in the grasp of the ample personification of government spending. *See* **deficit**.

Burton (R-Ind.) said, "If a guy pushes you around the schoolyard and you punch him in the mouth just one time, sometimes he gets the idea that it's better to work with you than against you." *See also* **bunker mode**.

delegates In addition to the 435 members of the House of Representatives, there are 5 delegates (one each from Puerto Rico, the Virgin Islands, Guam, American Samoa, and the District of Columbia) who may make speeches, serve and vote on committees and hold chairmanships. In 1993 they were given the right to vote on the House floor but only when their votes are not critical to the outcome. In response to a Republican suit challenging their vote privilege, U.S. District Judge Harold H. Greene said it was legal, but only because it was "symbolic" and "meaningless."

deliberative body *See* **world's greatest deliberative body.**

demagogue One who attempts to gain politically by appeals to emotion or prejudice. This term is also used as a verb, as in "Thou shalt not demagogue thy colleagues," an oft-cited congressional commandment. *Demagoguery,* the practice of the above, is an Americanism coined in 1855.

demagogue it To take a dramatic, **grandstanding** position on an issue without necessarily supporting or believing in the position; to mislead with spirit. The *New York Times* reported on September 16, 1982, that this "Capitol Hill verb" was introduced by Sen. Joseph Biden (D-Del.) when he remarked, "Ten years ago, I could sit in a closed committee meeting and say that I couldn't go along with something, but if they'd let me demagogue it for a while, I wouldn't stand in the way." However, *Times* readers questioned whether Biden was the originator.

Democrat A member of the Democratic Party, which emerged after the War of 1812 as an egalitarian response to Federalist notions of a centralized government. Democrats have drawn much of their strength from the South, from labor unions, and from urban ethnic minorities. In the 1980s, the party's association with welfare programs helped contribute to its decline nationally. Democrats have controlled Congress in recent decades, but they seemed incapable of gaining the White House until President Bill Clinton's election in 1992.

Democratic

1 Relating to government by the people.

2 Describing something related to the Democratic party by a Democrat; however, when a true-blue Republican speaks of something relating to the loyal opposition, it is often stated as *Democrat,* as in Democrat party or Democrat Convention. In their *Harper Dictionary of Contemporary Usage,* lexicographers William Morris and Mary Morris note without equivocation that " 'Democrat party' is the idiotic creation of some of the least responsible members of the Republican party."

Democratic Steering and Policy Committee A group of House members appointed by the speaker who meet to fill committee vacancies and make policy decisions, subject to the approval of the Democratic Caucus. Each region of the country is represented on the committee. This is a Democratic innovation, succeeding the former **Committee on Committees** in the early 1980s. It is the engine of Democratic control of the House and could one day be replaced by a Republican counterpart if the GOP gains control. *See also* **policy committee.**

Democratic Study Group (DSG) This coalition of reform-minded House Democrats grew out of mid-1950s efforts to strip power from autocratic committee chairmen. It continues to press for reforms and to keep members abreast of issues through daily bulletins and reports. One of its most popular publications is a listing of job openings on Capitol Hill. *See also* **policy committee.**

demonstration Demand for action or support by Congress. There are demonstrations of all sorts, with speakers, banners, songs, and slogans, almost daily on the Capitol steps.

demonstration project A project that is supposed to demonstrate the usefulness of a new transportation technology. In reality, such projects have become favorite mechanisms for **earmarking** funds for congressional districts. Hundreds of these projects, called *demos* by some but **pork barrel** projects by others, are traditionally sprinkled throughout House transportation bills. Most highway and mass transit spending is controlled by state governments, which have to come up with matching funds, but demos are exempt from matching requirements, thus their popularity.

Dems Short for Democrats, a term as beloved by headline writers as **GOP** is for Republicans.

denounce To condemn strongly in public. Being denounced by one's colleagues is a slightly milder rebuke than being **censured.** In 1975 the Senate denounced Herman Talmadge (D-Ga.) for using public and campaign funds for personal use. There are

Not all demonstrations are against something. Here, early 1970s Hill supporters of President Richard Nixon and his Vietnam War policy express their views. *See* **demonstration.**

All Democrats with impeccable credentials, from left to right, Senators Edward Long, Stewart Symington, Claiborne Pell, and Hubert Humphrey, greeting former President Harry S Truman in May 1964. *See* **Dems.**

no penalties beyond the public humiliation associated with this measure.

deperk To eliminate the **perks** of office, including cheap haircuts, taxpayer-funded trips, and the like. The term gained currency in the wake of the **House Bank** scandal of 1992, as public pressure grew to get rid of perks. Here is how the term was used by *USA Today* in its issue of April 9, 1992: "Despite congressional promises to 'deperk' special services for Congress remain."

deputy One who acts as a substitute or assistant for another; often referred to as "trusted deputy" or lieutenant.

deputy whip An assistant to a **whip**. The deputy helps the whip get an informal count of votes on important issues and stay in touch with party caucuses. There are chief deputy whips, deputy whips, and assistant deputy whips.

designated hitter A member of Congress who can be counted on to drive in political runs, or points, on a variety of issues, as opposed to a **gatekeeper,** who is limited by committee jurisdiction to a limited range of issues. "To be a designated hitter, you have to be playing above your pay grade," said Rep. Dennis Eckart (D-Ohio), who resigned in 1992. *Compare* **cleanup hitter.**

Etymology: The term comes from baseball, specifically the American League, in which since 1973 a player who does not take the field is designated as a hitter in place of the pitcher.

dilatory motion A motion that is made to kill time and obstruct passage of a bill. Such motions are usually based on a technicality and may be stopped by rulings of the presiding officer.

Dingellgrams Pentagon slang for frequent, lengthy letters from Rep. John Dingell (D-Mich.), one of the House's top investigators, who frequently roasts the Defense Department about procurement abuses.

Dirksen Doctrine Principle espoused in 1966 by the late Sen. Everett Dirksen (R-Ill.), who took the position that the nation needed more direct democracy. He believed that state legislatures (through the process of ratification) or the people (through a constitutional convention) should be given greater opportunities to make known their will.

Dirksen's Three Laws of Politics Oft-quoted during and after his time in the Senate, the late Sen. Everett Dirksen (R-Ill.) authored three bits of basic advice: (1) Get elected. (2) Get reelected. (3) Don't get mad, get even. Dirksen was one of the Senate's great aphorists; during the 1973 Arab Oil Embargo he authored the line, "The oil can is mightier than the sword." *See box,* "Beyond Dirksen: The Laws That Govern Those Who Govern."

BEYOND DIRKSEN: THE LAWS THAT GOVERN THOSE WHO GOVERN

While few politicians anywhere have lost sight of Dirksen's Laws, there are other rules, laws, and dictums, mostly lighthearted, that have been written to explain the workings of Congress and elective politics:

Foley's Political "Don'ts" (1) Don't go to spelling bees [uttered in 1992 shortly after Vice-President Dan Quayle had spelled potato with an "e" at a spelling bee]. (2) Don't shoot muzzle-loading rifles at targets. (3) Don't ride horses at rodeos. Don't even ride them in parades. (4) Never ride in a Rolls-Royce.
    —*House Speaker Thomas Foley (D-Wash.), quoted in the* Washington Times, *June 23, 1992*

Galbraith's Law of Junkets A junket is any business trip which if taken by anyone but yourself would be considered unnecessary.
Congressional Testimony: A lie at a congressional hearing gets you by for the moment at the cost of trouble later on.
    —*Economist John Kenneth Galbraith*

Hart's 13th Law of Political Economics Financial markets will tolerate a Republican deficit but will run screaming in panic from a Democratic deficit a fraction its size.
    —*Sen. Gary Hart (D-Colo.) in the* Houston Chronicle, *July 21, 1988*

Kelleher's Explanation The Congress is constitutionally empowered to launch programs the scope, impact, consequences, and workability of which are largely unknown, at least to the Congress, at the time of enactment; the federal bureaucracy is legally permitted to execute the congressional mandate with a high degree of befuddlement as long as it acts no more befuddled than the Congress must reasonably have anticipated.
    —*U.S. District Court Judge Robert Kelleher, Central District, California,* American Petroleum Institute v. Knecht, *August 31, 1978*

Korologos's Laws (1) The length of your answer in a public hearing has a direct and inverse ratio to the truth. (2) The closer you get to congressional recesses the better good government you get. (3) Congresses do two things best: nothing and overreact. (4) When 51 senators tell you they'll be with you if needed, you've got a problem. (5) "Thank God! They killed the prayer amendment."
    —*Lobbyist Tom C. Korologos, Great Falls, Va.*

---

dirty dozen An annual list, which received much attention in the 1970s, of congressional members with the worst environmental voting records, in the opinion of a group called Environmental Action.

dirty laundry Past misdeeds that can be damaging in later settings like confirmation hearings or election campaigns.

dirty tricks Political shenanigans employed by one party or candidate against another. Before **Watergate,** the crown prince of dirty tricks was Dick Tuck, a onetime Democratic campaign worker, who managed, during a rally for presidential candidate Barry Goldwater, to have a helicopter descend with an illuminated message saying, "In your heart, you know he's nuts," a take-off on Goldwater's slogan, "In your heart you know he's right." But dirty tricks developed a bad image during Richard Nixon's 1972 reelection campaign and have largely disappeared from the political scene.

disappearing quorum A quorum that vanishes when those present fail to answer. Apparently begun in 1832 by John Quincy Adams, this obstructionist tactic prevented the House from acting when members present in the chamber kept silent as their names were called. Speaker Thomas B. Reed, a Maine Republican, put a stop to it on January 29, 1890, when he simply counted those present. "I deny your right, Mr. Speaker, to count me as present," one man shouted. But Reed was firm. "The chair is making a statement of fact that the gentleman from Kentucky is present. Does he deny it?" The disappearing quorum disappeared.

discharge

1 A time-saving method, requiring unanimous consent, of moving noncontroversial bills to the House or Senate floor, discharging a committee from further consideration.

2 In the House, a discharge petition signed by at least 218 members, a majority, removes a bill from the control of a recalcitrant committee. Because it is seen as an affront to the chairperson of the committee—even though the bill has long languished there—the discharge route is rarely taken.

disciple   In politics, one who follows the teachings or philosophy of another.

discipline   The measure of a party's ability to keep members in line by meting out punishment for straying from the leadership's program. It is said to be waning in Congress as individual members gain in strength, but discipline is still used. Rep. Dennis Eckart (D-Ohio) said in a 1992 interview that when he voted against a congressional pay raise, a member of the Steering and Policy Committee, which controls committee assignments, told Eckart that his vote cost him a coveted seat on the Budget Committee.

The word *discipline* is also frequently used in talking about the budget; discipline is needed to keep legislators from violating budget agreements.

In an August 25, 1992, interview, House Speaker Thomas S. Foley (D-Wash.) said of his power to discipline: "It doesn't exist in the sense of a drumhead court martial or in terms of imprisonment, but it is true that most members have some interest in the good opinion of the leadership." As for punishing members by denying them choice committee assignments, Foley said this is more likely to happen after an accumulation of votes. "It's hardly ever a single vote," he said.

discretionary spending   Spending that is not guaranteed by **entitlements.** This increasingly shrinking authority was split into three categories—defense, domestic, and international—by the 1990 budget agreement.

dishonoraria   Derogatory term, created ca. 1990, for the **honoraria** paid to members of Congress.

dispose   To settle conclusively, but also to get rid of or throw away. Thus, the adage, "The president proposes, the Congress disposes," can be seen as either a positive or a negative power.

dissident triangle   This "power network," as Hedrick Smith calls it in his book, *The Power Game,* operates between the

Pentagon's internal critics, their allies in Congress, and the press, with news leaks about program failures or procurement scandals as the common currency.

distinguished   Common term of address used in Congress, not always sincere, as in "The distinguished senator from ——."

district

1   Members' geographical jurisdiction and the home grounds of their constituents. Representatives are concerned about their districts; senators about their states.

2   By extension and metaphorically, the House itself, as in this line from Christopher Matthews' book, *Hardball:* "For the leadership, the House is the district."

3   Washington, D.C., itself; the District [of Columbia].

district days/district work period   Time off from Washington to go home and work on constituent matters. The House has a periodic schedule of district work days; the Senate takes off one week each month. This practice has been abused by some members, who use it as vacation time.

district office   A satellite office located in a member's home district.

division vote   Procedure for counting heads in the House when a **voice vote** is inconclusive. Members are literally asked to stand and be counted. Now, with electronic voting, which can be ordered by one-fifth of a **quorum**, this procedure is practically obsolete, as is the **teller vote.**

Dixiecrat   Name given to the 1948 breakaway presidential candidate, renegade Democrat Strom Thurmond. It is still used to identify some conservative Southern Democrats or to describe the vestiges of segregationalist sentiment. The term is a blend of "Dixie" and "Democrat."

dogfight   A close and nasty political battle, not unlike the contests between fighter aircraft at close quarters or actual canine combat.

-doggle Suffix for that which is excessive and wasteful of public funds, from **boondoggle.** One example of its application is the term *moondoggle,* used by those who saw the Apollo moon program as a waste. It is, however, sometimes used in a strictly congressional context. In 1982 when the Senate was voting itself money for its third gymnasium, the *Washington Post* coined the term *gymdoggle.*

dome The white Capitol dome, capped by the **Statue of Freedom,** that was completed during the Civil War. President Lincoln had ordered work to continue on it during the conflict as "a sign that the Union shall go on." It is symbolic of Congress both as a term ("under the dome") and as an image.

domestic policy In Congress, all matters that are not foreign policy. President Harry Truman once warned that domestic policy can hurt you, but foreign policy can kill you.

done deal A deal to which all parties have agreed and about which there is no doubt it will be consummated.

donor states The states that pay more in federal highway taxes than they get back in transportation funds.

Do-Nothing Congress Democratic President Harry Truman's withering characterization of the Republican-controlled 80th Congress in 1948.

After the querulous 11-day **Turnip Session,** to which Truman summoned Congress in July 1948, ended in deadlock, a reporter asked: "Would you say it was a do-nothing session, Mr. President?"

"I would say it was entirely a do-nothing session," Truman replied. "I think that's a good name for the 80th Congress."

don't ask, don't tell A plan advanced by Senate Armed Services Chairman Sam Nunn (D-Ga.) as a compromise to President Bill Clinton's proposal to lift the ban on gays in the military. The compromise essentially keeps the ban but strikes a deal: the services may not ask about sexual orientation and the recruits may not talk about it. Rep. Barney Frank (D-Mass.), a leading advocate

The Capitol dome at night, with
the Robert A. Taft Carillon in the
foreground. *See* **dome.**

Rep. John D. Dingell (D-Mich.) listens to Rep. Lud Ashley (D-Ohio) after completing work on an energy bill. *See* **done deal.**

of homosexual rights, went a step further: Don't ask, don't tell, don't listen, don't investigate.

doorkeeper A House official who has various duties, such as announcing official guests—including the president—delivering messages from the Senate and White House and overseeing documents, publications, **cloakrooms**, and **pages.** Until recently the job was a patronage job handled by the Speaker. Reforms now going into effect will remove future doorkeepers from purely political control. *See also* **sergeant-at-arms.**

An illuminating paragraph on the role of the doorkeeper appeared in the September 15, 1989, *Washington Post* obituary for William "Fishbait" Miller, the doorkeeper who had just died at age 80: "The job of doorkeeper, especially under Mr. Miller, was not what one might expect. Not only did he keep track of who was admitted to the House floor, but he also ruled a fiefdom that included more than 350 employees and an annual budget of $3.5 million."

double dipper A person who takes dual compensation from the government; typically but not always a military retiree, who takes

"Our Congressman"

Totally unflattering view of
a congressman as multiple-
dipper from an 1883 *Puck* magazine cover by Joseph Keppler.
See **double dipper.**

a salaried government job or serves in Congress while receiving
a military pension.

ETYMOLOGY: Term originated at the old-fashioned ice cream parlor
for a cone loaded with two scoops (or dips) of ice cream.

dove Legislator who is generally against military intervention by
the United States and opposed to most increases in military spending of any kind. The dove's opposite number is the **hawk;** a well-
known congressional watering hole is the "Hawk & Dove."

The metaphoric meanings of the terms hawk and dove were established during the Cuban missile crisis of 1962, got much play during the Vietnam War era beginning in early 1966, and are still widely used. In 1970, *Washington Post* reporter Murray Marder wrote a short article on the moment the terms came into being. During the missile crisis, two groups were formed in the White House to draft opposing recommendations on how the crisis should be resolved. A **CIA** analyst, Ray S. Cline, asked, "Which group do you want me to join, the, uh, warhawks...or the, uh, Picasso doves?" National Security Advisor McGeorge Bundy saw the applicability of the names and he began using them. They were popularized in a *Saturday Evening Post* article by writers Stewart Alsop and Charles L. Bartlett, who also pointed out that the blended terms *dawks* and *hoves* were soon being used for those straddling defense issues.

The terms were revived in January 1966 when a group of American military officials unofficially and without using their names began a campaign to intensify the war against North Vietnam. These advocates were instantly labeled "hawks," and within days the White House leaked word that President Lyndon Johnson was displeased with the pressure they were putting on him.

dovish Having the nature or convictions of a **dove.**

down to the wire *See* **horse race.**

downtown Off the **Hill**; any in-town department of government, including the **White House.**

draft a bill To prepare a bill in proper legal form.

drive-by shooting Expression heard in 1992 for the random and sometimes unwarranted ousting of members of Congress by disgruntled voters.

drop-by A brief appearance at a fund-raising event or party by a member. When Congress is in session, a member may have as many as three drop-bys in an evening.

DSG *See* **Democratic Study Group.**

duck

1 A pest or nuisance on the Hill, sometimes a lobbyist.

2 To dodge a controversial vote on the House or Senate floor, a question from the press, or a meeting with a clamorous constituent.

dues Whether being paid, collected, or owed, dues are part of an informal system of favors bestowed by members of Congress.

dugout/dugout session About 15 minutes before the opening prayer in the Senate, the majority leader meets with reporters in the **well** near the leader's desk to discuss the day's schedule and other matters. Since the time allotted is finite, the leader can adjust the number of questions by his or her time of arrival. No cameras or recording devices are permitted. Some in the House use the term to mean the speaker's press conference before each session, but it has not stuck.

ETYMOLOGY: Dugout, a term originally applied to dugout canoes and wartime trenches dug out of the ground, was embraced by baseball in the early twentieth century when the teams' benches were positioned below ground level and sheltered.

dugout chatter A summary of what the majority leader said during a **dugout session**, as reported by a press gallery representative, and posted in the Senate gallery. It is not to be used for direct quotation either by members or by the press.

dumbbell district A congressional district shaped like a dumbbell. *See* **gerrymander.**

eagles Wall Street Republican campaign contributors, usually those who dispense large sums of money.

earmark Write provisions into laws that instruct the executive branch to fund legislators' **pet projects.** There were more than 500 instances of this in the 1991 transportation bill, prompting then Transportation Secretary Samuel Skinner to brand the bill as **pork.** Sen. Daniel P. Moynihan (D-N.Y.) called the provisions "tiny jewels." Research grants for particular universities are commonly earmarked.

ETYMOLOGY: The word comes from the identifying tag attached to the ear of a domestic animal to show ownership.

earned income Because it creates a clear conflict, members of Congress, officers, and senior staff may receive outside earned income equal to no more than 15 percent of their salary. Earned income is defined as income from actual work done, as opposed to unearned income, which is generally from investments—and is not limited.

As the House Commission on Administrative Review said in 1977, earned income may pose a threat to a legislator's integrity in several ways, "ranging from overt attempts to curry favor by private groups to subtle distortions in the judgment of members in particular issues."

East Front That side of the Capitol facing the Library of Congress, the Supreme Court building, and the eastern quadrants of the city

The new East Front of the Senate wing of the Capitol, as it appeared when it was under construction. It was completed in 1861. *See* **East Front.**

of Washington. A new East Front was begun in 1958 and completed in 1962. It replicated the original but was 32 feet 6 inches east of the old Front. The old walls were left in place to become part of the interior wall, which is now buttressed by the new wall.

eat the carpet Abase oneself; crawl. This is what contrite, and perhaps endangered, nominees are expected to do at confirmation hearings. It was the advice given in early 1993 to Zoe Baird, President Bill Clinton's first nominee for attorney general, after revelations about her hiring illegal aliens appeared likely to sink her nomination. Baird withdrew.

Education Congress The 88th Congress (1963–64), so called because it approved several new education programs. But the 88th, with most of its important committees chaired by conservatives, was also known as the "goof-off" or "stop, look, and listen" Congress because so many other bills were smothered in committee.

egghead/egghead vote A political intellectual, and the following he or she energizes. According to the *Dorsey Dictionary of American Government and Politics* (1988), egghead was "first used in American politics to derisively refer to Adlai Stevenson." Stevenson, a liberal Democrat, was widely regarded as an intellectual. But with the launching of the Russian *Sputnik*, the term "did a reverse spin in the American mind" and came to denote higher standards in education, Irving Stone noted in his book *They Also Ran*.

election The formal process of choosing between candidates for public office by ballot. Representatives must stand for election every two years, senators every six.

electioneering Actively taking part in gaining votes for a person or an issue.

election-proof Adjective applied to either house at times when the reelection rate is particularly high. Said the *Baltimore Sun* in late 1989: "The fact is, the House has become almost election-proof.... In 1990, of 408 members seeking reelection, 402 won."

The 1992 casualty list was much longer, with 19 incumbents losing primaries and 24 losing in November. These casualties also included losses due to retirements, resignations, redistricting, and running for other offices.

electoral college The body of presidential electors, equal in number to each state's representation in Congress, as chosen by the voters in presidential elections. *See box*, "Balloting for President."

BALLOTING FOR PRESIDENT

Every four years the final tally in presidential elections takes place in Congress. In keeping with the 12th Amendment to the Constitution, following the presidential election in November, the electoral votes of each state are opened and counted at a joint session of Congress in early January. If no one receives a majority, the House of Representatives decides. But instead of one vote per member, there is one vote per state, determined by a poll of the delegation. This has happened twice. The first was in 1800 when Thomas Jefferson and his choice for vice-president, Aaron Burr, received the same number of votes. There was then no distinction between president and vice-president on the ballot. After 36 ballots Jefferson prevailed, and Burr was given the vice-presidency.

In 1824 a four-way split between John Quincy Adams, Henry Clay, William H. Crawford, and Andrew Jackson threw the election into the House. The three top vote-getters—Jackson with 99, Adams with 84, and Crawford with 41—were placed in nomination. Clay, who had received 37 electoral votes, threw his support to Adams, who narrowly won. Clay was named secretary of state, stirring up a storm of protest that he and Adams had cut a deal to bar Jackson from the presidency.

---

electronic vote Vote by means of the computerized voting system in the House. **Roll-call** votes and **quorum calls**, with 435 members to tally, once went on interminably because they were oral. The speedier automated system, with its red and green tote board that lights up the wall above the speaker's desk, was installed in 1972. The Senate still uses verbal "ayes" and "noes," often indicated by thumbs up or down.

elevator phenomenon The predictable inflating of new senators' and representatives' egos when they realize that they have, among other perquisites, private elevators at their disposal. The phenomenon was first noted by Mark Green and Michael Waldman in their book *Who Runs Congress?* (1984). *See* **perk.**

Eleventh Commandment Respected political saw that holds: "Thou shalt not attack a colleague of the same party—at least not in public."

EMILY's List Acronym for the organization that took its name from the motto Early money is like yeast, and raises money for a list of female Democratic candidates. With the surge of interest in women running for office, the group's membership grew from 3,000 to 12,000 in 1992, with expected donations of more than $3 million. *See also* **wish list.**

empowerment The act of giving or conferring power. The word was popular among 1960s liberals who pushed for voting empowerment of minorities and among 1990s conservatives who sought to empower minorities through economic incentives.

enabling legislation A bill designed to give specific authority to a government official or unit of government to enter into agreements.

enact To **pass** legislation.

enacting clause The words in a bill that give it power. The clause starts with the words "Be it enacted that..." If a motion to strike the enacting clause succeeds, the bill is dead.

engrossed bill The official final copy of a bill that has been passed by the House or Senate. It includes any changes that have been made as a consequence of floor action. It must be certified by the secretary of the Senate or the clerk of the House.

ETYMOLOGY: The term goes back to the Declaration of Independence, which was to be "fairly engrossed on parchment." In this sense it means to write a final copy in large letters.

enhanced rescission authority A proposed modified **line-item veto** concept that would allow a president to make specific spending cuts if a majority of both houses approves.

enrolled bill A bill that has been passed in identical form by the House and the Senate, printed on parchment, and passed on for the signatures of the House speaker, the Senate president, and the president of the United States.

entitlements Programs, such as Medicare, Medicaid, and veterans' benefits, that must be provided to all eligible persons who seek them, with the added assurance of legal recourse if they are not. Total entitlements and other mandatory programs cost $766.8 billion in fiscal 1993, or more than half the federal budget. Cutting them has become an explosive issue—"a live third rail," an aide to Sen. Pete Domenici (R-N.M.) was quoted as saying.

"Suggestions to cut Medicare or other entitlements to pay for tax cuts will be rejected on a bipartisan basis, as they have in the past," Ways and Means Committee Chairman Dan Rostenkowski declared on February 4, 1992, responding to President Bush's plan to finance tax cuts with offsetting reductions in mandatory spending programs.

ERA Equal Rights Amendment. Failed constitutional amendment that would have prohibited discrimination based on gender.

errand boy A member of Congress who is distinguished not for legislative leadership but for helping constituents in their dealings with the federal bureaucracy. The term was invested with new meaning in the Senate's savings and loan scandal in 1990. Senators Alan Cranston (D-Calif.), Dennis DeConcini (R-Ariz.), and Donald Riegle (D-Mich.) were branded "errand boys" for former savings and loan kingpin Charles Keating, who was convicted of wrongdoing. In exchange for campaign contributions, it was charged, they made phone calls to federal regulators on Keating's behalf.

establishment Congress's first commandment is that it "shall make no law respecting an establishment of religion." But in modern times *establishment* has less to do with the church than with entrenched power. The Eastern Liberal Establishment, including Ivy League graduates and the press, was condemned by the political right for pushing social legislation. But in Congress, the establishment once consisted of mostly conservative committee chairmen.

ethics A code of official conduct by which members, officers, and employees are expected to abide. Generally, they are expected to reflect credit on the institution, avoiding conflicts of interest, declining lavish **gifts**, and not converting campaign funds for personal use. Nor may they discriminate in hiring or put **ghost employees** on their payrolls.

ethics thing, the A facetious term used to describe the widespread concern over Congressional ethics. At the time of the ethics investigation into Speaker James Wright's financial improprieties in 1989, members were heard to grumble that the "ethics thing" had gone too far.

"Ev and Charlie Show" Any exhibition that combines partisan politics with fatuous comedy. The term derives from the names of two former leaders of the Republican minority in Congress, Sen. Everett Dirksen and Rep. Charles Halleck, who made joint monthly television appearances during the 1960s. The show was a popular Washington institution, but author Robert J. Donovan dismissed it as "this harlequinade." It was succeeded by the "Ev and Jerry Show" when a new minority leader, Jerry Ford, replaced Halleck.

Everest Committee A congressional team organized to investigate something just because, like Mount Everest, it's there. Humorist Will Rogers once wrote of the compulsion to form committees, "I hear tell, Congress is a mite concerned with its members' tendency to form a committee at the drop of a hat. But everything's all right now. Congress has just announced it's forming a committee to investigate."

excess campaign funds Funds left over from congressional races; also known as *leftovers, leftover funds*; or **rainy-day war chest**. A **grandfather clause** allowed those who were members on January 8, 1980, the date the rules governing such funds changed, to leave Congress by the end of 1992 and pocket their leftover campaign funds. This was an added incentive for some older members to quit by the end of that year. Some who did had more than $500,000 in their campaign accounts. *See also* **cash on hand** *and* **kitty.**

Ev Dirksen (foreground) with Charles Halleck. *See* **Ev & Charlie Show.**

exclusion The process of preventing a member-elect from taking a seat in Congress on the grounds that the newcomer lacks the credentials for membership. Congress has used the polygamy practice of Mormons and the possible disloyalty of Southerners during the Civil War as pretexts for barring would-be members, but in 1967, when the House shut its doors to flamboyant Harlem Democrat Adam Clayton Powell, charging he misused public funds, the Supreme Court drew the line. In ordering Powell reinstated, the court said Congress must confine itself to the constitutional requirements of age and residency.

Had the House allowed Powell to be sworn in and then, by a two-thirds majority vote, expelled him for cause, there would not have been a constitutional question, scholars say.

exclusive committee The Ways and Means and Appropriations committees. House members assigned to either of these committees may sit on no other committee.

executive business Senate action that has to do with the executive branch, such as confirming nominees and ratifying treaties.

Executive Calendar List of actions such as treaty ratifications and confirmations of presidential appointments in which the Senate alone has constitutional authority.

executive privilege Doctrine under which the president or members of his cabinet may refuse to give information to Congress to safeguard confidential memos and protect the flow of ideas within an administration. The most dramatic clash occurred in 1974 over President Richard Nixon's refusal to provide Oval Office tapes to **Watergate** investigators. "Executive poppycock," drawled Senate Watergate Chairman Sam Ervin (D-N.C.). The Supreme Court ruled unanimously that Nixon must hand over the tapes.

executive session A legislative session or hearing closed to the public and the press. It is so named because the Senate once conducted **executive business** in secret. It is also called a **secret session**.

exemption

1 The long-established system by which Congress excuses itself from abiding by the laws it imposes on others (*see box,* "Do As I Say, Not As I Do"). In 1988, Henry Hyde (R-Ill.) said, "Congress would exempt itself from the laws of gravity if it could." In April 1992, President George Bush, warming to his anti-Congress theme, said, "Congress should govern itself by the laws it imposes on others. No more special treatment." At February 4, 1993, hearings aimed at reforming Congress, Rep. Jay Dickey (R-Ark.) said, "Voters are fed up with us being treated like we're some type of royalty up here."

2 A tax break for a particular person or company, or for a special class of people or companies, enacted by Congress.

exile Banishment from leadership posts, sardonically overstated.

ex officio By virtue of one's position. Committee chairmen may be ex officio members of each of the subcommittees of the main committee.

exposure Public awareness of a politician's positions, especially in the media. Members who take controversial stands may find the exposure uncomfortable.

expulsion Removal of a member for cause, requiring a two-thirds vote. Congress's equivalent of impeachment, expulsion is rare. On October 2, 1980, the House carried out its first expulsion since 1861 when it removed Michael "Ozzie" Myers (D-Pa.) after his conviction for taking a bribe from an FBI agent posing as an Arab sheik in the **Abscam** affair. *See also* **impeach**.

expunge To strike out or rescind an entry in the ***Congressional Journal.*** Both houses have the power, rarely used, to change entries in this official record of proceedings.

extended debate Euphemism for **filibuster** in the Senate. When it's late in the afternoon and a senator says it's time for some extended discussion, his or her colleagues decide it's dinnertime.

DO AS I SAY, NOT AS I DO

Congress is at least partly exempt from the following laws:

- Civil Rights Act of 1964
- Equal Employment Opportunity Act of 1972
- Equal Pay Act
- Fair Labor Standards Act
- National Labor Relations Act
- Occupational Safety and Health Act
- Social Security Act
- Freedom of Information Act
- Privacy Act of 1974
- Age Discrimination in Employment Act of 1967
- Title IX of the Higher Education Act Amendments of 1972
- Rehabilitation Act of 1973
- Age Discrimination Act of 1975
- Ethics in Government Act of 1978
- Civil Rights Restoration Act of 1988
- Americans with Disabilities Act of 1990

Source: Congressional Research Service.

Rep. Adam Clayton Powell, who was expelled from Congress, at a July 22, 1964, press conference. *See* **expulsion**.

TURKEY LOVERS

On July 21, 1992, the 28-page "Extensions" section of the *Record* included:

- **A tribute by Rep. Rod Chandler (R-Wash.) to Opal Chapman, his high school English teacher.**
- **Congratulations from Rep. Jerry Costello (D-Ill.) to the town of Red Bud, Illinois, on its 125th anniversary.**
- **A salute by Rep. Timothy Penny (D-Minn.) to the Minnesota Turkey Growers Association for its successful "June Is Turkey Lovers' Month" campaign.**

"Extension of Remarks" Name of the section in the back of the ***Congressional Record*** into which members insert newspaper articles, speeches, memorials, and proclamations. It is misleadingly named because members rarely use it to elaborate on their official remarks in the body of the record. As the *Congressional Quarterly's* primer *How Congress Works* noted, "Nothing is extended because no remarks are made."

Although the "Extension" section is usually less than a hundred pages long, there have been extreme examples in which a single extension has topped 500 pages. Since 1972, members seeking to make an extensive insert must get an estimate of the cost of printing it from the public printer. One incident that ushered in this restriction was the listing of each and every parishioner of a Youngstown, Ohio, church, which took up 5½ pages at a cost of $770. Still, in 1992, the government was spending upward of $2 million a year to insert **special-order** speeches and extensions into the *Record*.

In calling for the end of the practice, Rep. George Miller (D-Calif.) said, "I realize that there are Boy and Girl Scout troops, art exhibitions, 50-year anniversary celebrants, and Kiwanis/Lions/Rotary/Moose People of the Year who will not be honored in the 'Extension of Remarks' if this rule change passes. I think the Republic can survive the loss." *See box*, "Turkey Lovers."

extraordinary circumstances Reasons to delay a Senate **roll-call** vote beyond the permitted 20 minutes. On February 3, 1993, Senate Majority Leader George Mitchell (D-Me.) would only say what these were not: "Extraordinary circumstances will not include that a senator is on the way, that a senator is at the airport, at Union Station, on the subway, coming up the steps, or in the hallway."

eyeball-to-eyeball Term used to describe that moment when legislators confront each other with their differences and resolve them. The fuller metaphor has two individuals going eyeball-to-eyeball on an issue until someone blinks.

face-time

1 Public exposure, including appearances on television and at political rallies and parties. The fictional president in Joe Weber's novel *Defcon One* scoffed at congressional posturing over his actions. "They all want more face-time on the evening news, so let them bellyache for the time being."

2 Appearance before a congressional committee to give testimony, especially used by military witnesses. The term is included with this meaning in the glossary to Maj. Gen. Perry M. Smith's 1989 memoir *Assignment Pentagon*.

facilitator Politician who excels at getting things done. This has been called the main job of the Senate **majority leader.**

fact-finding trip Congressional trip sponsored by a nongovernmental organization for the express purpose of obtaining information. These trips may include an oil company's tour of its offshore drilling platforms, for instance, or a foreign foundation's look at its country's education programs. Such trips are permitted as long as they are directly related to the official business of Congress. But to prevent members from using them for personal pleasure or entertainment—a source of past abuse—rules require that reimbursements be disclosed. *See also* **junket.**

factotum One who is hired to get things done; a political operator. Most often, *chief factotum*.

fall on my sword To self-destruct politically. What a legislator tries not to do, especially by voting for an unpopular bill that would generate negative publicity back home. "Why the hell should I fall on my sword just to satisfy you," former Sen. Terry Sanford (D-N.C.) told a labor lobbyist seeking his support for a law prohibiting nonunion striker replacements.

fallout Reaction, usually negative, to one's actions or statements. This meaning derives from the standard sense of radioactive fallout from atomic explosions.

family matters Matters of personal concern to members of Congress: their committees, office assignments, loyalties, and friendships.

farm What a member of Congress calls a country estate in Gettysburg, Pennsylvania, or Middleburg, Virginia, if it is his own. An opponent's farm is a *country estate*, which turns into a *lavish country estate* in an election year. This distinction was pointed out in the 1970s by Merriman Smith, dean of the White House correspondents, who also observed that a *contribution* is the opponent's *slush fund*. Smith saw this trend to humble naming elsewhere. In 1963 he wrote, "Ever since Eisenhower called Truman's yacht 'a symbol of needless luxury,' presidents have been calling their yachts boats."

fast track The status legislation enjoys when leaders want it considered quickly. Some treaties, like the free-trade agreement eliminating most trade barriers with Mexico and Canada, are put on a take-it-or-leave-it fast track that does not permit time-consuming amendments.

fat Money contributed to a **pork barrel** bill or fund; also known as **sweetening**.

fat cat A big contributor to political campaigns. The figure that would qualify one as a fat cat is traditionally at least $10,000, some contend.

"The bosses of the Senate."

In this sardonic Joseph Keppler cartoon, the bosses are the trusts—truly fat cats. While Thomas Nast is often considered the cartoonist who best captured the down side of Congress, Keppler (1838–94) had an equally nasty eye when it came to depicting graft and corruption. *See* **fat cat.**

FEC Federal Election Commission, the agency that oversees all federal elections.

feed Network lingo for a live or taped segment sent from one location to another, by phone lines if audio, by satellite if video. The term becomes a verb when congressional press secretaries "feed" interview segments or video press releases to local stations.

feeding frenzy A vicious media attack, usually at the expense of a public official brushed by scandal. University of Virginia political scientist Larry Sabato, in his book *Feeding Frenzy* (1991), describes it this way: "The news media, print and broadcast, go after a wounded politician like sharks in a feeding frenzy." *See also* **death watch.**

fence-sitter One who is at least publicly—if not privately—undecided on an issue. *See also* **swing voter.**

fiefdom The staff and jurisdiction held by a subcommittee chairman—as opposed to a committee's *kingdom*.

field hearings Committee or subcommittee hearings held outside Washington, often in the state or district of the panel's chairman.

Fifth Amendment One of the original ten **amendments** to the Constitution, guaranteeing in part that no person may be compelled "to be a witness against himself." Witnesses before Congress in matters dealing with crimes have often "taken the fifth," refusing to answer questions on the ground that their answer might tend to incriminate them.

Fifth Amendment communists Expression devised by Sen. Joseph McCarthy (R-Wisc.) in the 1950s to describe witnesses who refused to answer questions on constitutional grounds during Congressional hearings; often considered slanderous. *See* **McCarthyism.**

fig-leaf Flimsy, unsubstantial solution to a political problem or controversial issue. Sen. Jim Sasser (D-Tenn.), during February 1992 debates over the economy, called President Bush's proposal a "fig-leaf economic growth plan."

ETYMOLOGY: The expression stems from the sculptural artifice for covering the private parts of a naked man or woman.

file The action of a committee in reporting a bill to the House or Senate.

filibuster

1 To delay or stop action on a bill in the Senate through constant talking.

2 A long speech or series of speeches used to delay or stop action on a bill by consuming large blocks of time.

This time-honored **delaying tactic** is almost always employed by a minority to defeat a measure favored by the majority. Some have so refined the art of the filibuster that the mere threat of

Sen. Hugh Scott of Pennsylvania is set to bed down for the night in his office during the filibuster over the Civil Rights Act of 1964. The Senate finally ended this filibuster, making it the first time in history that limitations were put on a discussion of civil rights legislation. *See* **filibuster.**

staging one can kill a bill or sidetrack it. It takes 60 votes to stop a filibuster (*see* **cloture**), and if a bill's sponsors cannot round them up, they are often forced to make a number of deals before having the bill considered.

The record for the longest filibuster is held by Sen. Strom Thurmond (R-S.C.), then a Democrat, who talked for 24 hours, 27 minutes, on August 30, 1957, in attempting to stop that year's Civil Rights Act. An earlier record holder was Huey Long (D-La.) who talked for 16 hours in l935. During his filibuster against the National Industrial Recovery Act, Long occupied the Senate's time by reciting recipes for southern "pot likker," the liquid left for gravy after meat and vegetables have cooked, and for turnip greens and corn bread. At one point he read from the Constitution, a tactic which humorist Will Rogers said fascinated other senators: "Many of them thought he was reviewing a new book!"

Predictably, the term has attracted a number of comic definitions (for example, the traditional "*filibuster:* throwing another monologue on the fire") and well-considered hyperbole (as Tom Wicker of the *New York Times* wrote in 1969, "The oldest established permanent floating case of futility in this citadel of frustration is the biennial efforts of liberals in the Senate to change Rule 22 which permits filibusters").

Historically, some filibusters have turned into highly organized efforts. In 1963 Senator Richard B. Russell (D-Ga.) put together what some called his "Dixieland Band" of Southern senators to block that year's civil rights legislation. As described in a UPI dispatch of July 6, 1963, if an attempt was mounted to break the filibuster by keeping the Senate in session around the clock, Russell had organized three squads of six senators on duty for 24 hours at a stretch. Each of the six-man squads would have three two-man units, each of which would work for 8 hours with one man speaking and the other acting as a "lookout" and helper.

Modern filibusters are much less colorful affairs. A senator simply informs the leadership that a filibuster is about to begin, the bill is temporarily set aside, and a cloture vote is scheduled for two days hence. If cloture is adopted by three-fifths of the Senate, a postcloture period of 30 hours for debate begins. If cloture fails, the bill is shelved.

USAGE: Filibusters were common in both chambers until 1841, when the House grew weary of long-winded debate and adopted its one-hour rule. Now the term belongs to the Senate exclusively.

ETYMOLOGY: The term has an odd and disreputable history. It began as the Dutch word *vribuiter*, which also evolved into the English *freebooter*, for pirate. Filibuster came into English by way of the French *filibustier* and then Spanish, where it became *filibustero*, which meant the same as freebooter. The term *filibustero* and then filibuster was first applied to the nineteenth-century tactic in which adventurers seized power in a nation through a false or faked revolution and then looted the country. Among the most notorious filibusterers was American adventurer William Walker, who invaded Mexico and Nicaragua in the name of democracy and the profit motive. He became dictator of Nicaragua in 1856 but was later unseated by railroad tycoon Cornelius Vanderbilt, who organized his own filibuster in conjunction with French and British interests.

The term was later applied to legislative piracy in which an issue is plundered by oratory. The first user in this context appears to have been Congressman John McQueen (D-N.C.), as quoted in 1858 (*Congressional Globe*, May 21, 1858), just three years after the Walker conspiracy.

Even if the term only dates back to 1858, the U.S. Senate practice is much older than that, with evidence of such talkathons dating back to the Continental Congress of 1789.

See also **extended debate** and **gag rule**.

filibuster extender Device attached to the body into which a member would urinate, thus enabling him to remain on the floor for longer periods of time. Also known as the "motorman's pal" (because it was also used by trolley car motormen), the device was usually strapped to the filibusterer's leg. It is said to be no longer used.

Sen. Estes Kefauver (D-Tenn.) once found himself on the floor after five or six hours with an ill-fitting filibuster extender. "Doc," his aide whispered to Senate Parliamentarian Floyd Riddick, "the senator wants to know what he can do. He is equipped with a bag to take care of the situation, but he's upset. He needs to go to the men's room to adjust himself."

Riddick, whose account is contained in an in-house oral history collected by the Senate historian in 1978, replied, "Just tell him to ask unanimous consent that he be permitted to call for a quorum without losing his right to the floor, and then he could go and adjust himself and come back." Riddick told the interviewer, "It was really entertaining, knowing what the situation was, to see him try to walk off that floor!"

financial disclosure Senators and representatives, as well as officers and key employees, must annually disclose their personal financial interests, including investments, income, and liabilities. This allows the public to judge whether their official conduct conflicts with their financial interests.

firestorm Political controversy. This Vietnam-era term originally referred to the actual firestorms caused by mass bombing raids. Firestorms have broken out in Congress on several occasions, beginning with President Richard Nixon's infamous October 1973 Saturday Night Massacre and the barrage of letters and telegrams generated by the dismissal of **Watergate** special prosecutor Archibald Cox, Attorney General Elliott Richardson, and his deputy, William Ruckelshaus, over the release of incriminating White House tape recordings. Equal to or worse than that firestorm was the one that took place when Nixon was linked to the cover-up with the release of the 64 tapes, including the **smoking gun** that led to his resignation.

fire wall A supposedly inviolable separation between Social Security funds and the rest of the federal budget. The difference between fire walls and walls, the slightly less unbreachable division between domestic and defense budgets, has recently become less clear. *See also* **walls up/walls down.**

Under the 1990 budget agreement, Congress could not—until 1993—reach over the protective walls and shift money from one budget category to another without breaking the agreement. In 1992, with the Cold War over and priorities shifting rapidly, Congress refused to tear the walls down.

first reading The first presentation of a bill before the House or Senate. In practice, bills are no longer read, even by title, the first time, but are merely printed by title in the House or Senate *Journal* and the *Congressional Record.*

fiscal year The 12-month period beginning on October 1 and ending the following September 30 during which federal spending is authorized. In other words, it is the government's book-keeping year. The years are designated by the year in which they end—for instance, the fiscal year that begins in October 1993 and ends at the end of September 1994 is fiscal year 1994—FY 1994, for short.

fishbowl Metaphor for political life in the public eye. The collective scrutiny of the media and the public and the unflinching eye of the other party are seen as major forces in the creation of the fishbowl of public office in which nothing is hidden or omitted. The ill-fated 1989 attempt to confirm former Texas Sen. John Tower as Secretary of Defense underscored the extent to which this metaphor had overtaken that of the protective **old boy network**, which embraced the tolerant view that if a politician could stay on a bar stool without falling off, he wasn't drunk. In the wake of the very public Tower defeat, Sen. John S. McCain III (R-Ariz.) declared, "The fishbowl has become larger." Others insisted it had become more transparent.

fishing expedition An open-ended investigation said by its targets to be in search of anything negative or defamatory, especially regarding nominees of the opposing party seeking Senate confirmation. Sen. John Danforth (R-Mo.) said that once it appeared that the hearing on Clarence Thomas's Supreme Court nomination was a fishing expedition, the situation would seem to "advertise for people to come forward with anything they have to dump on Clarence Thomas."

This term is also used by the subjects of investigations to denounce open-ended searches of their records by politically motivated prosecutors. In July 1992, when representatives Dan Rostenkowski (D-Ill.), Joe Kolter (D-Pa.), and Austin Murphy (D-Pa.) refused to testify before a grand jury probing a scandal in the House Post Office, they sent a letter to U.S. Attorney Jay Stephens, whose office was investigating the case, saying, "We can only conclude that the subpoenas for us are the product of an overall fishing expedition in an election year." *See also* **search and destroy mission.**

500-pound gorilla A political heavyweight or potent issue that must be dealt with because, like the proverbial simian of the rain forest, it will repose anywhere it wants to. "This is a 500-pound gorilla," Reg. Byron Dorgan (D-S.D.) said in a March 5, 1992, floor speech. "We are talking about deficits of enormous proportions."

five-minute rule After general debate ends, any member of the House may have five minutes to explain his or her amendment, with equal time going to an opponent.

five percenter An **influence peddler** of the late 1940s who introduced friends to powerful public figures in exchange for a 5 percent share of the resulting loans or contracts.

five pillars of incumbency Cornerstones of a successful campaign for reelection. According to political writer Hedrick Smith in his book *The Power Game*, these are: ric o **feeds**, computerized mail, **casework** appearances back home, and campaign contributions.

flack/flak A derogatory term for a **press secretary.** Like antiaircraft flak, a press secretary's efforts are supposed to be widely disseminated in hopes that some of the remarks will hit the target.

ETYMOLOGY: The word comes from the German *fhegerabwehrkanonen*, which really means anti-aircraft guns, but airmen also referred to the bursting shells as flak. The term was applied to public relations people who, when their clients were in trouble, whould throw up confusing information, or flak. Alternatively, public relations people are expected to catch flak when the going gets rough.

fleecing *See* **Golden Fleece Award.**

flip flop A vote or position switch (*see also* **back flip**). After President George Bush repudiated the 1990 budget agreement in which he approved tax increases despite his 1988 "no-new-taxes" campaign pledge, Senate Majority Leader George Mitchell (D-Me.) called it a "flop of a flip of a flop." In 1992, Democratic presidential candidate Jerry Brown uttered a classic explanation for one of his frequent position switches when he said, "That was then and this is now."

float Put an idea into play by talking to key members, their staffs, or the press to see how it is received. Floating has replaced "sending up a trial balloon" as the term of preference. But *floater*, according to linguist William Safire, is no longer a synonym for **swing voter.**

floor

1 The working area of the Senate or House chamber. *Floor action* is the consideration of legislation in either chamber. When

---

FLOORED!

In their 1965 book, *Washington: Magnificent Capital,* political commentators A. Robert Smith and Eric Sevareid described a typical view of the floor, which still remains current:

Most tourists witness the Congress during routine sessions, which are disappointingly deficient in entertainment value. The floor below is often as desolate as the lone prairie, with one or two coyotes baying at the stars. Attendance increases as a vote nears, but the scene never comes up to the expectations of the tourist who has just visited Statuary Hall. If only a few congressmen would stand proud, heads high, shoulders squared, scrolls outthrust in the manner of those bronze and marble statesmen who line the outer cooridor. Instead, the visitor encounters a melange of slouching, shuffling, leaning, hands-in-pockets figures, an artistic catastrophe, not unlike the familiar hometown figures encountered in courthouses, lodges, city halls, union temples, veterans' posts.

The floor of the House of Representatives, as seen in 1952 after a major remodeling. *See* **floor.**

staff aides say a member is **on the floor**, they mean that he or she is in the chamber. The expression invites such wordplay as "She can't come to the phone right now; she's on the floor with the senator." Sen. Terry Sanford (D-N.C.) said that a constituent, when told the senator was on the floor, replied, "For God's sake, what's wrong with him?"

2 The full Senate or the full House, as when one says that a bill is on the floor of the House. *See box,* "Floored!"

floor amendment An amendment offered **on the floor** rather than in committee.

floor fight An open debate on an issue argued **on the floor** of the House or the Senate. When disputes over bills or amendments cannot be settled ahead of time, the only thing left is a floor fight.

floor leader A party's leader on the floor of either house. The floor leader may plan the course of debate, decide in what order members of his or her party will speak and work, and—with the help of the **whips**—maintain party unity.

floor manager The member, usually the chairman of the committee or subcommittee that reported a bill to the floor, who steers it from introduction to final vote. The committee's ranking minority member often serves as floor manager of the opposition.

floor privilege Permission given not just to members of Congress but to the president and cabinet members, Supreme Court justices, governors, foreign ministers, former congressional members, and others to be on the floor of either chamber during sessions. While the House is in debate, a total of one clerk and four committee staff members are allowed on the floor at one time.

floor wisdom Aphorisms for legislators who want to play it safe with their constituencies: Always vote on the losing side of a controversial issue; if something goes wrong, you will not be blamed. If it is close and party leaders need your vote, vote yes; if the controversial measure appears to be passing comfortably, switch and vote no.

focus group Randomly selected group of potential voters who respond to questions about candidates and their ideas, with observers watching through one-way glass. The focus group is a popular alternative or supplement to polling in taking the measure of the electorate's interest in certain issues. Ideas or phrases generated in these sessions frequently find their way into political platforms and ads.

Folding Room The name for the House Publications Distribution Service, where much of the paper-handling work is done (including folding, cutting, and binding). The Senate equivalent is the **Service Department.**

The Folding Room is significant for the added reason that it has been a traditional place for patronage jobs to which relatives or political cronies of House members are appointed. Prior to his death in 1991, the $72,000-a-year job of director had been held by George F. Early, brother of Rep. Joseph D. Early (D-Mass.).

formality of address Tradition dictates that members of both houses refer to one another in public with respect, if not a high degree of veneration. Each level of veneration was puckishly decoded in a statement that has come to be known as "Cotton's Explanation." In his book, *In the Senate: Amidst the Conflict and the Turmoil* (1978), the late Sen. Norris Cotton (R-N.H.) wrote:

> One can usually tell from the degree of formality with which one senator refers to another what the nature of their personal relations may be. If the reference is made casually as "Senator Jones," they are probably close friends. If someone refers to a colleague as "the senator from Michigan," one may infer that they have a cordial relationship. If a senator refers to another as "the distinguished senator from Indiana," one may assume he does not particularly like him. And if he refers to him as "the very able and distinguished senator from California" it usually indicates that he hates his guts.

four bells

1 The number of buzzes or rings signaling the end of a session (*see* **bells**).

2 By extension, the number of rings signaling the death of a member. According to Speaker Tip O'Neill (D-Mass.), this use of the term is common among members. As he lamented in 1992 after the death of his old friend Rep. Silvio Conte (R-Mass.), "Poor Sil, four bells did ring for him."

fourth branch of government Alternately, the federal bureaucracy, lobbyists, or—most often—the **Fourth Estate**—the press. *See* **branch.**

Fourth Estate Members of the press, or the media as a whole. There were supposedly only three political **branches**—or estates of the realm (nobility, clergy, and commons)—but ever since British philosopher Edmund Burke, according to Thomas Carlyle, pointed in 1837 to the Reporters' Gallery in Parliament and called it "a Fourth Estate more important by far than them all," the press has been stuck with the title.

frank To use a real or facsimile signature in lieu of postage for official mail. Members may use the frank to respond to questions and send unsolicited copies of newsletters, surveys, reports, and press releases to constituents and other interested parties, but are not permitted to use it for campaign or personal business. The number of franked pieces—over 750 million in 1986—jumps dramatically in an election year. Franking is cited as one of the big advantages of incumbency, and efforts to curb it crop up from time to time. Its use goes back well into the nineteenth century, when members sent seed packets to constituents.

free conference *See* **conference committee**.

freshman A newly elected member serving his or her first term. In the House, freshmen regard themselves as a class, as in the

---

TEN COMMANDMENTS FOR NEW HILL MEMBERS BY EUGENE J. McCARTHY

New members of Congress usually get a lot of official advice upon arriving in the capital—most of it of little use in the real world of lawmaking. Those who are truly serious about accomplishing something might consider the following 10 commandments, which generally advise the opposite of what they will be told:

I. Vote against anything introduced with a "re" in it, especially reforms, reorganizations, and recodifications. This usually means going back to something that failed once and is likely to do so again.

II. Do not have a perfect attendance record. Any attendance record above 80 percent is evidence that you have been wasting time answering roll calls and quorum calls.

III. Do not master the rules of procedure. The Senate rules are simple enough to be learned, but they are seldom honored in practice. The House rules are usually applied, but they are too complicated to be mastered. Use the parliamentarian.

IV. Honor seniority. You may have it before you want it. Having a member with seniority assume a

position of power makes no reasonable sense, but as G. K. Chesterton said of the practice of having the oldest son of a king succeed his father on the throne, "It saves a lot of trouble."

V. Never trust a staff member who regularly gets to the office before you do and who stays after you leave.

VI. In evaluating your colleagues, remember that politics is much like coaching professional football. Those who are most successful are smart enough to understand the game but not smart enough to lose interest.

VII. Never be the only one, or one of a few, who are right on an issue (like a war) that will not go away. It is difficult to say to fellow members of Congress, "I am sorry I was right. Please forgive me." They won't.

VIII. Do not respond to an appeal to act in the name of "party loyalty."

IX. Remember that the worst accidents occur in the middle of the road.

X. As Ed Lahey, noted reporter for the *Chicago Daily News,* said to me soon after I came to Congress 30 years ago: "Never trust the press."

freshman class of the 100th Congress, and they elect class officers. The congressional "Class of '92," one of the largest in history, was expected to arrive in Washington demanding sweeping reforms, but this "freshman revolt" fizzled after minor concessions, like agreement on a pay freeze, were made. *See also* **Class of ——.** *See box*, "Ten Commandments for New Hill Members by Eugene J. McCarthy."

freshman lottery A drawing among new members of Congress for the choicest office suites among those that are left after senior members engage in a **space race** for offices vacated by departing members.

front burner Metaphorical place where issues tend to be placed when they are given high priority as presidents or constituents clamor for solutions. Sometimes they are moved there from the **back burner.**

front porch Nickname for Randall S. Harmon (D-Ind.), who, in addition to putting his wife on the payroll, used his front porch in Muncie as a district office and charged the government $100 a month in rent. "Front Porch Harmon" did not overcome his notoriety and served only one term, 1959–61.

front runner Person leading in a political race or contest.

full-court press All-out pressure applied by a member of Congress to a government agency. During 1990 hearings, senators were said to have employed such a tactic to get government regulators to go easy on Charles Keating's Lincoln Savings and Loan Association (*see* **Keating Five**).

ETYMOLOGY: The term derives from basketball lingo for defensive pressure that is extended over the length of the court.

fund-raiser An event staged for political supporters to raise campaign funds. For the privilege of dining on less-than-exotic food, shaking hands with the candidate, and rubbing elbows with like-minded politicos, attendees—often representatives of **PACs** (political action committees)—typically shell out from $100 to $1,000 apiece.

funny money Derogatory characterization of the funds Congress borrows to pay for government services. Iowa Republican H. R. Gross, a persistent budget gadfly, popularized the term during his 26 years (1949–75) in the House (*see* **gadfly's perch**).

fusion The bringing together of not-always-similar candidates or factions into a "fusion ticket" or party.

FY *See* **fiscal year.**

gadfly's perch A seat to the left of the Republican manager's table in the House where the party's conservative gadflies have long roosted, ready to pounce on real or imagined slightings of procedure or etiquette. Iowa's H. R. Gross began the tradition in the late 1940s, and a succession of outspoken conservatives have since occupied the same seat, including Robert Bauman of Maryland and Pennsylvania's Robert Walker.

gag rule Any official order or majority decision that limits debate or prohibits speaking on an issue. The strictly limited rules of House debates often provoke a cry of protest that a gag rule is being imposed. Democrats in Congress frequently clashed with President George Bush in the 1980s over his order prohibiting health workers in federally assisted family planning clinics from discussing abortion. They were unable to overturn this gag rule, but President Bill Clinton threw it out by executive order in 1993.

The original gag rule appears to have been the one passed in 1836 forbidding the House to receive antislavery petitions. After a long and bitter struggle, with former President John Quincy Adams leading the fight against Southern opponents, the House repealed the rule in 1844. Adams entered the House as a representative after his term as chief executive.

gallery Balconies overlooking either house where about 600 visitors can sit to watch the proceedings in the chamber below. Sections of the galleries are set aside for the public, press, staff, and

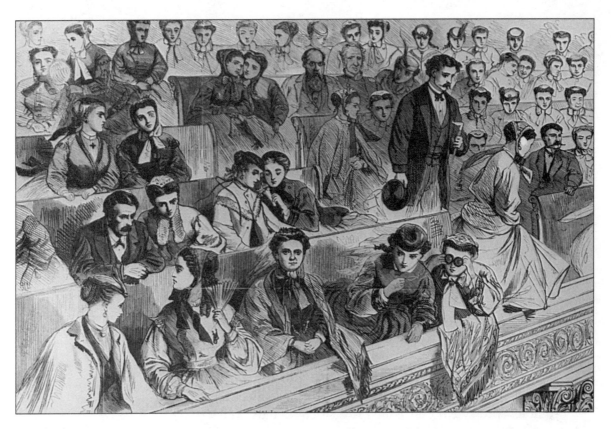

The Ladies' Gallery of the Senate during the March 1868 impeachment trial of President Andrew Johnson. *See* **gallery.**

family and friends of members. A pass, obtained from a member's office, is generally required. *See also* **press gallery.**

gallery pass Ticket that allows a visitor to observe the proceedings of either house from its **gallery.**

Gang of —— In Capitol parlance, gangs are groups of like-minded officials or lobbyists who swing considerable weight. Thus, House Speaker Thomas P. O'Neill, Sens. Edward Kennedy (D-Mass.) and Daniel P. Moynihan (D-N.Y.), and New York Gov. Hugh Carey—all Irish-Americans who pressured Britain to end its impasse with Ireland—were known as the Gang of Four. Both the "Baby Bell" telecommunication giants and the group of freshman Republicans who pressed for "full disclosure" of House check-writing abuses have been dubbed the Gang of Seven.

GAO General Accounting Office. An arm of Congress that monitors executive branch spending through program evaluations and financial audits. The GAO, headed by the comptroller general, has about 5,100 employees and a budget of $444 million. Members ask for and control the release dates of the newsworthy *GAO Reports*.

garbage Descriptive of committees in which a poorly connected legislator could get buried; legislation so meaningless that it is disposable.

gas Long-winded oratory. Sen. Daniel Patrick Moynihan (D-N.Y.) gave new meaning to this unflattering metaphor during a debate in June 1991 when Sen. Alan Dixon (D-Ill.) had wasted much of the Senate's time on an amendment renaming a local section of interstate highway. If they failed to accept his amendment, he shouted, senators would be voting for "chaos." Moynihan wryly noted that the English word *chaos* is derived from the Greek word for *gas*.

-gate The common congressional suffix used in naming scandals since **Watergate** burst on the scene in 1972. It has appeared in Koreagate, Iraqgate, and Irangate; Billygate; Gippergate; and, the ultimate, Gatesgate, the 1991 controversy over CIA nominee Robert Gates. There was even an Astrogate, following the revelation that

---

-GATE, GIVING 'EM THE

The extent to which the suffix -gate has grown in common usage was reflected in a December 4, 1988, cartoon in the *Christian Science Monitor,* that tried to find just the right label for the Iran-Contra arms scandal. The candidates included Northgate, Olliegate, Terrorgate, Syriagate, Swissbankgate, Naughtygate, Shreddergate, and *Your Name Here-*gate. Indeed, -gate scandals no longer have to originate in Washington; when it was discovered that the highly touted Vermont butter was churned out elsewhere, the folks in the Green Mountain state dubbed the flap "Buttergate." One of the wilder -gates that made headlines was *Zoogate,* a 1978 scandal at the San Francisco Zoo. This scandal is noteworthy because it involved a real "gate"— money stolen by a ticket-taker.

President and Mrs. Reagan relied on the pseudoscience of astrology. And then there was Russell Baker's 1987 entry for the various televangelist scandals involving Jimmy Swaggart and Jim Bakker: Pearlygate.

The original scandal was named for the Watergate apartment complex, site of the break-in at Democratic National Headquarters that first brought the illegal activities of the Committee to Reelect the President into public view, leading eventually to President Nixon's resignation. The widely used name for the bounced-check scandal that broke in 1992 and focused attention on individual members and the scandal-plagued **House Bank** was quickly dubbed **Rubbergate.** (*Compare* **-scam.**) *See box*, "-Gate: Giving 'em the."

gatekeeper   Generally a committee or subcommittee chairman, one who opens or closes the gate on legislation. The responsibility is both a power and a burden. "Gatekeepers have to make the trains run on time; they have to move their bills," said former Rep. Dennis Eckart (D-Ohio).

gavel-to-gavel   The period from the moment either house convenes until the moment it adjourns. Gavel-to-gavel coverage is what broadcasters provide when they stay on the air throughout a committee hearing, a session of Congress, or a party convention.

general orders   Bills and joint resolutions placed on the Senate **Calendar of Business.**

general pair   *See* **pair.**

gentle lady/gentlewoman   Formal terms of recognition given to female House members. Thus the elegant recognition: "For what purpose does the gentle lady from Ohio rise?" But, as the old Hill saw goes, "'Will the gentlewoman yield?' can get a gentleman in trouble."

Although she was not comfortable with the title, during the House Judiciary Watergate hearings Rep. Barbara Jordan (D-Tex.) became known as "the gentle lady from Texas" because that is how she was addressed by Chairman Peter Rodino (D-N.J.).

Georgia Mafia Former President Jimmy Carter's aides and confidants.

germane Relevant; bearing on the subject at hand. The term is commonly used to describe **amendments,** which, in the House, must be germane to the legislation to which they are attached. Senate amendments have to be germane only in certain instances, such as after **cloture** has been invoked.

The Senate's lax rules on germaneness leave the door open for extended, seemingly endless delays. Reformers have proposed that a senator be required to get 20 cosponsors in order to introduce a nongermane amendment.

gerrymander To design or redesign the boundaries of a congressional district to favor one party over another, usually by taking advantage of traditional voting patterns.

ETYMOLOGY: The term was created and first used in 1811 after Democratic Governor Elbridge Gerry of Massachusetts connived with the state legislature to readjust districts in Essex County to favor the Democrats. The resulting district was lizardlike or dragonlike in shape and inspired artist Gilbert Stuart to pencil in a head, wings, and claws and declare, "That will do for a salamander." Boston *Centinel* editor Benjamin Russell quipped that it would be better to call it a "Gerrymander" after the Governor.

Both the word and the practice long ago showed up in the British Isles. Lest there be any question, the term is still very much in use in newspaper headlines and text: A September 22, 1991, *Washington Post* headline for a piece on the late and legendary Rep. Phillip Burton (D-Calif.) says, MASTER OF GERRYMANDER LOOMS LARGE IN ABSENCE.

Over time a number of terms have been created to describe gerrymandered districts by their odd shapes, including dumbbells, shoestrings, saddlebags, turkey feet, and frying pans.

In his book *Loose Cannons and Red Herrings*, Robert Claiborne notes the extent to which districts around Boston have been gerrymandered, including one that was split into three pieces ("one on the far side of Boston Harbor, one in Boston itself, and the third several miles up the Charles River, in Cambridge"). When the late Mayor Richard Daley of Chicago tried to foist off an oddly

ALL that we can learn of the natural history of this remarkable animal, is contained in the following learned treatise, published in the newspapers of March, 1812, embellished by a drawing, which is pronounced by all competent judges, to be a most accurate likeness.

The horrid Monster of which this drawing is a correct representation, appeared in the County of Essex, during the last session of the Legislature. Various and manifold have been the speculations and conjectures, among learned naturalists respecting the *genus* and origin of this astonishing production. Some believe it to be the real *Basilisk*, a creature which had been supposed to exist only in the poet's imagination. Others pronounce it the *Serpens Monocephalus* of Pliny, or single-headed *Hydra*, a terrible animal of pagan extraction. Many are of opinion that it is the *Griffin* or *Hippogriff* of romance, which flourished in the dark ages, and has come hither to assist the knight of the rueful countenance in restoring that gloomy period of ignorance, fiction and imposition. Some think it the great Red Dragon, or Bunyan's *Apollyon* or the *Monstrum Horrendum* of Virgil, and all believe it a creature of infernal origin, both from its aspect, and from the circumstance of its birth.

The original Gilbert Stuart cartoon of "The Gerry-Mander" as it first appeared. *See* **gerrymander.**

configured district on Illinois Rep. Abner Mikva, the Democratic congressman retorted, "That's not a map, that's spaghetti."

See **Burton** and **Burtonmander** for modern versions of the term.

ghost employee   One who does no work but for whom payroll forms and salary checks are issued. Often, the absent employee kicked back part of his salary to his boss. The practice, also known as **payroll padding**, has largely died out. On October 4, 1988, Fofo Sunia, the House delegate from American Samoa, was found guilty of conspiracy to defraud the United States in such a scheme and was sentenced to 5 to 15 months in prison.

ghost senator A strong **AA** (administrative assistant) who performs many of the senator's duties. Now, more often, **gray ghost.**

ghost speech A speech that was never delivered but appeared in the *Congressional Record* (now identified by special symbols if not actually delivered). *See also* **revise and extend.**

ghost voting The unethical act of having one's vote recorded while absent. It was officially banned on January 5, 1981, after two unrelated Murphys, Austin (D-Pa.) and Morgan (D-Ill.), were accused of casting ghost votes. Austin Murphy was reprimanded. Speaker Tip O'Neill (D-Mass.) called for an investigation of why Morgan Murphy was recorded as voting while he was in Chicago. Murphy said it was a mistake and no further action was taken.

gifts Under Senate and House **ethics** rules, members are limited as to the value of gifts they may accept from people other than relatives. Gifts are anything of value, including food, lodging, entertainment, cash, reimbursements, or forbearances of debts. The most recent limit was $250 per gift from one person in the course of a year, but gifts of less than $100 are exempted. *See also* **hospitality** *and box*, "Valued Gifts."

VALUED GIFTS

The April 1992 *House Ethics Manual* provides the following examples to guide members and staffers in totaling the value of gifts:

Example 1: Over the course of one year, Company Z offers Member A the following gifts: in January, theater tickets worth $80; in April, a set of leather desk accessories worth $130; in September, a case of wine worth $120; and in December, a set of crystal stemware worth $200. The theater tickets do not count toward the $250 aggregate because they are worth less than $100. All the other gifts count. If Member A accepts the desk accessories and the wine, he must return the stemware to avoid exceeding the gift limit.

Example 2: An acquaintance of Member B has two theater tickets, worth a total of $300, that he is unable to use. He offers them to Member B. She cannot accept them as an outright gift because they are worth more than $250. By paying him $50 for the tickets, however, she may "buy down" to $250 the value of the gift to her, and (assuming no prior gifts to her from that source that year) she may then accept the tickets.

---

gimmick Characterization of former President George Bush's 1992 pre-election plan for economic recovery by both congressional critics and former Housing and Urban Development Secretary Jack Kemp. Kemp apologized to Bush for making the comment public, but he did not retract it. White House officials like Deputy Chief of Staff W. Henson Moore were not pleased. He told reporters on February 4, 1992, "Just let it be clear, by God, we don't think the president's economic program is a gimmick." *See also* **smoke and mirrors.**

globalony   Murky international thinking.

ETYMOLOGY: The late Clare Booth Luce's term for cosmic nonsense. She invented it for her February 9, 1943, maiden House speech in her role as representative from Connecticut. During the address she spoke of the views of Vice President Henry Wallace: "Much of what Mr. Wallace calls his global thinking is, no matter how you slice it, still 'globaloney.' " Within a week the term had appeared everywhere, was at the heart of a major debate on the postwar world, and had, by all accounts, become a word for the ages. A *San Francisco Examiner* editorial of February 15, 1953, said that she had brought a "new and meaningful word into the American language." Largely forgotten today is the fact that the specific notion that Luce was attacking was Wallace's vision of a "network of globe-girdling airways" operated by a United Nations "peace force."

goat   Derogatory slang for a constituent. In his "Heard on the Hill" column in *Roll Call*, Bill Thomas quotes the term in context from a Senate staffer: "We're here trying to save America, and some goat will come along and ask why we're not doing more in the district. It drives you out of your mind."

goat food   Shameless political posturing.

gobbledygook   Overblown language that commonly afflicts the bureaucracy. The word was coined during World War II by Rep. Maury Maverick of Texas when he was the chief of President Roosevelt's Smaller War Plans Corporation. Maverick became so furious with the bloated language of the memos that were landing on his desk that he wrote a memo of his own containing such lines as: "Anyone using the word 'activation' or 'implementation' will be shot." Maverick felt that bureaucratese sounded like a foolish old turkey who went around saying "gobble, gobble, gobble" and then ending with an emphatic "gook."

Over time a number of legislators have puckishly compiled their own "Gobbledygook Dictionary," including the late Senator Stephen M. Young (D-Ohio), who in 1962 first defined a *program* as "any assignment or task that cannot be completed by one phone call."

God Squad Top federal officials who decide which endangered species will be protected. The God Squad is formally known as the Endangered Species Committee and gets its nickname in part from the fact that it alone has the authority to override the Endangered Species Act, thereby "playing God." Membership on the committee is reserved for those holding specific positions, including the secretary of agriculture, the secretary of the army, the administrator of the Environmental Protection Agency, and the chairman of the president's Council of Economic Advisors. The God Squad meets infrequently and only for the most serious of issues. When it began meeting at the end of 1991 to consider the case of the northern spotted owl, it was the first time it had convened in 13 years.

gold bag *See* **orange pouch.**

Golden Fleece Award Sarcastic monthly prize awarded to a federally funded research project that on its face seemed to have

---

FLEECING THE PUBLIC

A sampling of Senator Proxmire's Golden Fleece Awards is presented here to underscore the diversity of waste:

- For government studies on how drunken fish behave and whether or not they can be driven to alcoholism. Proxmire wondered aloud whether or not the government wanted to know what it means to be "stewed to the gills" and what it really meant to "drink like a fish." This $102,000 grant was one of the senator's 1975 selections.
- To the Postal Service for spending $3.4 million in 1977 for an advertising campaign to get people to write more letters.
- To the U.S. Economic Development Administration for shelling out $700,000 for a set of limestone pyramids to attract tourists. The result was a pile

of rocks in a field 5 miles north of Bedford, Indiana.
- To the White House for using $1.8 million in taxpayers' money to provide 1,120 military chauffeurs, aides, and escorts for the 1981 inauguration of Ronald Reagan.
- To the Federal Highway Administration in 1981 for cost overruns totaling over $100 billion.
- To the Labor Department for shelling out $385,000 for a 1977 pet census in Ventura, California.

In 1979, Proxmire made headlines when he awarded the "Golden Fleece" to Congress itself because its spending for staff had risen 270 percent over the previous 10 years. The staff of Proxmire's Senate had gone from 3,400 to 6,800 during that period.

Sen. William Proxmire gleefully poses as a penny-pincher willing to put a coin back in the federal coffer. The Golden Fleece Award was his way of underscoring government waste and federal fascination with trivial research. *See* **Golden Fleece Award.**

little or nothing to do with the needs of the republic. It was created by Sen. William Proxmire (D-Wisc.), who gave the award for many years to projects with names like "Smiling Behavior of Primates" and to individuals like the Energy Department official who used a government jet to fly him at a cost of over $3,000 to Alabama to lecture Arkansas on the importance of fuel economy. In late 1988 Proxmire announced that he would continue to give the award from his new base as a director of the National Taxpayer's Union, where it reemerged as the Golden Wastebasket Award. *See box*, "Fleecing the Public."

gone goose Someone whose political situation is hopeless.

goodwill letter Unsolicited congratulatory letter sent to a constituent on the occasion of a wedding, anniversary, birth, birthday, award, and the like. Formerly, staffers watched local newspapers for such occasions so that these letters could be mailed. Recent limits on the use of the **frank**, however, have reduced such mailings. Franked, or postage-free, letters may be sent for public distinctions, such as a graduation or an award, but not for personal distinctions, such as birthdays or anniversaries.

goo-goos/googoos Forces of and for good government. The League of Women Voters is a perennial source of goo-gooism, as were the reformers attracted to Franklin D. Roosevelt's New Deal. Although the term sounds derisive, it is often meant to be affectionate. It has been in use for more than a hundred years and has been applied to many individuals and movements.

ETYMOLOGY: The term derives from the good government movements that sprang up in the 1890s. Reformer Jacob A. Riis was a salaried agent of the Good Government Clubs of New York City. Club A of the New York chapters was incorporated on February 28, 1893.

The term was applied to Teddy Roosevelt, a point that is made repeatedly in social critic Mark Sullivan's *Our Times (Volume II: America Finding Herself)*, in which on one occasion he footnotes as follows: "This epithet, by 1927, had become obsolete; during the 1880s and 1890s it conveyed rich meaning as a derisive diminutive for persons charged with thinking themselves better than ordinary politicians. Its derivation was probably from reform associations having the phrase 'good government' in their titles." Despite Sullivan's assertion, the term comes back from time to time.

Perhaps the most interesting commentary on the term appears in the book *New York Detective*, the 1938 memoirs of Ernest L. Van Wagner, a retired detective commander who worked for Roosevelt when he was police commissioner of New York City. The passage, which was collected by Peter Tamony, comes from the chapter entitled "I Become a Goo-goo":

> There was an old and portly policeman standing with another old and portly policeman at the door of Headquarters as I was passing out into the noisome odors of old Mulberry Street. Said the first to the second as I went by, "S'pose that's another of those Goo Goos from upstate looking for our jobs."

Goon Squad The dozen or so reporters who covered Sen. Joe McCarthy (R-Wisc.) during his heyday in the 1950s, reporting every outrageous charge the feared red-baiting senator made. *See* **McCarthyism.**

GOP Grand Old Party; time-honored nickname for the Republican Party.

Sen. Everett M. Dirksen speaks to fellow Republicans as Rep. Jerry Ford, then minority leader (1965–73), looks on. *See* **GOP.**

ETYMOLOGY: One of the early uses of GOP in Congress is found in the May 1, 1888, *Congressional Record:*

Rep. Charles T. Farrall, a Virginian who had served as commander of the Confederate cavalry in the Shenandoah Valley, invented the following dialogue between an old farmer and a federal tax collector who was bilking him for extra tax on his land:

Old Farmer: "Is this Democratic party doings or Republican doings?"

Collector: "O, it is the doings of the GOP — the Grand Old Party— the Republican Party."

Old Farmer: "Just as I expected. Well, sir, I am a Democrat and have been voting that ticket for many a year, but if Mr. Cleveland and the Democratic party don't bring about the old-time way of doing things and let every tub stand on its own bottom, I don't expect to vote anymore. Good day, sir." (Loud applause and laughter)

GOPAC Acronym for the Republican (**GOP**) political action committee (**PAC**) dedicated to electing conservatives to Congress.

go to conference Take different House and Senate versions of the same bill to a meeting, or conference, at which representatives of the two houses try to agree on a compromise version. Both chambers nearly always accept the resulting conference report.

go to the well Perform a favor for a colleague or a lobby at some personal cost. *See also* **well.**

Government-by- —— The efforts of one branch, group, or institution to supplant the democratic process: Government-by-Cabinet, Government-by-Crony, Government-by-Veto, Government-by-Press-Release. And, in the case of the **Gramm-Rudman-Hollings** plan to cut budgets across the board, "Government-by-Veg-O-Matic."

Government Printing Office Known locally as the GPO, this monstrous printing plant on North Capital Street in Washington, D.C., prints ***The Congressional Record*** and most other Hill documents. Completed in 1903, the red brick structure is listed in the *Guinness Book of World Records* as the largest printing plant in the world.

grab bag A bill with so many provisions that one could reach into it and find almost anything.

Gramm-Rudman-Hollings Act The 1985 law that set a timetable for achieving a balanced budget, largely through spending cuts. A *Washington Post* editorial called it "the little fellow who is supposed to cut the budget automatically if the president and Congress can't." But because Gramm-Rudman exempted **entitlements** and was silent on taxes, it was deemed unworkable.

grandfather clause Clause exempting existing structures or rights in new laws. In *Shoe*, a popular political comic strip, the "Senator" character is asked if there should be term limits. He replies, "I think we'll have to grandfather it." In the next frame he explains, "Meaning, it won't happen until you guys are grandfathers."

grandstanding Making a showy speech or gesture in order to gain the applause or attention of an audience or the media.

grass roots The folks back home; people who are not in the business of politics. "If you can organize the grass roots," said 1992 independent presidential candidate H. Ross Perot, "you could probably get a law passed saying the world's square." Traditionally, the grass roots have expressed themselves individually in letters and telegrams sent to Washington and collectively in polls.

ETYMOLOGY: In the political sense, the first use of note was at the Bull Moose Convention of 1912 when Sen. Albert J. Beverage said, "This party comes from the grass roots. It has grown from the soil of the people's hard necessities." In the mid-1930s the term was used by Republicans in their efforts to unseat Franklin D. Roosevelt.

In recent years, public-interest groups and lobby groups have made an art of generating "instant grass roots" responses by getting their members to bombard the White House or a congressional office with calls and letters. The slang term for this manufactured grass roots is *AstroTurf. See* **AstroTurf campaign.**

gray ghost The chief staffer of a senator or representative. *See also* **ghost senator.**

Meryl Streep plays gray ghost to Alan Alda, who portrays a senator in the 1979 film *The Seduction of Joe Tynan.* The movie focuses on behind-the-scenes political and romantic intrigue in Washington. *See* **gray ghost.**

Great Compromise James Madison's phrase for the deal that was struck in the Constitutional Convention of 1787 with small states who were afraid of being dominated by their larger neighbors in Congress. It granted each state, regardless of population, equal representation in the Senate, but retained proportional representation in the House.

Great Game

1 Politics.

2 How some politicians have described being in Congress. "There's a sense of being at the center of things. This is the Great Game!" Rep. Newt Gingrich (R-Ga.) told Hedrick Smith, author of *The Power Game*. Other adventures qualify. "That's the trade we're in, Adam. That's part of what Kipling used to call the Great Game," a British spy says in Frederick Forsythe's *The Devil's Alternative*. "Except this is no game," his contact replies, "and what the KGB will do to the Nightingale is no joke."

Great Society Name given to the array of social programs, nearly as ambitious as the **New Deal**, proposed by President Lyndon Johnson in 1964. Among them were medical care for the aged, voting rights laws, elementary and secondary education aid, housing assistance, job training, and efforts to end poverty.

green Adjective used to describe legislation, members, and programs that are pro-environment. *See* **greenies.**

Green Book The House **Ways and Means Committee's** annual overview of entitlement programs.

greenies Derogatory term for environmentalists. The term derives from the former West Germany's environmentally conscious Green party and the international Greenpeace movement. *See also* **tree-huggers.**

gridlock Political impasse between Congress and the White House. The term caught on in 1992 when the Democrats controlling Congress opposed numerous White House policies at the same time Republican President George Bush vetoed many

Democratic-sponsored bills. Many members of Congress resigned in disgust because of the resulting legislative impasse.

In his speech accepting the Republican party's nomination for a second term, President Bush tried to blame "the gridlocked Democrat Congress" for the mess. But congressional leaders returned the fire. Five days after the speech, House Speaker Thomas S. Foley said it was Bush who blocked the languishing laws through vetoes and veto threats. "The areas where we have had confrontation between the president and the Congress are in my judgment without exception those areas where the administration was trying to protect the tax preferences of higher-income Americans, which is a fundamental commitment of this administration." In March 1993, after the Senate passed his budget plan, President Clinton told Senate leaders, "Finally we've done something to break the gridlock."

Democratic presidential candidate Jerry Brown popularized the term in frequent blasts at the state of affairs in Washington during the 1992 campaign.

ETYMOLOGY: The term first appeared in print in 1980 to describe a "worst-case scenario" for traffic in New York City, in which the grids or cross-patterns of the city literally locked, tying up traffic in all directions. Although the term was clearly born in the exhaust fumes of New York City, its coiner has defied detection. In *What's the Good Word*, William Safire notes that one of the first people to use the term to good effect was former New York Police Commissioner Robert J. McGuire, who, upon hearing of an infant born in a taxi trapped in traffic, said, "We're checking out a rumor that the baby was born out of gridlock."

grip-and-grin Description of a quick photo session with a legislator or candidate and a contributor. The contributor gets an autographed copy.

GRPs Gross rating points (or "grips"), the number of times a political advertisement will be seen by a specific number of people.

guardians of gridlock President Bill Clinton's jibe at Republican critics of his budget proposals. On March 19, 1993, he said that their only pleasure was "to hear the gears squeal." *See* **gridlock.**

Gucci Gulch The polished marble hallway outside the House Ways and Means Committee room in the Longworth House Office Building where well-tailored lobbyists, who specialize in engineering tax breaks and loopholes for their clients, gather, especially while committee members are meeting in secret to deal with tax reform matters.

Although the term disappeared after the passage of the 1986 tax reform law, it was revived by 1989 as capital gains breaks were again proposed, and then again in early 1992, when sweeping tax code changes were being crafted by the House Ways and Means Committee and as many as 200 lobbyists camped outside the doors of Room 1100 of the Longworth Office Building during the committee's deliberations on major tax issues.

Despite the clear connection of this term with the Ways and Means Committee hallway, it has on occasion been applied to other locations where important action is taking place. It has been used to describe the area below the Senate Finance Committee as well as a room used by the House Ways and Means Committee in the North Corridor (East End) below the House Chamber.

ETYMOLOGY: The term came into being in 1986 and was a reference to the expensive Italian footwear favored by the nation's highest-paid lobbyists.

guerrilla politics Unorthodox methods of sneaking or getting controversial legislation past the legislative **gatekeepers** and onto the floor without alerting opponents. A favorite vehicle is the budget reconciliation bill loaded with hundreds of **riders.** As William Greider quotes North Dakota Rep. Byron Dorgan in his 1992 book, *Who Will Tell the People*: "If my provision is number 89 on the list and it's not very clearly described, it's likely you can get it passed with about seven and a half seconds of discussion."

Gulf of Tonkin Resolution A Congressional resolution in August 1964 approving President Johnson's use of naval forces against North Vietnam. The administration later contended that it was the "functional equivalent" of a declaration of war. To those who opposed the war, supporting the resolution was a grievous mistake.

gun issue The tactic of portraying an issue as one that will affect gun owners, thus animating the powerful National Rifle Association and its most powerful Congressional ally, Michigan Democrat John Dingell. The object is to arouse enough opposition to kill the measure. "If you make it a gun issue, it automatically brings John Dingell aboard," said Tom Korologos, a former White House/Congress insider and a leading Washington lobbyist.

gutter politics There's the high road, the low road, and then the gutter, apparently the lowest route a politician can take in trying to get elected. One candidate can engage in gutter politics, but the expression implies two candidates slugging it out with no holds barred. One can be lured into the gutter by a mudslinging opponent and turn off voters in the process. That is probably what cost former North Carolina Governor Jim Hunt the election in his 1982 Senate campaign against Republican Sen. Jesse Helms, according to the state's other senator, Democrat Terry Sanford. "He threw it away by getting in the gutter."

gym group Informal, bipartisan fraternity of members who regularly work out in the House and Senate gyms.

gypsy moth A Republican moderate. According to William Safire in his syndicated column "On Language," the term was created by Rep. Lawrence DeNardis (R-Conn.), who said that the gypsy moth is as much a nuisance in New England and the Great Lakes as the **boll weevil** is in the South. The gypsy moths, mostly from the Northeast, opposed several Reagan policies, thus defying their party's leadership. One frequent point of disagreement was the environment.

Hall of the House Official name for the House Chamber. In the original 1815 design by architect Benjamin Latrobe, it was called the Hall of Representatives.

hammers Special rules written into many bills describing how and when a law is to be enforced. The rules go into effect automatically if the agency that is supposed to implement the law fails

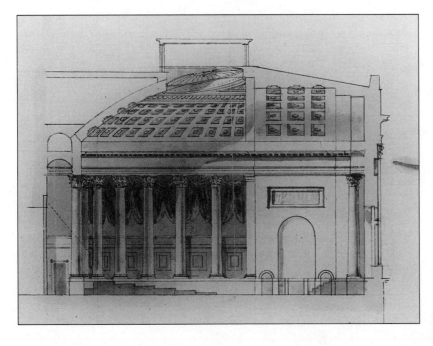

A sketch from Benjamin Latrobe's proposed 1815 design for the Hall of Representatives, showing a section from north to south. *See* **Hall of the House.**

to do so by a prescribed date. In other words, hammers force a reaction, just as the hammer in a gun ignites a cartridge.

Handholder Caucus Derisive nickname for members of the House who, on difficult votes, watch the computer monitor from the back of the chamber to see how others are voting before casting their own vote. "They hold each other's hands and say 'I'll vote this way if you vote that way,'" said Rep. Dennis Eckart of Ohio in an interview with the authors before he retired in 1992.

handler The advisor—usually assigned by the White House— to nominees during **confirmation** hearings. This term originally applied to trainers of boxers, dogs, and horses.

handout A press release, fact sheet, speech copy, or press clipping accompanying a press release, to bolster a lawmaker's case. Meant primarily for the press, handouts are given to anyone who asks for them.

hand-walk To move a bill through the legislative maze with uncharacteristic speed; to actually walk it through the process. This

Judge David Souter, with handlers in the background, during the 1990 confirmation hearings that led to his being seated on the Supreme Court. *See* **handler.**

kind of attention is normally reserved for wartime or economic emergencies, although it is sometimes used for "hot" or emergency legislation. An extraordinary example of hand-walking for reasons of compassion was a 1989 bill that released Dr. Elizabeth Morgan from jail after 25 months. Morgan had refused a judge's order to send her daughter on an unsupervised visit to see the girl's father and was jailed for contempt.

hangers-on Political **cronies** or former associates who tend to overstay their welcome at congressional offices.

hardball A big-league political play. In *Hardball*, Christopher Matthews' book about congressional politics, he defines it as "clean, aggressive, Machiavellian politics. It is the discipline of gaining and holding power, useful to any profession or undertaking but practiced most openly and unashamedly in the world of public affairs."

hard-liner One who takes an aggressive, unyielding stance in politics to the right or left, but most often a conservative. In 1992, congressional hard-liners forced President George Bush to toughen his stance on tax legislation.

hash A confused muddle, as legislation often is, with ingredients from many sources.

ETYMOLOGY: This motley mix of meat, vegetables, and seasonings came into English in the mid-seventeenth century from the Old French word *hachier*, meaning "to chop." In nineteenth-century America, cheap restaurants were known as hash houses and those who worked in them were hash-slingers.

Hatch Act Laws passed in 1939 and 1940 limiting the ability of federal employees—and state employees paid from federal funds—to engage in partisan politics. Authored by Democratic Sen. Carl Hatch of New Mexico, this "Act to Prevent Pernicious Political Activity" also shields employees from being forced to contribute to or work for a candidate.

After two decades of partisan combat, the House and Senate in July 1993 approved changes in the Hatch Act to allow federal

Known for their good food, the kitchens and cooks of the Senate have also been used metaphorically. This is Thomas Nast's view of the senators who opposed the policies of Nast's hero, President Ulysses S. Grant. In this June 22, 1872, *Harper's Weekly* cartoon they are depicted as meddling cooks creating political hash and stews. *See* **hash.**

workers to engage in political activity during off-duty hours. The amendment would permit nearly three million civil service and postal workers to hold political party office, distribute literature, solicit votes, and organize political meetings. A similar bill passed in 1990, but Congress failed to override President George Bush's veto. As of late July 1993, President Bill Clinton was expected to sign the bill.

hat trick Political coup of appearing within a brief period of time on "Meet the Press," "Face the Nation," and "This Week with David Brinkley," the three most important political interview television programs.

ETYMOLOGY: The term is based on the hockey feat of scoring three goals in one game.

having the floor Controlling the floor of the House or Senate by virtue of being the recognized speaker. In a **debate**, the person who is speaking has the floor and does not have to surrender it or even **yield** for a question if he or she does not wish to.

hawk One who tends to favor military intervention and increased military appropriations. (*See* **dove** for a discussion of how these two opposing terms emerged.)

hawkish In the manner of a **hawk**.

head count An estimate of the number of votes lined up in support of or opposition to a particular bill or amendment. In a September 1981 article in *Washingtonian* magazine, lobbyist Tom Korologos said a good lobbyist "never gives an honest answer. If you're behind, you look ineffective, and if you're ahead, your opponents will work harder. Besides, head counts never turn out right, even the supposedly firm ones called 'hard counts.' " *See also* **whip count.**

"Heard on the Hill" Insider column of Capitol Hill scuttlebutt published in the newspaper ***Roll Call;*** also known as *HOH.*

hearing An information-gathering session held by a congressional committee. After opening speeches, of which there are often many, witnesses—often government officials or outside experts—present testimony. Committee members follow up with questions. The hearing forms the basis of committee reports or legislation. *See box,* "Congressional Speaking?"

heat Political pressure. Members "take a lot of heat" for controversial positions. Some live by former President Harry Truman's oft-stated slogan, "If you can't stand the heat, stay out of the kitchen."

heat-seeking missile Insider description of a member who is willing to take on unpopular tasks.

heavy hitter A congressman or lobbyist who wields great influence among members of Congress. Also known, in the plural, as *heavies.*

> **CONGRESSIONAL SPEAKING?**
>
> **In their March 11, 1993, hearing on the confirmation of Janet Reno for attorney general, members of the Senate Judiciary made speeches lasting far longer than the testimony of the nominee, even cutting her off occasionally to make their televised points. Commented ABC News anchor Peter Jennings: "Why do senators call it a hearing when they do so much talking?"**

Scene in the hearing room on the last day of the Army–McCarthy hearing in June 1954. The transcripts of the deliberations are piled in one place for effect—and for the benefit of the television cameras in the room. *See* **hearing.**

heavyweight *See* **heavy hitter.**

held at the desk Status of a bill that has not been assigned to a committee. Holding a bill may stall it or speed its passage by having it taken up directly without committee assignment.

If a bill is passed by the Senate and sent to the House, and if a similar bill has already been considered by a House Committee, the Senate bill goes directly to the speaker's table for consideration by the House. *See also* **at the desk.**

hereby Word common in bills, amendments, and other forms of legislation. It has been said that Congress would have to cease operation if this word were deleted from the language. *See also* **whereas.**

hessians Paid political workers, named for the mercenaries who fought for the British during the Revolutionary War.

hideaway offices Private rooms with unmarked doors in the Capitol. They were made a little less secret after the 1971 bombing of the Capitol when *Newsweek* reported, "The explosion that rocked the Capitol last week also blew away the curtain of privacy that had shrouded the Congress's so-called 'hideaway offices'—a warren of odd, unplanned rooms and suites scattered throughout the old building and parceled out to ranking senators and congressmen for whatever purpose they might wish to put them."

When William "Fishbait" Miller, the legendary House **doorkeeper**, worked for minority whip John McCormack (D-Mass.) in 1947, he was given a basement office, which he dubbed "Hernando's Hideaway," after the name of a popular song of the pre-rock'n'roll era.

Before he left the Senate, Lyndon Johnson had seven hideaways on two floors of the Capitol, known collectively as "LBJ Ranch East."

hierarchy Leadership, party, or committee structure, in order of authority; also listing of bills by priority.

high crimes and misdemeanors Offenses against law so grave as to warrant impeachment of the president, vice president, judges, or any public official. These offenses include treason, bribery, and other crimes; at the discretion of the House, they can be extended to include personal habits and misconduct. The articles of impeachment against President Andrew Johnson in 1868 included "intemperate, inflammatory, and scandalous harangues." *See* **articles** and **impeach.**

high muck-a-muck An important, prominent person, often the highest-ranking individual in a group or agency.

high roller Legislatively, one who gambles frequently, for high stakes.

This drawing of the U.S. Capitol as it appeared in 1800 clearly illustrates that the Capitol is indeed on a hill. The Hill was chosen as the site for Congress by Pierre Charles L'Enfant, a French architect who was appointed by George Washington to plan the city. *See* **Hill, the.**

Hill, the

1 Insider's name for Congress. One goes to it, works on it, testifies on it, takes one's case to it. On a weekday, this "village" counts 15,000 temporary residents, the number of congressional employees.

2 The neighborhood surrounding the U.S. Congress.

Hillite Traditional term for any Washingtonian who lives on Capitol Hill.

hip pocket Figurative place in which one has stashed enough votes or pledges of votes to pass a bill.

Hispanics in Congress The first Hispanic delegate to the House of Representatives was Joseph Hernandez, from the Territory of Florida, who served from 1822 to 1823. The first full representative was Romualdo Pacheco, a California Republican, who took his seat in 1877. In 1993, the number of Hispanics in Congress rose to 17.

hit list A group targeted for removal from office. The group could be legislators whom the White House would like to see defeated in the next election or government officials the administration would like to get rid of. In 1983, reacting to the belief that only Republicans were being charged with using hit lists, Rep. Robert H. Michel (R-Ill.) commented, "But when a Democratic administration performs the same function, we say it is 'engaged in helping the president to carry out his mandate.'"

Many of the groups inside and outside Congress hoping to change the makeup of the House or Senate have had hit lists. The expression has a brutal connotation associated with underworld hit men who are hired to hit—or kill.

HOB House office building, of which there are three: Rayburn, Longworth, and Cannon—all named for former speakers of the House. *See box*, "House Room Numbers Decoded."

hobgoblins A frightening apparition or bugbear, incorporated in political speeches to arouse voters. Said H. L. Mencken in 1921, "The whole aim of practical politics is to keep the populace alarmed (and hence clamorous to be led to safety) by menacing it with an endless series of hobgoblins, all of them imaginary."

HOH Short for "**Heard on the Hill.**"

hokum Insincere, overly sentimental speech.

hold An informal request, usually honored, to keep a nomination from being approved, to "hold" it on the calendar. As explained by the Senate Republican Policy Committee in its 1987 *Glossary of Senate Terms*, "'holds' are not in any way official; they are simply a part of the unwritten code of 'Senatorial courtesy,' and can be

> **HOUSE ROOM NUMBERS DECODED**
>
> Room numbers with three digits are in the Cannon House Office Building. Those with four digits beginning with one (1) are in the Longworth House Office Building, and those with four digits beginning with two (2) are in the Rayburn House Office Building.

overridden by the majority leader, who has broad discretion to set the Senate's program."

"Holds have been part of the Senate since day one," Republican Leader Robert Dole of Kansas said in a March 3, 1992, news release. "They are an essential tool to preserve the rights of the minority and the wide-open democracy of the U.S. Senate." But in May 1993 majority leader George Mitchell of Maine declared that although holds would be allowed for a "reasonable time" to allow for consultation with the nominee, they would not be honored indefinitely.

Hole, the The secure conference room inside the Senate Intelligence Committee room where top-secret conversations are held. Senators' notes may not be taken out, but are sealed in individual safes, according to Sen. William Cohen (R-Me.), in his book *One-Eyed Kings*.

hollow laws Symbolic legislation of little substance, often enacted in election years to convince the public that something is being done. In William Greider's book *Who Will Tell the People?* (1992), former House aide Richard Fortuna describes such measures as "laws in name only."

home rule The right to self-rule and to elect legislators; local power. Home rule was long kept from the District of Columbia by Congress. It was a cause during the 1960s when Rep. John McMillan (D-S.C.), chairman of the House District Committee, was the virtual mayor of Washington, D.C., and refused to relinquish power until it was taken from him in the 1967 reorganization act. D.C.'s cause, in recent years, has shifted to statehood.

honeymoon Short period after an election during which Congress and the press refrain from criticizing the president. David Cushman Coyle, in *The United States Political System and How It Works*, says the period lasts until the supply of political patronage jobs, which a president allocates to friends in Congress, runs out.

honorable Like **distinguished**, this adjective is an overused and not always sincere term of flattery. It is also a form of address for lawmakers and judges.

The District of Columbia Committee Room of the Senate as it looked in the early 1950s. This room and its House counterpart long stood as testament to the fact that the city lacked the authority to govern itself. *See* **home rule.**

honoraria Fees formerly paid to members of Congress, usually by favor-seeking lobbies, for speeches, articles, briefings, broadcasts, or simply showing up for a convention or "power breakfast." As Bill Thomas of the newspaper *Roll Call* pointed out, a member could earn an honorarium "by simply walking from point A to point B," and a House aide told *Newsweek* in 1989, "Two thousand dollars is the going rate for a bran muffin."

Members could command up to $2,000 an appearance. Total honoraria paid all members ran into the millions—$2.6 million in 1988, according to the *Washington Post*—and were a source of long-running controversy until Congress outlawed them in 1989. The chief argument against honoraria was that they created the perception that members of Congress were beholden to the lobbies that paid the fees. During 1988 hearings on salaries and honoraria, Common Cause President Fred Wertheimer said, "Honoraria has become one of Washington's most striking misnomers—there is no 'honor' involved on either end of the bargain." Honoraria are among the last vestiges of a system in which Congress members were said to be "bought."

In late 1989, Congress voted to phase out honoraria by 1991. Starting in 1991, House members and staff were barred from keeping such fees although they can and do accept them and give them to charity. The Senate, which held on to a token $23,000-a-year limit, ended honoraria on August 14, 1991, when salaries for senators were raised to equal those of their House counterparts.

hopper   The box on the clerk's desk in both chambers where bills are placed upon introduction.

By extension, a bill that is *in the hopper* is in play.

horse   The member who agrees to be chief **sponsor** of a major bill or advocate of a position. "Who's our horse?" is an often asked question.

horse and jockey   Candidate who is also his or her own campaign manager. An axiom in politics is that one cannot effectively be both.

horse race   An election that is turning out to be close, usually confounding the experts. Other turf expressions, *down to the wire*, *stretch race*, and *photo finish*, denote elections that are too close to call.

horses   Valuable assets in an election or legislative contest. Having the horses means having the votes or the power to win. "If you've got the horses, then why make a big deal of it?" Democratic National Chairman Ron Brown said, explaining his preference for not gloating over a victory.

horse trading   Swapping political favors.

hospitality Euphemism for food, lodging, and travel offered by outsiders. It is permissible for members of Congress and their staffs to accept the personal hospitality of friends for a few days, but beyond that it gets ethically sticky, especially if one's friends have a legislative ax to grind. If an invitation is for a week, the home or lodge should be the host's, not his or her employer's, and the costs of the visit should not be written off as a business expense. If a member is invited to a condo in Aspen, with air fare, lift tickets, and ski rentals provided, the costs fall under the $250 minimum **gift** rule. Anything over, the member pays.

hot air Inflated, insincere rhetoric.

hot button Describing that which is value-intense and controversial. Hot-button issues are invariably those in which the electorate is most interested: abortion, gun control, Social Security changes, and congressional pay. For a while, flag burning was a very hot button.

ETYMOLOGY: Language columnist William Safire has traced this term to the 1970s, when it was first used in the field of consumer marketing. He quoted *Fortune* for September 11, 1978: "The marketers are searching for what they call 'consumer hot buttons'—needs to be satisfied, desires to be slaked—and the means to push those buttons."

Hotline A daily electronic newsletter containing political intelligence from across the country, including poll results, advertising campaigns, and predictions and analysis from pundits. It is published by the American Political Network.

house Either "house" of Congress, but, if capitalized, specifically the **House of Representatives.**

House Bank A loosely managed check-cashing facility in the Capitol that proved to be a debacle for many House members in 1992, a year of historic public disgust with Congress. After the General Accounting Office reported rampant overdrafts by hundreds of members, a House ethics panel disclosed the names of 325 present and former members who had overdrawn their accounts. The worst offender had written 996 checks for insufficient funds over a 39-month period.

The flap, which came to to be known as **Rubbergate**, temporarily undercut Democratic Speaker Thomas Foley's reputation as a deft leader and manager, ruined the political careers of several members, forced the resignation of Sergeant-at-Arms Jack Russ, who oversaw the Bank, and even reached across the Potomac to embarrass Defense Secretary Richard Cheney, a former member.

The Bank was not run by commonly accepted banking practices. It routinely posted deposits late, hand-listed overdrafts on the back of daily tally sheets, not bothering to inform the transgressor, and often covered the overdrafts with funds credited to other members' accounts. Foley declared the Bank "an anachronism" and closed it.

Even so, the scandal would not die. A special counsel, Malcolm R. Wilkey, was appointed to look into possible crimes and convinced a federal grand jury to issue a sweeping subpoena of House Bank records. That might have provoked a standoff based on the balance of separation of powers, but the politically battered House voted 347–64 to comply. Wilkey eventually cleared all but a handful of members of any criminal wrongdoing.

House gym   A well-equipped health facility for members only in the Rayburn Office Building basement. It contains a steam room, basketball and paddleball courts, a golf driving cage, treadmills, and weights. "Amid the steam and sweat, members of Congress engage in bipartisan bonding and quiet deal-making," Eleanor Clift of *Newsweek* wrote in January 1990.

housekeeping amendment   Punctuation or syntax change that does not alter the meaning of a bill. It is usually passed by **voice vote.**

House office building   *See* **HOB.**

House of Representatives   The legislative body designed by the Founding Fathers as the most directly connected to the American people, with members elected every two years and the sole authority to initiate tax and spending legislation. The House went into session in 1789 with 65 members. Now it has 435, with over 150 committees and subcommittees. Compared to the freewheeling Senate, the House is run with almost military discipline, with strict rules of decorum and debate. Each state is guaranteed at least one seat in the House, with additional seats awarded on the basis of population. *See box*, "The People's House."

House Rules Committee *See* **Rules Committee.**

House Un-American Activities Committee (HUAC)

(pronounced "hue-ack") House panel set up in 1938 under the chairmanship of Martin Dies, Jr. (D-Tex.), who zealously used it to pursue suspected Communists and other alleged subversives. The Dies committee, which became the HUAC in 1945, had a reputation for leaking unsubstantiated charges, issuing contempt citations for uncooperative witnesses, and inspiring blacklists: most were rosters of actors and writers who were kept from working because of supposed subversive ties. It was "almost like a dress rehearsal for the McCarthy era," said Michael Wreszin in the anthology *Congress Investigates, 1792–1974*. One of its most famous investigations was that of Alger Hiss, a former State Department official accused of being a communist. Then-Congressman Richard Nixon (R-Calif.) played a major role in pursuing Hiss, who was convicted of perjury and jailed. The panel survived several attempts to put it out of business and changed its name to the Internal Security Committee in 1969, but finally was put to rest in 1975.

In an April 29, 1959, lecture at Columbia University, former President Harry Truman said of the committee, "I've said many times that I think the Un-American Activities Committee in the House of Representatives was the most un-American thing in America!"

HR Abbreviation used before a bill number to indicate that it originated in the House of Representatives.

HUAC *See* **House Un-American Activities Committee.**

hundred days The crucial first three months or so of a president's term—for example, the March–May 1933 stretch for Roosevelt, when more far-reaching legislation was enacted by Congress than had passed in decades before. Sixty years later, the first 100 days of President Bill Clinton's term was subjected to intense analysis, underscoring the degree to which this period had become a media benchmark.

hurry-up spending Using appropriated funds quickly before the **fiscal year** comes to an end. Some agencies furiously exhaust their budgets in the final days of the fiscal year, "practically shipping the money out of the Treasury in wheelbarrows," Sen. William Cohen (R-Me.) once remarked.

hustings Where election speeches are made—i.e., before the electorate; not in the Capitol. The term comes from Hustings Court in London's Guildhall, where candidates for Parliament once addressed the voters. Candidates are said to be "out on the hustings."

ETYMOLOGY: The original hustings were assemblies and date back to the old Norse *husthing*, a compound word meaning "house assembly," which became *husting* in Old English. The editors of *Webster's Word Histories* suggest that the first husting may have been a body acting as a means of settling disputes between Danish and English merchants. In Norman times hustings were civil courts (a court of hustings still exists in the City of London), and over time the word was also applied to the place where officials were seated and spoke from—including political speeches. On both sides of the Atlantic the term was eventually applied to the political process itself.

hype Slang for exaggerated publicity generated by public relations representatives or **flacks** in advance of an event in an effort to assure greater coverage. The media itself can also hype an event by giving it more attention or treatment than it deserves.

hyperbole Exaggeration, to which legislators and most other politicians are especially given. Witness the comments by Sen. Alan Simpson (R-Wyo.) on the charges of sexual harassment against Supreme Court nominee Clarence Thomas: "this foul, foul stack of stench."

idiot sheets List of questions for witnesses in congressional hearings prepared for not-always-knowledgeable lawmakers by their staffs.

immunity

1 Privilege enjoyed by members of Congress, under the Constitution's "speech or debate" clause, which prevents them from being prosecuted for most things said while in office. Courts have ruled that certain activities, such as libelous press releases, non-legislative use of classified documents, or evidence of bribery, are not shielded from inquiry.

2 Exemption from prosecution given to a witness before a congressional committee in order to secure that person's testimony.

impeach To bring charges against a public official for **high crimes and misdemeanors.** The House impeaches and the Senate tries the charges. *Impeachment* is the actual bringing of charges against a public official, *not* the hearings or trial on those charges.

The only president to be impeached was Andrew Johnson, in 1868, but he was acquitted by the Senate. President Richard Nixon, under investigation for his role in the **Watergate** cover-up, resigned on August 9, 1974, as the House prepared to begin debate on impeaching him.

President Gerald Ford, who pardoned Nixon on September 8, 1974, even though he had not been convicted of any charges in the scandal, once said about the definition of impeachable violations,

The impeachment of President Andrew Johnson in 1868. A scowling Johnson is in the foreground of the engraving. *See* **impeach.**

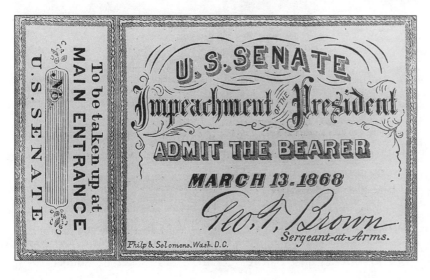

This ticket to the impeachment trial of President Andrew Johnson was almost as hard to come by then as it is now. An original ticket would be worth thousands in today's market for rare political ephemera. *See* **impeach.**

Demonstrators demand the impeachment of President Nixon in October 1973. *See* **impeach.**

"The honest answer is that an impeachable offense is whatever a majority of the House of Representatives considers [it] to be at a given moment in history."

See also **expulsion.**

imperial presidency The accretion of power in the executive branch. Arthur M. Schlesinger, who wrote his study *The Imperial Presidency* just before Richard Nixon's fall in August 1974, was concerned that the president had taken away Congress's war powers responsibility, withheld information, intimidated the press, refused to spend congressionally appropriated funds—all under the guise of national security. "It was as much a matter of congressional abdication as of presidential usurpation," he wrote. After Nixon's resignation, the pendulum swung the other way, with Congress passing the War Powers Act, the Budget and Impoundment Control Act, and asserting itself in other ways. Power has also swung toward an *imperial judiciary* and an *imperial press. Compare* **congressional government.**

impoundment Action taken by a president to delay or avoid spending sums approved by Congress for specific programs. The practice goes back at least to Jefferson, but stirred perhaps its biggest controversy when Nixon refused to spend billions of dollars for programs he did not like. Congress reasserted its control by passing the Budget and Impoundment Control Act of 1974, which created the **Congressional Budget Office.** *See also* **rescission.**

The act specifies that the president may ask that specific funds be rescinded—and may impound those funds for 45 days. But both houses must approve the rescission within that time or the funds must then be spent.

impropriety Act committed by a politician or a public official that oversteps ethical bounds. The House Committee on Standards of Official Conduct, in its report on the financial transactions and gifts of transportation of a congressman in 1987, cautioned all members "to avoid situations in which even an inference might be drawn suggesting improper action" *See also* **conflict of interest.**

in conference Expression used to describe the status of a bill after it has been referred to a committee but before it has been considered.

incumbent Member who currently holds office. The term is often invoked in an election year when the incumbent is challenged.

Incumbents, with their ability to get free publicity and keep constituents happy by doing constant favors, and blessed with voter apathy, were almost unbeatable until recent years. In 1988,

INCUMBENTS RETIRED, DEFEATED, OR REELECTED

Year	Retired*	Running	Defeated	Reelected	Percentage Reelected†
1980 House	34	398	37	361	90.7
Senate	5	29	13	16	55.2
1982 House	40	393	39	354	90.1
Senate	3	30	2	28	93.3
1984 House	22	409	19	390	95.4
Senate	4	29	3	26	89.6
1986 House	38	393	8	385	98.0
Senate	6	28	7	21	75.0
1988 House	23	408	7	401	98.3
Senate	6	32	4	23	85.2
1990 House	27	406	16	390	96.0
Senate	3	32	1	31	96.9
1992 House	65	368	43	325	88.3
Senate	6	24	3	21	87.5

*Does not include those who died or resigned before the election.
† Of those seeking reelection.

Source: Congressional Quarterly and authors' research.

98 percent of all incumbents who sought reelection were returned to office. Cornell University political scientist Benjamin Ginsberg asserted in *USA Today*, June 18, 1990, that more die in Congress than are defeated. "If God didn't vote, they would be there forever" (*see also* **permanent Congress**).

In 1992, a near-record 110 representatives were elected, and the incumbency rate dropped to 88 percent. *See box*, "Incumbents Retired, Defeated, or Reelected."

ETYMOLOGY: A press release on political words from the Merriam-Webster Co. issued during the 1988 election season noted, "'Incumbent' was added to the English vocabulary in the fifteenth century. The original denotation of the Latin word it came from was to lie down."

independent expenditure Campaign funds provided by an outside organization not affiliated with a candidate's campaign or with a political party. Such funds support a candidate with television, radio, or direct mail advertising. This arrangement enables a group to support an individual without running afoul of the campaign financing laws. Such support must be made wholly independently without collaboration or consultation with a candidate's campaign operation. According to an article on campaign financing in *The Economist*, "The National Rifle Association and the American Medical Association work this way." *See also* **campaign finance.**

industry representative Term often used by **lobbyists** to describe themselves.

infighter Politician who is not afraid of a political battle and, in fact, may relish one. A classic application of the term showed up in this line from a *San Francisco Chronicle* article of April 27, 1952, describing a battle between President Harry S. Truman and former Secretary of State James F. Byrnes: "Two tough political infighters, both Democrats, paused for breath last week after pummeling one another in public."

ETYMOLOGY: Originally, the term denoted a style of fist fighting at close quarters in which a smaller fighter—an infighter—would have a better chance with a larger opponent.

infighting Squabbling within political ranks, often stated as *political infighting* and often described as bitter. Although there are exceptions, infighting is described as a negative—as in the headline DIRTY IN-FIGHTING COULD SPLIT PARTY (*San Francisco Call-Bulletin*, July 7, 1952)—whereas an individual described as an **infighter** is respected as tough and wily.

influence Pull; the ability to help things happen or not happen. It is this commodity that lobbyists assert, to their clients at least, they have on the Hill.

influence peddler Lawyer, lobbyist, or anyone else who seeks special privileges from Congress for his or her clients, usually by acting as a middleman or a **facilitator.** The term is reserved for those who are paid for their brokering skills, some of which can be illegal. In 1970 Martin Voloshen and an aide to Speaker John W. McCormack (D-Mass.) were indicted and later convicted of

See also **broker**; *see box*, "Pipelayers and Wirepullers."

PIPELAYERS AND WIREPULLERS

Influence peddler is just one of many phrases describing those who make their livings guiding legislation. Here are a few from *The American Thesaurus of Slang* (1953), by Lester V. Berry and Melvin Van Den Bark:

- dress-suit burglar
- finagler
- highbinder
- legpuller
- lobby member
- pipelayer
- wirepuller

using the speaker's office to obtain favors for Voloshen's clients. Voloshen, who reportedly once bragged he "could do anything in Washington short of murder," carried the appellation "influence peddler" until his death in 1971. *See also* **broker**; *see box*, "Pipelayers and Wirepullers."

ETYMOLOGY: Although the term was doubtlessly already in use before 1951, it did not come into wide public use until the spring of that year, when a series of highly visible and shocking hearings concentrated on the role of influence peddlers. On the one hand, there was the Senate Investigating Subcommittee under the leadership of J. William Fulbright (D-Ark.) that looked into the near-bribery and influence selling in the deals of the Reconstruction Finance Corporation, and on the other hand, there was the subcommittee under the leadership of Chairman Clyde Hoey (D-N.C.) that looked into the general business of influence peddling. Both committees found many examples—then legal except in cases where a criminal conspiracy could be proven—but none so odd as the man who was pulling down a six-figure income selling "inside information" on the government's plan to spend millions to build underground shelters in case of nuclear attack.

influence peddling What an **influence peddler** does; the act of selling one's clout. At an April 29, 1986, hearing on legislation to discourage federal employees from entering the "revolving door" of government–private employment, Sen. Howard Metzenbaum (D-Ohio) said, "The plain truth is that Washington has become a sink-hole of influence peddling."

ink

1 To sign one's name.

2 Publicity, particularly in the printed media. "To get a lot of ink" is to be widely covered in the press.

in-kind contributions Political gifts other than an outright contribution of money. Once a favorite way to skirt campaign contribution limits, these gifts of services such as plane rides and use of office space or equipment are now treated the same as cash contributions.

inner circle A loyal group of insiders who quietly surround and advise a person in power.

Inner Club The phrase was coined by writer William S. White to describe those members of Congress who play by unwritten rules of devotion to the institution by serving a long apprenticeship before making speeches, and by settling differences in the back rooms rather than in public. "The inner life of the Senate," White says, "is controlled by the Inner Club." But Nelson W. Polsby, in his 1969 essay, "Goodbye to the Inner Club," discounted this notion because it "vastly underplayed the extent to which *formal* position—committee chairmanships, great seniority, and official party leadership—conferred power and status on individual senators almost regardless of their clubability."

inoculated candidate A politician who becomes immune to damage after surviving repeated attacks—like president Reagan, for example.

inquiry *See* **parliamentary inquiry; resolution.**

insert To place something in the ***Congressional Record***, either in the middle of a speech or in the **Extension of Remarks** section in the back pages.

insider Politician or political advisor who is in the ranks of decision makers or is well connected with those who are. Such a person is often called a *Washington insider*.

inside strategy A method of getting something accomplished by working within the system, lining up support among colleagues, and generally playing by the rules. For lobbyists, this strategy includes buttonholing members and staff for support. *Compare* **outside strategy.**

inside the Beltway The area outlined by the interstate highway that rings the city of Washington (*see* **Beltway**). The term is a popular metaphor for the parochialism and political intensity of Washington; it was coined in the 1970s by *Washington Post* columnist Mike Causey. *Compare* **outside the Beltway.**

insist Action by the Senate or House in refusing to accept the other body's version of a bill, thus triggering the formation of a **conference committee.**

instant majority An unexpected uprising in favor of a new amendment that undercuts the leadership's position. House leaders, with their penchant for predictability, wish to prevent this situation; that is why the rules of debate on major issues—including the number and language of amendments—are tightly controlled.

instructions Directives given to conferees in a House–Senate **conference committee** by their parent body requiring that they adhere to that body's position—in other words, that they not budge, even as they presumably work to compromise.

insults One of the reasons House and Senate rules require members to address the chair, even in debate with each other, is to minimize personal attacks. But scathing insults were once a congressional staple. As Sen. Robert Dole describes in his *Historical Almanac of the United States Senate*, another Kansan, John J. Ingalls (*see* **amen corner**), once caught Sen. Joseph E. Brown of Georgia changing the substance of their previous debate in the *Record*. Ingalls compared Brown to a "thug stabbing a sleeping enemy" and called him the "Uriah Heep of the Senate . . . a sniveling political Pecksniff." Alas, such rich and quotable rhetoric is now proscribed by House and Senate rules.

insurgents While this term applies to any rebellious group in Congress, it refers specifically to House members who on March 19, 1910, wrested control of the Rules Committee from autocratic Speaker Joseph Cannon by removing him from the committee. Three days later George Norris of Nebraska, a **Progressive** Republican who led the uprising, received a telegram from an admirer telling him to "keep on insurging." *See* **Cannonism.**

integrity A relentless adherence to a moral or political code. Former Rep. Frank D. Smith (D-Miss.) said this is "one of the favorite words members of the House use in assessing one another." But the real measure is power.

interested constituencies Voters in congressional districts with a predominant interest in a major area of legislation like agriculture, manufacturing, or urban affairs.

interest groups Groups that represent a set of policies. There are hundreds of these in Washington. Because politicians receive large campaign donations from these groups, they are accused of being bought and paid for by interest groups.

interrupted by applause Measure by which politicians rate major speeches such as the president's State of the Union address. An incumbent attempts to see how many times he or she can get interrupted after uttering a platitude about the economy, American jobs, or the sanctity of the Social Security system.

in the hopper *See* **hopper.**

in the loop Being on the distribution list for certain kinds of political information. In what Hedrick Smith calls the "national security power fraternity," you are in the loop if you are on "the short list" to receive daily intelligence documents. Members of congressional intelligence committees are in the loop if they have been consulted about sensitive military or intelligence operations. George Bush repeatedly claimed that as vice president (1981-89) he was "out of the loop" during discussions of secret weapon sales to Iran and the conversion of the proceeds into aid for Nicaraguan contras (*see* **Iran-Contra**).

introduce To bring legislation before the House or Senate for the first time. Bills are delivered to the House speaker or Senate president and then referred to committees. *See also* **lay down.**

investigation In the congressional context, the gathering of evidence and questioning of witnesses. With its oversight and confirmation responsibilities, Congress is constantly running investigations. It investigated un-American activities in the 1950s, racketeering in the 1960s, **Watergate** and assassinations in the 1970s, and **Iran-Contra** in the 1980s, and it is investigating Supreme Court nominees, military waste, and insurance fraud in the 1990s.

Crime boss Joseph Valachi prepares to testify at a sensational September 1963 Senate subcommittee hearing on crime. *See* **investigation.**

Congress has formidable power to hire investigators, subpoena witnesses, and issue contempt citations. Besides regular committees with oversight authority, it has several investigative committees. Occasionally, it ends up investigating itself. In the January 1, 1956, *New York Times Magazine*, humorist Will Rogers was quoted as having said, "About all I can say for the United States Senate is that it opens with prayer and closes with an investigation."

invisible government Any group of nonelected people who seem to have strong—but not commonly understood—powers. Variously, the term is applied to party bosses, consultants, think tanks, and lobbyists. The term was more broadly used as the title of a 1964 book by David Wise and Thomas B. Ross, in which the authors gave a disturbing view of the unchecked activities of the Central Intelligence Agency.

involuntary retirement Euphemism for defeat in an election.

IOUs Favors owed by one legislator to another.

Iran-Contra The popular name for wide-ranging hearings into the secret sale of arms to Iran to raise funds for the illegal funneling of cash and weapons to contra rebels in Nicaragua. The

Rep. Lee Hamilton of Indiana is seen with staff following a session of the Iran-Contra hearings on May 6, 1987. *See* **Iran-Contra.**

House and Senate held extraordinary joint hearings for 12 weeks beginning in November 1986 to investigate the scandal.

But the star of the televised proceedings was not an investigator, but rather Marine Lt. Col. Oliver North, whose forceful defense of the illicit policy gave him matinee-idol status and fostered a state of mind called "Olliemania." By contrast, North's accusers were seen as bullies. Even though the panel concluded that the Reagan administration broke the law, the message of guilt was muddled and the hearings failed in one of their most important purposes—to educate the public.

iron triangle The mutually reinforcing linkage of a government agency or program, the private industry or special interest it serves, and the congressional committee(s) that oversees it. There is such a well-entrenched triangle for most major federal programs. These triangles are so tightly bonded that they are said to be welded like iron.

In 1987, near the end of his term in office, President Ronald Reagan warned of the influence of the iron triangle; however, he substituted the news media for government agencies in his particular version.

See also **triple alliances.**

irreconcilables A group of isolationist senators who repeatedly and vociferously opposed America's entry into the League of Nations after World War I.

item veto *See* **line-item veto.**

itemized appropriation Amount of money **earmarked** and stipulated for a specific purpose or project, in contrast to a **lump-sum** or general appropriation for an agency or program.

Jackson Democrat A Democrat who favors a strong defense as well as liberal social policies, like the late Henry ("Scoop") Jackson (D-Wash.), for whom the term is named.

Jefferson's Manual A collection of procedural rules and customs of the English Parliament, developed by Thomas Jefferson for his own use when he presided over the Senate as vice president from 1797 to 1801. They form the basis for the many rules of Congress.

Jessecrats The antiliberal followers of Sen. Jesse Helms (R-N.C.). In his *Hard Right: The Rise of Jesse Helms*, Ernest B. Furgurson wrote, "In Carolina today the once solidly Democratic tractor-cap vote is called collectively 'Jessecrats.' "

Joe Six-Pack An average working-class voter—presumably one who likes beer. The term is used with a certain degree of affection. After Delaware Gov. Pierre S. du Pont, a patrician millionaire, sought to ally himself politically with such "Joe Six-Packs," a Wilmington cartoonist in January 1978 christened him "Pierre S. Six Pacque IV."

First Used: Columnist Arthur Hoppe of the *San Francisco Chronicle* was one of the first to use this personification (albeit spelled differently) in a September 6, 1972, piece entitled "Joe Sikspack Loves a Fight." It was an open letter to President Nixon that began with the lines: "DEAR PRESIDENT: I, Joe Sikspak, American, take pen in hand to get it off my chest. Congratulations to you and the Mrs. and Spiro, too." *See also* **Six-Pack Republican.**

Joe Six-Pack Republican *See* **Six-Pack Republican.**

Johnson Rule In 1953, while Lyndon B. Johnson (D-Tex.) was Senate minority leader, he made it a policy to assign junior Democrats to at least one major committee before allowing senior Democrats to preempt all the seats on such committees. The Republicans adopted a similar practice in 1959.

joint Describing that which involves both chambers of Congress, such as a **joint committee**, **joint resolution**, or **joint session.**

joint committee A House–Senate panel with a common purpose, such as a major investigation. Some, like the Joint Committee on Printing, have purely housekeeping functions. In 1992, in the midst of what some called institutional **gridlock**, Congress set up the Joint Committee on the Organization of Congress.

joint resolution A policy statement passed by both houses that has the force of law and is subject to the veto of the president. A similar resolution passed by both houses but lacking the force of law is known as a **concurrent resolution**. It usually expresses the "sense of Congress" regarding a pending issue of policy. *Compare* **simple resolution.**

joint session A gathering of both House and Senate, always in the larger House Chamber, to hear speeches by the president or foreign leaders, to count electoral votes every four years, or to consider the president's request for a declaration of war.

joker

1 A **rider** or **amendment** to a bill that has nothing to do with the subject of the bill—akin to a joker in a deck of playing cards. *See also* **clinker.**

2 A provision added to a bill that changes its meaning.

Usage: Seldom used today, this was once the common term for an extraneous rider.

Vice President Richard M. Nixon and Speaker of the House Sam Rayburn congratulate President Dwight D. Eisenhower at a January 10, 1957, joint session. The occasion was that year's State of the Union message. *See* **joint session.**

Journal   Short for *Congressional Journal.*

judge   Appellation once bestowed on chairmen of the House Rules Committee, even if they had no judicial background.

judicial review   The principle by which the Supreme Court exercises its authority to determine whether acts of Congress are constitutional. It is an actual review or examination of laws and acts by the Court.

jugular   One of two large veins in the neck carrying blood from the brain to the heart. To "go for the jugular" is, figuratively, to kill. Someone who lacks the "jugular instinct" has no stomach for political **infighting** and combat. The term is used in descriptions of Congressional campaigns.

juice bill   Any piece of proposed legislation that causes lobbyists on either side of the issue to spend lots of money—in other words, a bill ripe for squeezing.

junior senator

1 The most recently elected of the senators in a state delegation.

2 Facetiously, a senator's **AA** (administrative assistant).

junket Derogatory term for an expenses-paid, **fact-finding trip** made by a member of Congress. A trip is a junket if paid for by public funds or by a special-interest group. In recent years Congress has spent more than $4 million a year on foreign travel. Junkets have a negative image, but they have proven useful. *Newsweek* noted that a tour of the Philippines in 1985 alerted members of the House to the impending fall of the Marcos regime.

The late Sen. Jacob Javits (R-N.Y.), who once led a delegation to China, put it this way: "We spend billions of dollars in preparing for war. To suggest that we should not spend thousands for peace is absurd." Still, according to *Newsweek*, Asia remains a favorite

Members of a congressional delegation investigating ancient ruins in Persepolis, Iran, in 1976. *See* **junket.**

pre-Christmas port of call for congressmen who buy their gifts in Hong Kong.

Domestic junkets may be almost as exotic. In 1989 the *Washington Post* took a look at preferred destinations for expense-paid trips and found a proclivity for Florida (particularly Palm Beach) and California (particularly Palm Springs).

ETYMOLOGY: Junket is from the Latin word *juncus*, for the rush used to make the rush baskets in which one brought cream cheeses to market. The term came to mean cream cheese, and then more generally "feast" or "banquet," and then "roistering celebration." To English author Hugh Walpole, in an 1837 letter, it stood for fun. "You are as junkettaceous as my lady Northumberland," he wrote.

The word is a boon to political cartoonists, who can caricature members visiting the Folies Bergere, as well as to reporters, who have long delighted in writing provocative reports about globe-trotting legislators (as in "Members of Congress continue to display a disturbing indifference to public opinion as they take off on extended junkets all over the world at public expense"—a wire service dispatch, *San Francisco Examiner*, November 24, 1972).

junketeer Member of Congress given to travel outside of his or her district. All too often, the junketeer is more than willing to give up precious winter days in Washington, D.C., to discuss Atlantic–Pacific relations under the hot Hawaiian sun or to address the issue of Caribbean cooperation at poolside in Montego Bay.

junk vote Slang for the practice of taking stands on both sides of a controversial subject. For instance, in 1987 the House voted against a pay raise that had taken effect the day before. This junk vote allowed an individual to pocket the pay raise while going on the record opposing it. A vote for a gun-control amendment to a bill that has no chance of passing is another example.

jurisdiction The range or sphere of authority of a committee. Occasionally, when there is overlapping jurisdiction with a second committee, the speaker will refer a bill to different committees, which in turn handle different parts of it. Sometimes committees have jurisdictional battles, or **turf wars**, during which they try to broaden their spheres at the expense of other panels. Weak chairmen give ground. Strong ones do not.

Efforts to clarify committee jurisdictions and eliminate overlap have been contentious. "We could not even resolve who had jurisdiction of the walls, the floor, and the toilets," Sen. Mark Hatfield (R-Ore.) said of past attempts to reform the system.

justification Documents submitted by federal agencies to the **appropriations** committees in support of budget requests.

kamikaze Democrat Member of an uncompromising left-wing Democrat tribe, originally hailing from Texas. According to *Washington Post* columnist Edwin M. Yoder, Jr., kamikaze Democrats characteristically "despised conservative allies more than they liked beating Republicans."

ETYMOLOGY: A Japanese term meaning literally "divine wind," *kamikaze* was applied by the warlords of World War II to an elite corps of men willing to make suicidal attacks on enemy ships in explosives-laden aircraft. Since 1945, the term has been used in English for anyone or anything displaying recklessness.

kamikaze mission Tactic or motion sure to fail, but attempted anyway for political effect. Sen. Jesse Helms (R-N.C.) was credited with offering hundreds of "kamikaze amendments" on issues like busing, sex education, abortion, and school prayer, that while failing to pass, served to force opponents to cast embarrassing votes—and to generate contributions to his political causes from C-SPAN viewers.

kamikaze tactic A destructive strategy employed for political gain, such as trying to engineer a budgetary crisis in order to gain a tax increase. It is a tactic that one party frequently accuses the other of employing.

Kasten plan Name for precinct-organization plan designed to turn out the conservative vote, pioneered by former U.S. Sen.

Robert Kasten (R-Wis.) when he ran for the state Senate. It sets specific vote goals for a network of precinct leaders.

Keating Five Name given to the five senators accused of intervening in 1987 with banking regulators on behalf of former savings and loan executive Charles H. Keating, Jr., who had contributed more than $1.3 million to their campaigns and causes.

Four of the senators—Dennis DeConcini (D-Ariz.), John Glenn (D-Ohio), John McCain (R-Ariz.), and Donald Riegle (D-Mich.)—were found by the Senate ethics committee to have used poor judgment in their contacts with Keating. Sen. Alan Cranston (D-Calif.) was "condemned" by the Senate for engaging in an "impermissible pattern of conduct in which fund-raising and official activities were substantially linked."

key resources people *See* **KRPs**.

kickback An illegal arrangement by which an employee gives back a portion of his or her salary to an employer. Several members and their aides have been prosecuted over the years for kickback schemes under federal fraud statutes.

kicker A hidden, unsuspected section of a bill. There are often dozens of kickers in supplemental **appropriation** bills. Sen. Robert Byrd (D-W. Va.), the chairman of the Senate Appropriations Committee, was reputed to be the master kicker, especially when his state benefitted. Without a hearing, Byrd had the 2,600-job FBI fingerprint center moved from Washington, D.C., to Clarksburg, West Virginia, by inserting the appropriate language into the 1990 Commerce, Justice, State and Judiciary appropriation bill.

kill To recommit a bill to a committee, thus effectively killing it for floor consideration.

killer amendment An addition that either completely rewrites a bill or destroys its effectiveness.

killer bee Description by Sen. Robert Byrd (D-W. Va.) of a **balanced budget** constitutional amendment. Byrd, chairman of the

"Killed in committee."

The spider in this 1906 *Puck* cover illustration is Nelson Aldrich (R-R.I.). *See* **kill.**

Senate Appropriations Committee, called it "a killer bee amendment that we and our children and grandchildren will rue for generations to come and for which we in this Congress would be blamed as long as men remember our names."

king cash The reign of special interests over legislators by means of political contributions and lobbying.

king caucus The system under which party leaders could impose their views on the House through powerful caucuses. When Democrats took over the House in 1910 and dethroned "Czar" Joseph Cannon (R-Ill.), they declared that a two-thirds vote in a caucus bound every party member to vote in lockstep on the floor (*see* **Cannonism**).

kingfish A person who wields absolute power. The late Gov. Huey Long (D-La.) was the most famous holder of that nickname.

kingmaker *See* **broker.**

king of the mountain A House rule providing that the last amendment adopted for a given bill is the one that prevails. Thus, an amendment that might have passed by a substantial margin can later be cut off at the knees by a subsequent one that passes by the narrowest of margins.

kingpin Like the center pin in bowling, the leader or essential person in a group. A political kingpin is a leader or top party official, especially the head of a political machine.

Kitchen Cabinet Ordinarily used to describe informal—thus "kitchen"—advisors to a president, but the term can also describe key staffers or influential friends and **cronies** of a member of congress.

Etymology: The term was first used in reference to the Andrew Jackson administration (1829–37).

kiting Writing checks without the funds on deposit to back them up. This expression was used interchangeably but erroneously with "bouncing" in news reports of the 1992 **House Bank** affair.

kitty

1 The campaign fund or **war chest** accumulated by a politician for an upcoming election.

2 An appropriation category.

knee jerk One who, like the reflex action of a knee being tapped by a doctor's hammer, reacts predictably. "The most notorious Congressman from Iowa is cranky old H. R. Gross, a seventy-year-old knee-jerk best remembered for castigating the Reverend Bill Moyers for dancing the frug in the White House ..." Larry L. King wrote in *Harper's*, March 1952.

knife thrower A **lobbyist** who knows who the decision makers are and how to get to them.

Koreagate Scandal of the mid-1970s in which Congress members were indicted for taking gifts from Korean lobbyists. *See also* **-gate.**

KRPs U.S. Chamber of Commerce initialism for *key resources people,* who have close personal relationships with their senator or representative.

K Street The wide, glass-box boulevard in downtown Washington where many lobbyists and law firms have their offices. By extension, an allusion to the many high-powered industry representatives who put pressure on Congress.

LA Legislative assistant. The person in a congressional office who is in charge of legislation. *See also* **AA.**

lady lobbyist Term used in the nineteenth century for women who were employed by those wishing to influence legislation and whose hospitality and charm were offered to members of Congress as bribes. In some accounts, seduction was part of the package.

In his 1938 history of gambling in America, *Sucker's Progress*, Herbert Asbury points out that these women were used by lobbyists as a fallback to the gambling den. "To influence Congressmen who were immune to the fascinations of Faro, [one lobbyist] utilized the services of women who were politely referred to by journalists as 'lady lobbyists,' a term which by no means fully describes their activities."

lame duck

1 An incumbent member who has lost an election but whose term has not yet expired. Originally, lame duck sessions of Congress were the rule rather than the exception. The Constitution required Congress to convene on the first Monday in December of every year, but those elected in November of even-numbered years did not take office until March 4.

The Twentieth ("Lame Duck") Amendment, ratified in 1933, set January 3 as the date for terms and sessions to begin, partly curing the problem. January 3, 1934, was the first time Congress met under the new system.

The term is also applied to presidents who have been defeated at the polls or cannot run again because of the two-term limitation.

ETYMOLOGY: The term was borrowed from British financial slang and was used as far back as the early nineteenth century to de-

---

LAME DUCK SESSIONS

The passage in 1933 of the 20th Amendment to the Constitution, establishing noon on January 3 as the time and date for beginning terms and sessions, created the possibility that Congress could be in session after the November election while some retired or defeated members were still in office. Such "lame duck" sessions have been held 10 times.

1940–41. War threatens. Although President Roosevelt said it was unnecessary, Congress elected to "stand by" in case of emergency. It met regularly through mid-October, then less often until January 3. Little was accomplished in this session and quorums were hard to raise.

1942. War. Congress remained in session until December 16, but the election that year sharply reduced the Democratic majority, putting a damper on the lame duck session. During this session, Congress approved the draft of 18- and 19-year olds, but other items, including a war powers bill and expansion of the Reconstruction Finance Corporation, were left to the next Congress.

1944. War. Congress recessed for the November election, but returned on November 14 and stayed until December 19. It delayed a Social Security tax increase, renewed the War Powers Act, and increased the clerk-hire allowance by $3000 to $9500. The Senate confirmed Edward R. Stettinius as secretary of state.

1948. Formalities. During a special session called by President Truman that summer, Congress agreed to reconvene on December 31. During the minisession—lasting only an hour and a half—it approved several minor resolutions and swore in new members. The House Un-American Activities Committee resumed investigation of alleged communist espionage in government.

1950–51. War. The conflict in Korea dominated the November 27–January 2 session. Several items on President Truman's "must" list were approved, including new rent controls, a far-ranging civil defense program, and famine relief for Yugoslavia. Statehood bills for Alaska and Hawaii were delayed in the Senate and eventually shelved.

1954. McCarthy. The House adjourned prior to the November election, but the Senate reconvened on November 8 for the sole purpose of considering a resolution to censure Sen. Joseph McCarthy (R-Wis.) for improprieties in his communist-hunting investigations. By a 67–22 vote, the Senate acted to "condemn" McCarthy for his behavior, then adjourned.

1970–71. Unfinished business. Seven regular appropriations bills, along with other major issues—electoral reform, family assistance, clean air, equal rights for women—brought Congress back on November 16. Several major items were blocked by filibusters. President Nixon chided Congress for seemingly losing "the capacity to decide and the will to act," then vetoed several measures that were passed.

1974. Succession. Delayed by the Watergate investigation, President Nixon's resignation, and the succession of Gerald Ford, Congress reconvened on November 18 with much unfinished business. Before going home on December 20, it approved the vice-presidential nomination of Nelson Rockefeller, a mass transit bill, and a foriegn aid package. It also overrode two Ford vetoes: one broadening the Freedom of Information Act, and another providing educational benefits for Korean and Vietnam War veterans.

1980. Unfinished business. Congress returned on November 12 to act on the budget and appropriations, as well as many other pending measures. It passed Alaska lands and "superfund" cleanup bills, decorated a continuing appropriations bill with more than 100 "Christmas tree" amendments, including a $10,000 pay raise. It turned out the lights on December 16.

1982. Economy. Congress convened on November 29 upon President Reagan's request to handle 10 appropriations bills. A worsening economy overshadowed a session marked by filibusters in the Senate and disagreements with Reagan policies in the House. Measures increasing the gas tax and approving a 15-percent pay raise were passed. The House adjourned on December 21, the Senate on December 23.

scribe a stockbroker who could not cover his losses and was said "to waddle out of the alley like a lame duck." It is one of a number of "animalisms" that originated in British financial markets, along with *bull* and *bear*, which drive markets to this day.

First applied to politicians in 1863, it was not widely used to describe congressional losers until about 1924. It was applied to President Eisenhower in 1959 when he could not run for a third term. A typical newspaper headline of that year read IKE, THE "LAME DUCK," IS FLYING HIGHER THAN EVER (*San Francisco News*, August 17, 1959). In this context, the *Encyclopedia Britannica* lists it as a neologism for 1958–59 in its *Yearbook*. There were earlier applications, however; on December 8, 1910, *New York Post* reported that a portion of the White House, "where statesmen who went down in the recent electoral combat may meet," was being referred to as "lame duck alley."

2 Adjective applied to Congresses after November elections and before the convening of a new Congress in January. *See box*, "Lame Duck Sessions."

language

1 The wording, hence the specifics, of a piece of legislation. It is possible to have general support for a bill but not for its language. Through tinkering amendments that change the crucial language of a bill, opponents can derail it.

2 Prepackaged administration reaction to an issue or question that clarifies the issue at hand. This second meaning may have emerged from the State Department 30 years ago or more as the need was felt to give the White House and Congress "language" on a given issue.

Columnist Art Hoppe of the *San Francisco Chronicle* first ran into the term in 1962, and got this reaction from "somebody" in the State Department press section:

> Here at State we supply material on foreign issues to any Government official, elective or appointed, who wants to make a speech or write a letter to a constituent. Now we have three kinds of material. At the top are Position Papers and such. Very official. Next down are texts of speeches by Mr. Rusk or Mr. Ball and the like. You call this semi-official. And at the bottom comes Language.

Hoppe goes on to explain:

Language? ...If a crisis pops tomorrow morning, obviously we won't have a Position Paper on it without Study. Nor will we have texts of official speeches for at least several days. But several Congressmen may want to make speeches immediately. And naturally they want to know what position to take. So as soon as each new crisis breaks, we draw up Language. You might call Language unofficially semi-official.

languish Condition of bills that are long ignored: they tend to lose vigor or, as in one definition from *Webster's New World Dictionary*, "suffer with longing."

lap dog Person or organization that willingly does the bidding of a political master. *Washington Post* television critic Tom Shales, referring to the Clarence Thomas confirmation hearings in 1991, wrote, "Some devoted White House lap dogs who'd become attack dogs for the nomination were still snarling even though victory was at hand." The name is not applied just to people, however, as Sen. Kit Bond (R-Mo.) illustrated in a March 3, 1992, news release in which he asked, "Is the General Accounting Office an independent watchdog or a pet lapdog?" *Compare* **attack dog.**

lard bucket Humorist Dave Barry's description of the **pork**-filled 1991 Transportation Bill.

late night During busy times, the Congress often stays in session far into the night to finish its business. In his poem "To the States," Walt Whitman was moved to ask:

Who are they, as bats and night-dogs, askant in the Capitol?
Are these really Congressmen?

laundry list List of a party's or administration's legislative goals.

law An act of Congress that has either been passed and signed by the president or that has been passed, vetoed by the president, and overridden by Congress. Laws are listed numerically, with the number of the Congress as a numerical prefix (a law enacted during the 103rd Congress, for instance, begins with the number 103).

lawyer's bill Any bill that would create a lot of confusion and litigation if enacted.

lay down To **introduce**, as a bill or resolution.

lay on the table *See* **table.**

leader Title for a member of Congress who has risen to leadership rank. There are **majority leaders** and **minority leaders** in both House and Senate. **Whips** are sometimes called **assistant majority leaders/assistant minority leaders.**

ETYMOLOGY: The term, in its political context, was first applied to the chief spokesman for the government in the British House of Commons when the prime minister was a member of the House of Lords and thus could not speak in the House of Commons.

leadership, the Collective term used by Congress to refer to its officers and ranking committee members. The term has a certain vagueness, however, that was addressed by Rep. Jerry Voorhis (D-Calif.) in his book *Confessions of a Congressman:*

> "The Leadership" is a term constantly used in conversation among House members. It can mean the Speaker alone or the Speaker and the majority leader, or those two gentlemen plus their unofficial advisers among the older members. No one ever knows, without asking, just what "the leadership" does mean.

> Former Senate Majority Leader Mike Mansfield's comment on the term was, "The leadership has no special powers to lead"— alluding to the fact that certain individuals like Sam Rayburn and Lyndon Johnson created their own "powers to lead."

leadership ladder Steps on the path to power in Congress. In the House, the first rung is generally deputy whip or caucus chairman. Once on the ladder, a member may begin a long— often interminable—rise to the speakership. The Senate has no similar route to the top rung. In fact, leaps from **whip** to leader have been the exception rather than the rule.

leak The release of confidential information primarily to the media. Leaking is endemic to Congress and in fact to the entire

Left to right: Senators Jacob Javits,
Warren Magnusen, Philip Hart,
Thomas Kuchel, Everett Dirksen,
Hubert Humphrey, and Kenneth
Keating strike the traditional
pose of leadership in front of
the Capitol dome in the 1960s.
See **leadership, the.**

Washington establishment. It is routinely used by the executive branch to test or prepare public opinion before going to Congress for a solution. When government bureaucrats see their pet projects are about to be savaged by budget cutters, they invoke what *Washington Post* reporter John Yang called "the classic Washington rule of bureaucratic infighting: When you think you're losing, leak."

One of the most notorious leaks in Senate history turned the 1991 Supreme Court nomination of Clarence Thomas into a major televised event. University of Oklahoma law professor Anita Hill alleged, in private affidavits to the Senate Judiciary Committee, that Thomas, while director of the Equal Employment Opportunity Commission, had made improper sexual advances toward her. The committee failed to take the charges seriously until they were leaked to members of the media. Sensational hearings, complete with explicit details, were the result.

The displeased senators voted for an investigation of the leaks and turned the matter over to a special counsel, Peter E. Fleming, who subpoenaed the reporters to disclose their sources. They refused, and a constitutional crisis was at hand. Had Fleming gotten permission from the Rules Committee to compel testimony, the reporters could have been cited for contempt and jailed.

Sen. Daniel Patrick Moynihan (D-N.Y.), who opposed the move, exclaimed, "Surely we're not daft enough to bring these journalists before us in chains when they've done nothing wrong. What the hell is going on here? Are there not enough self-inflicted wounds around here without this?"

National Public Radio reporter Nina Totenberg, one of those who broke the story, said the disclosures may have been an "embarrassment" but "not a crime." She added that "to subpoena reporters—and thus to threaten them with prison—in order to force disclosure of their sources, is, I think, very much akin to the Sedition Act of 1798." That law set stiff penalties for malicious writings about public officials or the government.

ETYMOLOGY: As early as 1832, *Webster's Dictionary* described this verb as "to escape privately from confinement or secrecy; as a fact or report." In 1840, Richard Henry Dana, in his novel *Two Years Before the Mast*, wrote of "rumours of such a ship to follow us, which had leaked out from the captain."

Thomas Nast chose to depict Sen. David Davis as a roly-poly toy to show the senator's many leanings. Davis, on the other hand, considered himself an independent. *See* **leaning.**

THE MANDARIN IN THE SENATE.

leaning Status of a legislator who is still uncommitted on a major upcoming vote but tending—or leaning—toward one side or the other. As Daniel Shorr of National Public Radio put it, "Leaning gets you on TV."

leave to address the House Phrase used by a member desiring to schedule a speech on a subject not involved in a House debate. In asking for leave to address the House, the legislator requests a specific date and time to make the speech.

leaving the station From the metaphor "The train is leaving the station," this is said of a bill about to be passed. It is given as a warning to members to get their **riders** on board or miss out on the **gravy**. Promptness is advisable in the House, where **nongermane** amendments can be declared out of order if offered later on the floor. Thus members are advised to insert their amendments in committee before the train gets under way. In the Senate, where there is no germaneness rule, the train always has a head of steam and every day is Christmas. Lobbyists, like those for the health care industry in 1993, used this expression when it was clear that a bill would pass and that it was wiser for them to work with lawmakers than against them.

A legislative train that is leaving the station has so much momentum that it cannot be stopped. And getting on board is not always a good idea, especially if it is loaded with political freight. "It appears that the tax train is leaving the station and the middle-income people have been left behind," House Majority Leader Richard Gephardt (D-Mo.) declared on February 11, 1992, in chiding President George Bush for loading his tax proposals with tax breaks for business and well-to-do investors.

left/left wing The liberal side of a party or chamber. The term originally referred to the position of seats in a legislative chamber—on the left side of the aisle—held by members holding liberal views.

leftovers/leftover funds *See* **excess campaign funds.**

leg counsel (pronounced "ledge counsel") Short for **legislative counsel.**

legislation A proposed change, or changes, in the law.

legislative assistant *See* **LA.**

legislative counsel A term that some **lobbyists** use to describe themselves.

legislative dance The intricate series of steps that a bill must undergo before becoming law.

legislative day The time between the moment either house convenes and the moment it adjourns. The House normally adjourns at the end of every day, but the Senate rarely does. Senate majority leaders prefer instead to recess because of the time-consuming procedures need to crank up the Senate. The **morning hour,** for instance—which lasts for two hours, not one—must be endured before legislative business can be conducted. Legislative days in the Senate, in fact, may last several weeks or even months. On May 24, 1993, for instance, the Senate calendar still read April 19. *See also* **adjourn.**

legislative history The hearings and debates that take place when a bill is considered. Members often engage in debate over legislation to clarify their intent so that when legal questions arise—and they always do—lawyers and judges will understand their intent in approving or opposing the law.

legislative intent The purpose of a bill or resolution. Intent is frequently spelled out in hearings and reports that courts later comb when laws are challenged.

legislative liaison

1 Lobbying as performed by those who euphemistically call themselves legislative liaisons.

2 The relationship between the executive branch and the legislative branch. The purpose of legislative liaison is pursuing presidential programs on the Hill.

legislative oversight Formal term for **oversight.**

Legislative Service Organization The correct and official name for special-interest **caucuses** within Congress—for instance, the Congressional Black Caucus and the Senate Children's Caucus.

legislative veto Process by which Congress overrules the actions of federal agencies. It was deemed to be an invasion of legislative authority on the executive by the Supreme Court on June 23, 1983, and was ruled unconstitutional. *See also* **veto.**

legislative work "Not what congressmen do; euphemism for lobbying," according to the June 20, 1988, issue of *Newsweek*.

level playing field Fairness on the part of the majority toward a minority. This favorite, and therefore widely used, expression on Capitol Hill is often invoked by a minority on a particular issue, when it is usually prefaced by, "All we're asking for is a..."

liberal In current usage, one who is to the **left** of center politically and desires to improve social conditions through actions of government. Before the presidency of Franklin Delano Roosevelt (1933-1945), liberalism was associated with individual liberty and limited government. Roosevelt stretched the concept to embrace social well-being for the majority rather than liberty for the few

Ray Milland hunts for microfilm in the main reading room of the Library of Congress in the 1952 film thriller *The Thief.* *See* **Library of Congress.**

The Main Reading Room of the Library of Congress, shown here before an early 1990s renovation replaced the card catalogs with computer terminals. *See* **Library of Congress.**

and firmly planted his party in that soil. Since the late 1960s many Democrats have sought to shed the liberal label, while opponents have sought to attach it to them. In a demonstration of pique against congressional critics, President Bush on January 15, 1992, said that he was tired of "hearing one of these carping little liberal Democrats jumping all over my you-know-what."

Library of Congress Created by Congress in 1800, it is now the world's biggest library, with 97 million items. The library, with its three imposing buildings on the Capitol complex and reposi- tories around the country, has a collection that includes 27 million books, 4 million maps, 12 million prints and photographs, and 7 million musical pieces. It had a $267 million budget in 1990, with a staff of 5,000.

lieutenant A congressional **aide** or **deputy.** This individual is counted on to carry out the will of a **chairman** or **leader.**

limousine conservative Label applied to conservatives with expensive tastes, most recently to former White House Chief of Staff John Sununu, who made a habit of using government transportation for personal business.

limousine liberal A wealthy political liberal. It is used in the pejorative sense to describe a rich politician who would blithely tax the middle class to fund programs for the poor or one who talks about the importance of public schools but sends his or her children to the most exclusive private schools. The slur was used with telling force by conservatives to criticize former New York City Mayor John Lindsay, a liberal Republican.

line-item veto The power to delete individual items in **appropriation** bills—often loaded with pet congressional projects—rather than vetoing entire bills. Presidents often say they need this power to curb reckless spending in Congress.

In 1992 Sen. John McCain (R-Ariz.) proposed letting the president, within 20 days of signing an appropriation bill, strike out individual items. These **rescissions** would take effect unless Congress passed a resolution of disapproval by a two-thirds majority. Appropriations Chairman Robert C. Byrd (D-W. Va.) called this proposal "quack medicine which would be better denominated as snake oil." Democratic President Bill Clinton, who favors the line-item veto, said in November 1992 that he was "intrigued" by a proposal to tie the line-item veto to majority vote approval by Congress.

See also **enhanced rescission authority.**

litmus test A position or vote so closely associated with a political philosophy that it immediately classifies a politician or movement. The litmus-test issue for some feminist groups may be abortion rights; for conservatives the issue may be capital gains taxes. In 1990 when President George Bush nominated David H. Souter to the Supreme Court, he said, "There was no single issue, no litmus test or standard dominating my decision to nominate…"

ETYMOLOGY: Litmus derives from a Scandinavian word for a coloring matter taken from lichens that turns red in acid solutions and blue in alkaline solutions. It is infused into unsized paper and used as an acid/base indicator. Over time litmus came to mean a single factor that is decisive. *Webster's Ninth New Collegiate Dictionary* lists the date of origin for litmus paper as 1803 and litmus test as 1952.

little band of willful men/little group of willful men

President Woodrow Wilson's exasperated characterization of a group of isolationist senators who filibustered to death his bill to arm merchant ships. By extension, this has come to mean a small, fanatical minority bent on preventing the enactment of legislation.

little legislatures President Woodrow Wilson's description of the standing committees of Congress. It was coined to reflect Wilson's oft-quoted view that "Congress, in its committee rooms, is Congress at work." The term is still commonly alluded to in books and articles on the working of Congress and was, in fact, the title of a book on the standing committees by George Goodwin, Jr.

live pair An arrangement under which a member who is present and one who is absent, and who are on opposite sides of an issue, agree not to vote, thereby canceling each other out. They are recorded as "paired." *See also* **pair.**

live quorum A real **quorum** of members, as opposed to the usual *pro forma* quorum, when hardly anyone responds. The signal of two **bells** for a quorum of the Senate is simply a device to stall for time.

lobby

1 To seek to influence legislators in the passage, amending, or defeat of legislation.

2 A group united to exert pressure in favor of a particular industry, issue, or point of view.

Etymology: The term derives from the First Congress held in New York City's Federal Hall in 1789, when merchants, farmers, and others with a first-hand interest in the outcome of legislation were forced to wait outside in the lobby. They were originally called *lobby agents*, and they typically came to ask for personal favors, charters, contracts, jobs, patents, and copyrights.

lobbyist A person, usually a paid professional, who seeks to influence legislation for a client or employer. Under law, lobbyists are required to register as such with the **clerk of the House.** In reality, few lobbyists call themselves lobbyists and are likely to use a business card description such as *industry representative, trade group representative* or *Washington representative,* and *legislative counsel*. A 1992 study by Sen. Carl Levin (D-Mich.) indicated

"The lobby of the House of Representatives during the passage of the Civil Rights Bill."

The civil rights bill referred to is the Civil Rights Act of 1866, which was designed to protect the rights of freed men. It nullified laws passed in the Southern states that restricted the rights of freed slaves, including, in some cases, the right to appear in public. *See* **lobby.**

"Congressional pests—lady lobbyists importuning senators at the Capitol, Washington, D.C."

The original caption (above) to this mid-nineteenth-century engraving expresses a popular contemporary attitude toward the highly charged issue of women lobbyists. *See* **lobbyist**.

that only about one out of four professional lobbyists bothered to register.

Columnist Jack Anderson wrote: "Every two years, Congress listens to the people. Every day, Congress listens to the lobbyists." In 1978, columnist Sydney Harris said, "Laws by themselves are ineffective tools for reform: consider that the state constitution of California (now 100 years old) made 'lobbying' a felony."

Starting in 1947, lobbyists were required to report their activities, and a summary is published in the *Congressional Record*. The first such report appeared in May 1947, identifying nearly 800 lobbyists (including two clergymen, a former congressman, and a man who had served Franklin D. Roosevelt as a speech writer and confidant). By 1979 there were more than five times that number registered, but some observers think this figure is low.

By 1983 there were anywhere from the 5,000 officially registered lobbyists to an estimated 80,000 who in one way or another try to influence legislation. Responding to public mistrust of lobbyists and their influence in Congress, the Senate in May 1993 approved the most far-reaching overhaul of lobbying laws in half a century. The Senate resolution would prohibit gifts of more than $20 to lawmakers or their staffs and require that all lobbyists register and file semi-annual reports disclosing whom they represent, how much they spend and on what issue, and whom they contact. *See* **PAC**; *also box,* "In the Lobby."

ETYMOLOGY: By 1829 the term "lobby-agent" had emerged from the term **lobby** and was soon modified to lobbyist. It was one of several nineteenth-century terms for **influence peddler**, including "boodler" and "striker."

lock it up   Get all sides to agree to a compromise.

loco-foco   Legislator said to be in the pay of outside interests. Charges that corporations and trusts were able to buy legislators helped bring about the passage in 1913 of the 17th Amendment, which requires the popular election of the Senate. Also, anti-**Tammany** Democrat. The term is rarely used; Irving Stone lumped it with "other mementos of our rich political past" in his 1966 book *They Also Ran*.

logjam   An oversupply of items crowding a legislative calendar, usually at the end of a session; from the logging term describing the pileup that results form too many logs in a stream.

logrolling   Trading votes to get important—or pet—bills passed, especially those benefitting one's congressional district. Briefly, it is an exchange of favors, in which politician X agrees to vote for politician Y's measure with the understanding that Y will help X on another measure. A politician may also add amendments to a bill in order to attract another's support.

ETYMOLOGY: The term is said to come from an event common to the American frontier in which one settler would help another in clearing (rolling) immense trees from the land. It appears to have been transferred to politics as early as 1821 (according to R. H. Thornton's *An American Glossary*, 1912) as individuals and cliques worked with one another to "roll" a certain measure through the legislature.

IN THE LOBBY

Although some reports put the total of all Washington lobbyists as high as 80,000, the 1992 edition of *Washington Representatives* indicates that there are close to 14,000, including:

- 4500 officers of trade and professional associations and labor unions
- 2200 advocates of special causes, from handgun control and the environment to saving whales and protecting unborn children
- 2800 lawyers representing clients in legal and regulatory matters before the government
- 2500 public and government relations consultants
- 200 officers of political action committees and 250 policy research "think tank" group analysts.

OFF THE FLOOR: There was a period earlier in the twentieth century when the term *logrolling* was used to describe the practice of writers or critics praising another's book, play, or other work (no matter how bad), with the understanding that the praise would later be returned in kind.

lollipop Sweet-tasting but insubstantial gifts made by politicians to favored interests. The term most often applies to tax matters. On June 30, 1992, the *Washington Post*'s editors declared that President Bush was holding out tax lollipops to gain approval of his economic plan. Presidential candidate Jerry Brown, in criticizing his 1992 Democratic primary opponents, said, "One gives tax lollipops to business, the other to something he calls the middle class. All economists acknowledge they'll do nothing to stimulate jobs and increase investment or saving."

long minute This ironic term is invoked when an indulgent speaker lets a windy legislator take more than the allotted 60 seconds to speak.

lords of the Hill Name used in April 1990 by *Business Week* to describe three powerful committee chairmen: Rep. John Dingell (D-Mich.), Rep. Dan Rostenkowski (D-Ill.), and Sen. Lloyd Bentsen (D-Tex.). All committee chairmen have a certain amount of power by virtue of their positions, but these three were singled out because they wielded power most effectively. *See also* **bulls and lions.**

love fest Any overt display of bipartisan cooperation.

lower body/lower house The House of Representatives. This time-honored distinction between the House and the Senate has led to an ample share of wordplay. "The House is termed the lower body, because of the example it sets," proclaimed a comic almanac back in 1905.

"The senatorial round-house."

Thomas Nast cartoon of 1886 depicting the Senate as the mouthpiece of the railroad industry — the honorable body of loco-focos. *See* **loco-foco.**

House Historian Ray Smock says the term dates at least to the Tudor period in England, when the House of Commons represented the lower class, and it spilled over to the American colonies, where there were upper and lower legislative houses. The signers of the Constitution had no such intention in creating the House of Representatives. Instead, because it was to represent the people, they called it the "First Branch." But the slippage was inevitable, and by the 1790s the press had labeled the House the "lower" of the two bodies.

low profile A non-boastful stance rare to politicians but one regarded as laudable for junior members or for members hoping to downplay a controversial position. *Keeping a low profile* means staying out of the public eye and avoiding publicity.

loyal opposition The other party, usually the minority.

loyalty Faithfulness to a party or president, often measured as a percentage of party-line votes or White House support. The increasing independence of members and the decline of party discipline have diluted the concept.

L-word Liberal, especially in negative context, as one who is soft on crime, drugs, and wasteful government spending.

Lyndonology The science of figuring out what Lyndon Johnson, the former Senate majority leader and president, was up to. *See* **treatment** for an explanation of why this was a necessary science.

mace A symbol of authority, brought onto the floor of the House each day by the **sergeant-at-arms** and placed on one of two pedestals next to the Speaker's desk. If on the upper pedestal, it signifies that the House is in regular session; if on the lower, that the House is in the **Committee of the Whole.** Any member coming onto the floor need look only at the mace to determine which. The mace also leads the House onto the platform during presidential inaugurations and remains on display during the ceremony. It is composed of a bundle of 13 ebony rods—one for each of the original colonies—tied together with silver thongs and topped with an eagle and a globe.

The mace was pressed into practical rather than symbolic use during the First Congress of 1789 when, according to the official *Rules of the House of Representatives,* "Extreme disorder arising on the floor, the speaker directed the sergeant-at-arms to enforce order with the mace."

machine politics Politics dominated by well-organized parties or factions, usually in urban centers. Usage has declined in modern times along with the big-city political organizations that inspired the term. But it continues to resurface. When former Rep. Elizabeth Holtzman (D-N.Y.) failed to get the endorsement in 1992 of a group that supports liberal Democrats, she charged that their choice was influenced by their close ties with her primary opponent for the Senate, Geraldine Ferraro. She complained to the group's president: "What bothers me most about your rush to

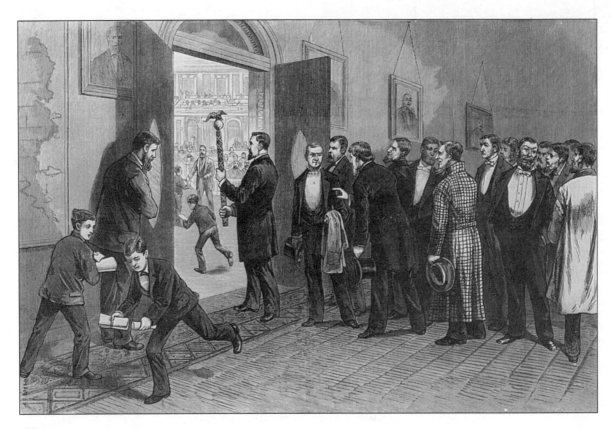

"The sergeant-at-arms carrying the mace and leading absentee members onto the floor."

This nineteenth-century illustration originally appeared in *Frank Leslie's Illustrated Newspaper. See* **mace.**

judgment is it harkens back to the same machine politics all of us have fought long and hard to defeat."

ETYMOLOGY: According to H. L. Mencken in *The American Language*, the first American to apply the term *machine* to politics was Aaron Burr.

Madam Chairman   Form of address for a woman who chairs a committee or subcommittee. The masculine form is **Mr. Chairman.**

Mafia   In politics, a powerful group of loyal legislators or members of a president's **inner circle** who mostly hail from the same state or region. Typical examples of this usage are former President Jimmy Carter's Georgia Mafia and the late President John F. Kennedy's Irish Mafia. The regional identification blurred with former President Richard Nixon, who drew his inner circle from Southern California to Florida. Writer Angele de T. Gringras called it a "Southern Rim German Mafia."

magic asterisk A budgetary sleight of hand attributed to former Budget Director David Stockman in which unidentified future "savings" are claimed but never realized. It is similar to saying, "We'll come up with something later."

major committees Committees with major responsibilities in the legislative process. *See box*, "Committee Assignments," p. 63.

majority

1 More than half the voting members of either chamber.

2 The group that controls more than half the votes, such as the Democratic majority or a conservative majority.

majority leader Legislator elected by members of the majority party to lead them in their legislative efforts. In the House, the majority leader is second in power to the speaker and is generally responsible for legislative strategy. In the Senate, the majority leader does not rank above the vice president or president pro tempore, but he or she holds the most power. The majority leader decides, in consultation with the minority leader, what legislation goes to the floor and when it will be considered. He

Sen. Daniel Patrick Moynihan (D-N.Y.), Majority Leader Sen. George Mitchell (D-Me.), Sen. Alan K. Simpson (R-Wyo.), and Sen. David F. Durenberger (R-Minn.) during a conference on the 1991 Clean Air Bill. *See* **majority leader.**

or she normally serves as chief spokesperson for the majority's policies.

majority-minority district Term used for a congressional district in which a minority group is in the majority and where a black or Hispanic can win. The Census Bureau said in March 1993 that the number of majority-black districts increased from 17 to 32 since the last redistricting in 1982; majority-Hispanic districts went from 9 to 20.

manager Professional administrator hired to oversee the non-legislative activities of the House following multiple scandals in 1992, including those of the **House Bank** and the House post office and restaurant.

mangy dog Description of legislation that has as many flaws as a dog has fleas.

man in the green hat A shadowy figure who quietly performs personal favors for members. The term originally referred to a Prohibition-era bootlegger who supplied intoxicating liquors to members of Congress. By all accounts, he operated out of a basement office in the Capitol.

marginal district Like a **swing district,** one not firmly in the grasp of either party. In an interview in *Nation's Business* magazine in November 1991, political scientist David Mayhew said the "rise of the vanishing marginals" was discouraging potential challengers. Before redistricting in 1992, few House districts were competitive.

markup A session in which a committee prepares a **bill** for floor action by editing, amending, and drafting its **language.** It is literally marked up as a committee goes through a draft version and votes on each **title,** with members permitted to offer and argue over amendments.

Mastergate Title of a 1989 play by Larry Gelbart, a political satire set in a congressional hearing room. *See* **-gate.**

max out Contribute the legal limit in a political campaign.

MC Short for *member of Congress*. Some MCs like to have this designation on their license plates.

McCarthy, Eugene J. *See box*, "Ten Commandments for New Hill Members," p. 128.

McCarthyism Eponym, coined by *Washington Post* cartoonist Herblock in 1950, for the character-assassination methods used by the late Joseph McCarthy, the Republican senator from Wisconsin, in his crusade against what he saw as Communist infiltration into every sphere of American life. (At one point McCarthy went so far as to charge that as many as 205 card-carrying Communists had infiltrated the State Department.) Political writer Richard Rovere called the term "a synonym for the hatefulness of baseless defamation, or mudslinging." *Webster's New World Dictionary* defines it as "sensationalism, inquisitorial investigative methods, etc., ostensibly in the suppression of communism." *See box*, "The Army vs. the Senator."

THE ARMY VS. THE SENATOR

Like grainy, black-and-white phantoms, the images of accuser and accused snapping at each other day after day haunts America's political memories. Here were the insulted but proud U.S. Army and the feared but slipping Joseph McCarthy in a fight to the finish, live on national television.

The hearings began on April 22, 1954, without even the veneer of civility. The stated purpose: to decide which of the two, McCarthy or the Army, was telling the truth. Did McCarthy and his staff improperly pressure the Army to give special treatment to Pvt. David Schine, a McCarthy staffer who had been drafted? Or was the Army, as McCarthy charged, involved in a "conspiracy" to thwart his investigation of supposed espionage? As commentator David T. Bazelon put it in *Point of Order!*, a 1964 CBS documentary of the hearings, the "circus train" of the Army–McCarthy hearings was "on the rails and rolling."

For 88 televised hours from April to June, millions watched the drama, the humor, and the menace of the hearings. American public affairs would never be the same. By the time the cameras finally fell slient, the feared Communist-hunter's days would be numbered.

The charges and countercharges are not as vividly remembered as the cast of characters, including Army Secretary Robert Stevens, Army Special Counsel Joseph Welch, McCarthy committee counsel Roy Cohn, and Pvt. Schine. And, of course, McCarthy himself, frequently under attack, intoning again and again, "Point of order, Mr. Chairman."

Few who watched the drama would even forget Welch's anguished plea to McCarthy to stop his "cruelty" and "recklessness" in besmirching the name of Welch's young assistant. "You've done enough. Have you no sense of decency, sir, at long last? Have you left no sense of decency?"

As Bazelon put it, McCarthy "never regained his former menace." That fall, a special committee recommended that McCarthy be censured for "personal contempt" of the Senate. The vote was 67 to 22 in favor of the motion. McCarthy died on May 2, 1957, from the effects of excessive drinking.

Sen. Joseph McCarthy points to areas of alleged Communist infiltration while Army counsel Joseph Welch listens incredulously. After McCarthy attacked the Army in 1954 as part of his scattershot indictment of institutions supposedly penetrated by Communism, his crusade began to flounder. *See* **McCarthyism.**

McGovern Democrat A liberal whose beliefs are so far to the left that he or she is out of the mainstream of American politics. The reference is to Sen. George McGovern (D-S.Dak.) and his 1972 presidential candidacy, in which he strongly opposed the U.S. war in Southeast Asia and won only one state—Massachusetts—on election day. The term was still in use in 1988, when Republican presidential candidate George Bush tried, apparently with some success, to pin the McGovern Democrat label on his Democratic opponent, Michael Dukakis, former governor of Massachusetts.

meat ax Popular—and graphic—congressional metaphor for across-the-board budget cutting; it is often used in the context of the **Gramm-Rudman-Hollings** budget reduction act, which calls for bringing the meat ax down evenly on domestic and defense expenditures. The opposite of meat ax cuts would be **selective cuts.**

The term became very popular after World War II when Congress was seen as wielding a meat ax to keep the economy in balance in the face of the growing cost of government. A most interesting manifestation of the phenomenon was a secret operation known as "Operation Meat Ax," run by Rep. John Taber (R-N.Y.), then chairman of the House Appropriations Committee, in 1946 and 1947. Thirty outside accountants and tax experts were put into government agencies to look for waste and ways to save money. The outsiders were paid $25 a day and were credited with saving millions. Three "Operation Meat Ax" consultants were also responsible for slicing $70 million from the $189 million Civil Aeronautics Bureau budget.

USAGE: A telling example of the term in use is this line from a *San Francisco Chronicle* article of April 10, 1955: "Though Senator Joe McCarthy is now on the sidelines, the work he did in meat-axing the State Department's propaganda work and the Voice of America is being carried out by like-minded people and friends."

media filter The mechanism with which the putatively all-powerful media decide what is news and what is not. This was a popular assumption in 1992, when so much of the presidential campaign coverage was on personal issues. In a May 12 interview with television journalist Bill Moyers, Kathleen Hall Jamieson, dean of the Annenberg School of Communications at the University of Pennsylvania, said, "What gets through the media filter is not the substance but the attacks."

MEGO Acronym for "My eyes glaze over"; bored. The all-too-common Washington response to obtuse subjects has become a popular bit of Hill shorthand. Columnist William Safire has noted that an apt subject for MEGO is Mexican debt.

member Short for *member of Congress*. This term of address can refer to those in either house, but it is more commonly used to mean a member of the House. As the book *Capitol Jobs* points out: "As with most other congressional nouns, the word is usually capitalized ('Member') when written by those on the Hill and elsewhere in government; hardly anyone else follows this practice." Some staffers refer to their boss as "my member," as in "My member is changing committees."

member bills Small tax proposals approved by **unanimous consent** as favors to members of the House **Ways and Means Committee.** Upholding a committee tradition, Ways and Means Chairman Dan Rostenkowski (D-Ill.) approved 13 members' bills in 1992, reported them out of his committee, and sent them directly to the House floor for passage. Among them: a bill to exempt small fishing boat operators from withholding federal payroll taxes for crew members.

Explaining the system, a Rostenkowski aide told the *Washington Post* on July 9, 1992, "It's payoff time for the members in return for having shown some restraint."

member of Congress *See* **MC** *and* **member.**

member of the club A senator. *See also* **Men's Club.**

memorials Resolutions of state legislatures and assemblies asking Congress to take specific actions.

Men's Club/All-Male Club Formerly a term applied to the Senate, which for most of its history has been an exclusive male bastion. In his book *Long-Distance Runner,* Michael Harrington describes the Senate as "the most sexist institution in American politics." In 1991, at the time of the confirmation hearings for Supreme Court nominee Clarence Thomas, the club was 98 percent male. Even more evident to the public was the exclusively male Judiciary Committee, whose members grilled University of Oklahoma law professor Anita F. Hill, who had accused Thomas of sexual harassment. "I guess if I were on the outside looking in, I might think this place is not as sensitive as it should be to women and women's rights," Sen. James Exon (D-Neb.) said during the hearings. The percentages changed markedly in the 1992 elections, with four new women members, making a total of six. In early 1993, two women, Carol Moseley Braun (D-Ill.) and Dianne Feinstein (D-Calif.), won Judiciary appointments.

mentor

1 A senior member who has brought along a junior one.

2 A member who has overseen the hiring and promotion of a **patronage** employee.

Message Board A weekly publication listing polling results, upcoming events, and the status of pending bills, published by the House Democratic Caucus.

message meeting Fifteen-minute gathering in current Majority Leader Dick Gephardt's office every Tuesday and Thursday morning to decide on the Democratic message of the day or week. The message, designed to reinforce what party or House leaders want to emphasize, is dutifully trumpeted by junior representatives in one-minute speeches. Republicans employ a similar strategy but have not named their sessions.

me-too Describing members who seek to identify with popular issues advanced by their opponents. Thus there are *me-too Republicans* and *me-too Democrats.*

Mickey Mouse Term for something requiring substantial effort for meager results—like the Walt Disney mouse, whose name became synonymous with that which is petty or insignificant. President Reagan used the phrase in describing **continuing resolutions** in Congress.

middle of the road Describing a politician who is a **moderate** in his or her views. By extension, such a politician is known as a *middle-of-the-roader.* The middle of the road can be a dangerous place in today's world of special-interest marksmanship. Former Texas Agriculture Commissioner Jim Hightower is credited with the saying, "The only thing you'll find in the middle of the road is yellow stripes and dead armadillos."

Etymology: The expression was associated with the Populist movement of the 1890s. "If the Bryan faction predominates, the middle-of-the-roaders will bolt and nominate another candidate," said the *New York Tribune* on July 21, 1896.

midnight judges The jurists appointed by John Adams the night before the inauguration of his successor, Thomas Jefferson, to keep the circuit courts under Federalist control. The term has now come to mean any presidential appointees commissioned just before a turnover in office.

midnight pay raise The late-night, briefly debated salary hike that was approved by the Senate in January 1991. The vote—actually held at 9:50 P.M.—increased Senate pay from $101,900 to $125,100. At the same time, the senators agreed to give up a maximum of $23,068 in honoraria. The phrase has come to mean any pay raise sneaked through Congress with little or no debate. *See also* **congressional pay.**

midsession review An administration evaluation, due by July 15 every year, of budget targets and deficits. President George Bush planned to use it in 1992 as campaign ammunition against congressional Democrats who scuttled his proposals.

mid-term elections *See* **off-year elections.**

Millionaires' Club Sardonic nickname for the Senate in the 1890s. Even today, a large percentage of senators are millionaires. *See also* **rich man's club.**

mindless cannibalism Phrase used by Speaker Jim Wright (D-Tex.) in his resignation speech in June 1989 as a condemnation of the interparty accusations of ethical misconduct that had contributed to his downfall. The phrase evoked what many saw as the lack of **comity** and mutual respect that characterized the early days of the 101st Congress (1989-90).

minicommittees The most powerful subcommittees of the House, like the Health and Environment or Energy and Power subcommittees of the Energy and Commerce Committee.

minority

1 Less than half the voting members of either chamber.

2   A group that controls a small fraction of the vote, such as the liberal minority.

minority leader   Leader of the minority party in either house.

Mr. Chairman   Form of address accorded to a man who chairs a committee or subcommittee. *Washington Post* columnist David S. Broder had this to say about the title in a March 1992 column: "[The House] has spawned so many subcommittees that almost any third-term member can be called 'Mr. Chairman,' enjoying additional staff and perks, even though this undergrowth of subcommittees interferes with the work of legislation."

The correct form for a female chairman is **Madam Chairman.**

mixed trips   Washington big shots, like cabinet secretaries, frequently combine official business with political visits, so the taxpayers frequently share the costs of sending them out to campaign for the president or for members of Congress.

moderate   In politics, one who holds moderate or tempered views. The moderate position may be slightly **left** of center in that it is more dynamic than **middle of the road.** The term is frequently used to describe a less-than-conservative Republican, one who is in the moderate wing of the party.

modified rule   House term for the most common debate rule under which bills are considered. *See* **rules.**

money chase   The constant pursuit of campaign contributions that members of Congress find, to their dismay, they must engage in to stay in office. The alarming word on Capitol Hill is that in the two years prior to their re-election races, senators must raise an average of $20,000 a week.

Rep. Dennis Eckart (D-Ohio) quit in 1992 partly to get out of the chase. "You get tired of walking around with your hand out—either to shake hands or ask for money," he said.

money committees   Committees that control the purse strings: Ways and Means and Appropriations in the House; Finance and Appropriations in the Senate.

moral high ground A place from which unpopular but morally elevated political decisions are defended. To occupy it one must stake it out. Some find themselves on the high ground after an unpopular vote and are forced to defend it on the grounds that it was right.

morning business Any House or Senate activity, such as introducing bills, filing committee reports, and receiving messages from the other body, taken during the early hours when Congress is in session.

morning hour The hour before legislative business begins in the Senate, reserved for speeches and announcements. Frequently during the day a senator will ask unanimous consent—always granted—to "proceed as if in morning hour" and then make a speech unrelated to the business at hand. Thus morning hours can take place at any time and often last longer than an hour.

mossback A hidebound conservative, one resembling an aged shellfish or turtle with algae growing on its back.
ETYMOLOGY: The term originally referred to a settler or pioneer farmer, but acquired a conservative, do-nothing connotation. "He's mossbacked and close to a fascist, but he's perfectly sincere," one character said of another in George V. Higgins's novel, *A City on a Hill.*

motherhood bill Any measure evoking patriotism and the eternal verities that few politicians would dare assail.

mother of all perks The House and Senate recording studios, where video press releases and other electronically transmittable messages are prepared for distribution to hometown media. Jack Anderson's June 11, 1992, column in the *Washington Post* is headlined: HILL STUDIOS CALLED "MOTHER OF ALL PERKS." *See* **perk.**
ETYMOLOGY: The term is a play on Saddam Hussein's 1991 characterization of the impending Gulf War land battle as "the mother of all battles."

motion A proposal to proceed or take action. There are motions to **table**, **adjourn**, **recess**, postpone debate, substitute,

reconsider, and bring to a vote. In making a motion, a legislator "moves" that the Senate or House take certain action.

motion to instruct Accompanies a motion to refer a bill back to its committee, with instructions to revise it.

motive Something that one member may not question of another. To accuse a colleague of hypocrisy, lying, demagoguery, or racism can be a censurable offense. Any member so accused is entitled to the floor on a **point of personal privilege.**

motor voter Name of bill favored by Democrats to allow voters to register when obtaining or renewing a driver's license. It died in 1991 under threat of a Republican **filibuster,** was passed by **party-line vote** in 1992, and was then vetoed by President Bush. A compromise bill was passed in 1993.

mouthpiece A spokesperson or publication representing the views of another, usually for a fee. The term has an unsavory connotation because of the association with another kind of mouthpiece: a lawyer who represents underworld figures.

moveable feast This allusion to, among other things, an Ernest Hemingway novel of the same name, describes a long-lasting argument. Referring to political finger pointing over economic growth plans, Sen. Nancy Kassebaum (R-Kans.) said on February 20, 1992, "Actually, the Democrats started early in January with criticism of the president, and then our side answered, and it started going back and forth and it keeps on going. Both sides want to get out their side of the story. One thing leads to another, and then it's a, well, it becomes a moveable feast."

muckraking The practice of digging down in the muck for real or alleged corruption and publishing or leaking it.

ETYMOLOGY: The term is widely attributed to Teddy Roosevelt who, in a 1906 speech critical of the "excess" of journalists, alluded to the muckrake in Bunyan's *Pilgrim's Progress:* "The men with the muckrakes are often indispensable to the well-being of society; but only when they know when to stop raking the muck."

This cartoon by William A. Rogers, which originally appeared in the *Washington Post* in April 1924, was accompanied by these lines:

> Whither old woman, whither so
>   high,
>   To rake cobwebs from the sky?

See **muckraking.**

Although there is little question that Roosevelt popularized it, the term was being used in political circles in the nineteenth century. It appears in Maximilian Schele de Vere's *Americanisms,* published in 1872, as "a slang term...for persons who 'fish in troubled waters.'"

mudfest All-out political warfare in a close race, complete with **attack ads**, unfavorable **leaks**, unproven charges, and equally unsubstantiated countercharges.

"Mugwump!!
The Tribulation Trio—
Who said Mugwump? There
aren't any Mugwumps! Go
away! Who's afraid?"

This illustration appeared on a
Puck magazine cover in 1886. *See*
mugwump.

mudslinging   The act of making unscrupulous, malicious attacks against an opponent.

mugwump   A self-important leader who is aloof from party politics and claims to hold superior views. The term is derived from an Algonquian Indian dialect word for great chief or great man. It was applied generally to Republicans who bolted from the candidacy of James G. Blaine in the 1884 presidential campaign. Former Rep. Wright Patman (D-Tex.) in *Our American Government and*

How It Works said a mugwump was a "person educated beyond his intellect." In April 1936 Rep. Albert J. Engel (R-Mich.) defined mugwumpery as "fence-sitting with one's mug on one side and one's wump on the other."

In a March 1977 *Playboy* interview, former U.N. Ambassador Daniel P. Moynihan described how he revived the word in the midst of Third-World criticism of the United States: "You're sitting here, asking us for bread; you're sitting here, asking us for food; you're sitting here, asking us to help you against your traditional and mortal enemies, the mugwumps on the other side of the border; and there's your guy back there voting against us. How can we help you if you're not going to help us out." And suddenly, these ambassadors were getting cables from home saying, "What in the hell are you doing? You need help against those mugwumps."

ETYMOLOGY: The term, according to the sleuths who prepared *Webster's Word Histories,* came originally from Natick, a dialect of the Massachusetts Indians. In 1643 Roger Williams translated the Natick word *muckquomp* as "captain."

munch and crunch Term for a Capitol Hill lunch in which two or more staffers or lobbyists try to overmatch an opponent and change that person's views.

Murtha's corner A section of the House floor—the left-hand corner at the back—where the Pennsylvania delegation gathers under the leadership of 20-year veteran John P. Murtha.

mushroom treatment According to an item in Bill Thomas's "Heard on the Hill" column in *Roll Call,* this is Pentagonese for keeping congressmen in the dark and "feeding them crap."

"must" list Legislation that in the view of the list-maker must be passed during a session. As Congress began its November 1950 **lame duck** session, President Truman sent up a "must" list of 13 matters, 5 of which he said were of the "greatest urgency." Five *were* passed, but not all of them were "urgent" measures: extension of rent controls, an excess profits tax, a civil defense program, $38 million in famine relief for Yugoslavia, and an $18 billion defense appropriation.

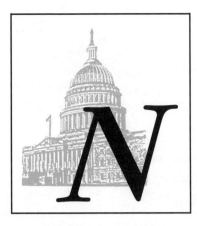

named bill A bill carrying the name of its prime **sponsors.** *See box,* "In the Law of the Name."

name recognition The ability of constituents, measured as a percentage, to recognize their representatives. An incumbent or otherwise well-known figure is thought to have a better chance at being elected than a relative unknown.

narrow bill One that accomplishes one mission and carries no other legislative baggage.

National Conservative Political Action Committee *See* **NCPAC.**

IN THE LAW OF THE NAME

Most laws have only their captioned names: the Civil Rights Act, the Clean Air Act, and so on. But occasionally one or two members become so identified with a legislative proposal that their names become inseparably attached to the law.

The otherwise obscure Rep. Fred Hartley, Jr. (R-N.J.), was briefly chairman of the House Education and Labor Committee and he, along with Sen. Robert A. Taft (R-Ohio), became best known for the 1947 Taft–Hartley Labor Relations Act. Likewise, Sen. Reed Smoot (R-Utah) and Rep. Willis Hawley (R-Ore.) were immortalized by the Smoot–Hawley Tariff Act of 1930.

Both are two-name laws, with one representative and one senator filling the bill. But there are no rules in this game and plenty of one-name laws have been enacted: Sen. Robert F. Wagner (D-N.Y.) wrote the 1935 law setting up the National Labor Relations Board that bears his name; Rep. James R. Mann (R-Ill.) put his name to the 1910 act barring interstate transport of women for immoral purposes; Sen. Carl Hatch (D-N.M.) is best remembered for his 1939 law restricting political activity by government employees.

Even amendments have names, especially those pushed so often by prominent lawmakers that the media make the connection. Rep. Henry Hyde (R-Ill.) is known for the amendment limiting federal spending for abortions. And Rep. Edward Boland (D-Mass.) put his name to the measure ending financial support for the Nicaraguan Contras.

nattering nabobs... Usually with "of negativism," an alliterative label coined in the late 1960s by former Vice President Spiro Agnew in denouncing the scolding princes of bad news, the media.

nature-fakers President Teddy Roosevelt's term for overly zealous environmentalists. Now supplanted by **tree-huggers,** and expressions like "the nuts and berries crowd."

NCPAC The National Conservative Political Action Committee, also called Nick-Pack. NCPAC spent $3,307,962 in 1980 for conservative Republican candidates, including $1,859,168 for Ronald Reagan. The committee distinguished itself as the nation's most negative political advertiser by spending $1,435,232 to discredit office holders targeted for defeat and attacking the morality and patriotism of liberal incumbents. NCPAC should not be confused with the National Citizens Political Action Committee of the 1940s, which supported progressive candidates.

negative campaign Aggressive campaign featuring **attack ads**, **mudslinging**, **gutter politics**, and the like.

neighborhood guy A representative who closely identifies with his or her district, a decided advantage in a race against someone with more powerful connections but out of touch with the voters.

neoconservatives The label that Michael Harrington, a democratic socialist, applied to those who staged a right-wing revolt among liberals. As E. J. Dionne, Jr., defines them in *Why Americans Hate Politics* (1991), they were "newly conservative ex-liberals" who continue to have a powerful impact on American politics. Also called *Neocons.*

new breed The younger generation of congressmen who came to Washington in the mid-1970s after **Watergate,** and who, says political writer Christopher Matthews, "ran for Congress as reformers: partisans of clean environment and cleaner government."

Author Hedrick Smith says new-breed Democrats have looser ties to party than the old, are good at playing television-age "video politics," disdain political machines, and tend to be "bright, articulate, energetic." He quotes former Rep. Richard Bolling (D-Mo.), who referred to them as "this brand new bunch."

New-breed Republicans, many from the **freshman** class of 1978, have similar intellectual qualities and media savvy, but they are on the right-wing political cutting edge: against taxes and social programs they brand "the welfare state."

New Deal Franklin Roosevelt's slogan for the hundreds of programs designed to end the Great Depression. They included the Civilian Conservation Corps, the Public Works Administration, the Securities and Exchange Act, and the Social Security Act. At the 1932 Democratic Convention, FDR called his programs "a new deal for the American people."

ETYMOLOGY: The term was coined by two of Roosevelt's speechwriters, Raymond Moley and Judge Samuel Rosenman, and was said to blend elements of Woodrow Wilson's "New Freedom" and Teddy Roosevelt's "Square Deal."

New Democrats The moderate-to-conservative members of the Democratic Party, many of whom voted for Bill Clinton in 1992 but, at least in the early part of his administration, were disappointed. They identify with the Democratic Leadership Council, a centrist group that Clinton headed while governor of Arkansas. Michael Kelly of the *New York Times* said the president's advisors sought to redefine him as a "New, New Democrat."

New Frontier John F. Kennedy's **New Deal** sequel, articulated in his 1960 acceptance speech. It was not so much a series of programs but a range of problems that needed to be addressed: "uncharted areas of science and space, unsolved problems of peace and war, unconquered pockets of ignorance and prejudice, unanswered questions of poverty and surplus."

New Left The counterculture political movement of the 1960s and early 1970s that pressured liberals to pass civil rights laws and end the war in Vietnam.

In a *National Review* piece on December 8, 1989, Robert Bork described the New Left as "a congeries of radicals" who "collapsed as a political movement, but its adherents are still with us and arguably have more effect on our politics and policies than ever."

new paradigm A concept that appeared in politics in the early 1990s favoring a conservative approach to dealing with social problems. Empowerment of low-income families is one of its cornerstones. A *paradigm shift* is a political movement toward these principles. Developed in the early 1960s by physicist-historian Thomas S. Kuhn as a new model for scientific research, the idea was expanded by Bush White House adviser Jim Pinkerton and Republican Whip Newt Gingrich of Georgia to embrace a market-oriented approach to problems.

new politics Term created in the late 1980s to describe the political viewpoints of young House Democrats who were strong on environmental issues, **dovish** on defense, and pro–free trade.

New Right Conservative activists who rebelled against traditional conservatives of the Old Right, drawing their inspiration from the social resentments aroused by George Wallace, the former Alabama governor who ran for president in 1976. As observed by political writer Kevin Phillips, these included "public anger over busing, welfare spending, environmental extremism, soft criminology, media bias and power, warped education, twisted textbooks, racial quotas, various guidelines, and an ever-expanding bureaucracy."

New South A late 1960s–early 1970s description of a progressive South liberated from the politics of race and exemplified by such political figures as North Carolina Gov. Terry Sanford and Georgia Gov. Jimmy Carter, both Democrats. Arkansas Gov. Bill Clinton inherited the New South mantle in the mid 1970s.

night callers Members of Common Cause, a citizen lobby, who mobilize **grass roots** support in selected parts of the country with evening phone calls.

"No comment" Phrase used by politicians to duck uncomfortable questions. It is rarely heard on the Hill, where far more sophisticated methods of evasion are cherished. William Safire reports that after meeting with President Truman in 1946, former British Prime Minister Winston Churchill avoided questions with, "I think 'No comment' is a splendid expression. I got it from [American diplomat] Sumner Welles."

nod, get the To be chosen or nominated for a post.

No man's property... The ultimate warning about Congress and all other legislatures, attributed to Gideon J. Tucker, a surrogate judge, in an 1866 report of a New Yorker's estate: "No man's life, liberty, or property are safe while the legislature is in session."

Woodrow Wilson echoed the warning when he observed that "the nation breathes easier when the Congress adjourns." The *Washington Post*'s editors repeated the theme in a March 16, 1992, editorial condemning Congress for offering tax breaks on top of a crippling deficit. "The risk of bad legislation from the session is much greater than the likelihood of any good. Go home."

No new taxes Candidate George Bush's seemingly unequivocal "Read my lips" pledge, repeatedly made during his 1988 acceptance speech. This promise disintegrated during the 1990 budget agreement with Congress, provoking a revolt among conservatives and terrifying others who had to face the voters that year.

nonfrankable Items a member may not mail without postage under Congress's free mailing privileges. *See* **frank.**

nongermane Not relevant; the opposite of **germane.** The House does not allow nongermane amendments during floor consideration. The Senate does.

nonpaper A briefing paper that is circulated around the Hill but does not carry the author's name.

nonpartisan Without regard to party or philosophical differences.

Northern Democrat A supposed evil, synonymous with **liberal,** much to be loathed by Southern conservatives in the 1960s. The term is now rarely used in its original pejorative sense.

notch babies People born between 1917 and 1921 who receive less in Social Security benefits than those born before 1917. They complain, sometimes bitterly, to Congress about the discrepancy. A powerful movement has built to get Congress to restore the lost benefits; but Congress has balked because of the tremendous cost of equalizing the payments. *See also* **babies.**

not voting Designation in the *Congressional Record* that a member neither voted nor abstained, suggesting absence.

no-year appropriation Budget authority in an **appropriation** act for funds to be spent for an indefinite period of time.

number cruncher An accountant. Almost every bill Congress considers has a price tag that must be offset by revenues, so legions of accountants populate the Hill and the affected government agencies, working overtime to make the numbers work.

oath The vow that presidents, members of Congress, state legislators, judges, and executive officers must take to preserve and defend the Constitution and to faithfully discharge the duties of office.

obligation As authorized by Congress, this is an order placed, a contract awarded, a service received, or a similar transaction that will require payments now or in the future.

obstructionist One who stands in the way.

October surprise The theory pushed by former Carter administration national security advisor Gary Sick that Ronald Reagan's campaign officials sought to postpone the release of U.S. hostages in Iran until after the 1980 presidential election, thus avoiding an October surprise that could swing the outcome in favor of Jimmy Carter. House and Senate task forces were asked to investigate and concluded there was no credible evidence of such a conspiracy.

off-budget The state of being excluded from budget totals, as are certain accounts like those of federally guaranteed mortgages and the money-losing Postal Service.

office, the A member's office, consisting of a minimum of three rooms and a few nooks and crannies.

Office of Technology Assessment *See* **OTA.**

office wife Female spouse who works for a member of Congress. Under current law, spouses who work for members must be unpaid unless their employment predated the marriage.

off the record An arrangement with the media in which a member or congressional staffer consents to an interview on the condition that he or she not be revealed as a source. In some cases, the news reporter reports the information obtained with no attribution. In others, the reporter agrees not to disclose the information at all. This differs from a **background** briefing or interview, where the information can be used freely and even quoted, but not attributed to a recognizable source. *See also* **backgrounder** and **on the record.**

off year Any year in which there are no regular federal or legislative elections, such as 1993.

off-year elections Elections held for House members and one-third of the Senate in even-numbered years, when no presidential election is held. These elections occur every four years and fall in the middle of a presidential term. Beyond their importance to Congress, they are watched as a barometer of the president's popularity. It is seen as a troubling political omen if the number of representatives from the president's party declines significantly in these elections—although some slippage is normal.

Also known as *mid-term elections.*

Ohio Clock The interesting but inaccurate name for the large mahogany clock in a wide corridor outside the Senate Chamber, where press conferences, especially with visiting dignitaries, are frequently held. The clock, 11 feet tall from the floor to its spreading eagle's wings on top, has 17 stars carved on the shield of its lower case. Since Ohio was the 17th state admitted to the Union, some assumed the clock was made to commemorate that event. But Ohio was admitted in 1803 and the clock was not built until 1816—after the 18th and 19th states had already joined—so Senate historians say the legend is apocryphal. It was built by Thomas Voight of Philadelphia at a cost of $392.50.

oilies Nickname for oil industry lobbyists.

Mark A. Hanna, the very powerful senator from Ohio from 1897 to 1904, talks to reporters in front of the Ohio Clock. *See* **Ohio Clock.**

old-boy network A clubby fraternity of men with similar back-grounds who tend to look after each other's interests in politics and diplomacy. It has long been said that both houses of Congress have been run by such male networks. The original old-boy

233

network goes back to the playing fields of British public schools in the mid-nineteenth century. It extended throughout the financial and diplomatic worlds and was exported to America.

old bull A senator or representative who, through seniority and territorial toughness, has attained and held on to power. An **old bull** is the opposite of a **young Turk.** *See also* **bulls and lions.**

old-girl network An informal but growing body of women who have been elected to office in the United States and are expected to become increasingly prominent in national politics. The term was frequently used by reporters in describing the large crop of female congressional candidates in 1992.

old guard Any long-established political group that is not comfortable with change—for instance, old-guard Southern Democrats. The term was originally applied exclusively to the conservative element in the Republican party.

ETYMOLOGY: The term is a translation of the French term *Vielle Garde*, dating back to 1804. It refers to Napoleon's Imperial Guard, the elite troops of the French military.

old oaks Old-line committee chairmen so-nicknamed by Speaker Thomas P. O'Neill, Jr. (D-Mass.): Claude Pepper (D-Fla.), Jack Brooks (D-Tex.), Jamie Whitten (D-Miss.), Peter Rodino (D-N.J.), and John Dingell (D-Mich.).

old Turk A play on the term **young Turk**, a political insurgent. Old Turks, too, seek to overthrow entrenched elders. William Manchester in *Goodbye Darkness* applies the term to a regimental commander for whom "the years had shrunk his slabs of muscle to gristle, and he had a grooved, windbitten face with wattles that turned crimson when he was enraged, which was often."

old walrus *See* **walruses, old.**

omnibus bill Any piece of proposed legislation that deals with a wide variety of subjects. Today, the term is used mostly to describe a mammoth bill like a **continuing resolution**, in which many controversial measures may be concealed.

one-House bill Legislation created for its publicity value only, and never intended to be signed into law.

one man, one vote/one person, one vote Principle established by the Supreme Court's *Baker v. Carr* decision in 1962: that all legislative districts, federal and state, be virtually equal in population. This decision began the decennial battles over **redistricting.**

one-minute/one-minute speech, a A speech that lasts no more than 60 seconds, made by a member of the House on any topic before the official start of business. "One-minutes" can be about any subject. But in recent practice, Democrats and Republicans have used them to hammer away at partisan themes.

one of their own/one of its own Phrase invoked when a member of the House or Senate is either protected by colleagues or disciplined by them. When the Senate denounced Sen. Dave Durenberger (R-Minn.) in July 1990 for violating its rules and forced him to repay $123,000 for fees he received improperly, the Associated Press reported: "The somber judgment marked the 24th time in 201 years that the Senate disciplined one of its own."

on the floor Spoken importantly by an aide, this phrase means that a congressman or senator is involved in some activity within the House or Senate chamber. But it can be momentarily confusing to constituents who do not understand why their representative is "on the floor." *See also* **floor.**

on the order of/on the order of magnitude Terms commonly used in a budget to signify a rough estimate. During the Kennedy years, Russell Baker defined this phrase as a way of "estimating costs which may later prove to be $1 billion to $5 billion higher." Nowadays the spread may be $15–20 billion higher.

on the record Describing conversations or information shared with reporters that may be used in full, with no restrictions on identifying the source. *See also* **backgrounder** and **off the record.**

open rule One of several procedures, or rules, set down for debate by the House Rules Committee, it allows the bill to be debated in full and amended from the floor.

open seat One for which an **incumbent** is not running, generating more-than-usual interest among would-be office-holders.

operative

1 A political worker who toils behind the scenes for an official or candidate.

2 The language in a bill that accomplishes its objectives.

opposition research The investigation, often highly organized, of an opponent's record in hopes of uncovering damaging or seemingly damaging information. Any public document is fair game.

orange pouch Mail sack marked for expedited delivery to a member's home district or state. It is also known as a *gold bag.*

orders *See* **general orders; special orders.**

organizing Congress What Congress does when it begins a new session, especially swearing in new members and making committee assignments.

originate To begin; in reference to a piece of legislation, to begin legislative life as a **bill.** A bill originates in the House or Senate or in a committee. Tax bills, for instance, always originate in the House.

OTA The Office of Technology Assessment. An arm of Congress that studies and evaluates public policy issues to gauge their technological impact. OTA was asked, for instance, to evaluate various proposals for improving auto mileage during consideration of a national energy bill. It employs about 150 people and costs Congress about $21 million annually.

OTE Acronym for the phrase *overtaken by events*. It is said of a bill, report, or concern that has been rendered obsolete by time.

other body, the What the House calls the Senate and vice-versa. The phrase sometimes has a ring of contempt when used in lines like, "If the members of the other body would stop debating and start voting, this issue would be resolved by now."

However, as House historian Ray Smock points out: "The term may be used with contempt but its origins are just the opposite. It is part of the language of gentility and politeness that parliamentary bodies often adopt to neutralize passions and provide for regular order." He adds that the rules of the House were changed a few years ago to allow for direct reference to the Senate, but most members still use "the other body" most of the time.

other chamber, the Where the **other body** meets.

other end of Pennsylvania Avenue, the One of the ways that Congress refers to the White House and vice-versa. *See* **Pennsylvania Avenue.**

Ottinger effect The phenomenon of not living up to an image. It stems from former Rep. Richard Ottinger's 1970 Senate race. The New York Democrat's television ads were considered effective, but in a live debate the candidate fell short of his televised image and eventually lost the election.

out front The condition of being in a leadership role. It is the place to be on certain issues, but the phrase also implies danger if one is out front too often or too soon, especially on controversial matters. As Sen. Timothy Wirth (D-Colo.) put it in an October 1992 *New York Times Magazine* interview, "Anyone who gets out front on something here is going to take flak."

outlays Budget jargon for money spent.

outside income Money earned by employment outside of Congress—by "the sweat of one's brow," as former Rep. Bill Frenzel (R-Minn.) put it. It is forbidden by House and Senate rules,

View from the Capitol dome, looking west down Pennsylvania Avenue to the White House. At the time this photograph was taken, about 1900, Pennsylvania Avenue was still very much a street of commerce. *See* **other end of Pennsylvania Avenue.**

except for book royalties. But unearned income, such as interest or stock dividends, is permitted.

outsider Politician who has been a sufficient distance from public office, especially membership in Congress, to not be tainted by the association. Hundreds of candidates, even some relative **insiders**, sought to identify themselves this way in 1992. As outsider Sonny Bono, the singer-turned-Palm-Springs-mayor, said of his bid for the Senate, "I know I could do as good as those guys."

outside strategy A method of achieving one's ends by seeking to enhance one's image outside Congress. This strategy involves frequent speeches, press conferences, and news releases— **playing to the galleries.** *Compare* **inside strategy.**

outside the Beltway Beyond the heavily traveled interstate highway circumference—the supposed outer limit of Washington's self-absorbed concerns—where real Americans, not bureaucrats, consultants, or politicos, are said to reside. The *Washington Post* defined "outside the beltway" as "the so-called Real World, as perceived by those unfortunate souls doomed to live east of Seat Pleasant [a suburb in Prince George's County, Maryland] and west of the moon." *See also* **Beltway** and **inside the Beltway.**

outyear In budget parlance, a year beyond the budget year for which revenue and spending projections are made.

oven, the The House's temporary quarters in the south wing of the **Capitol** from 1801 to 1804. The tight, hot, oval brick structure was known unaffectionately by this nickname.

overdraft A withdrawal from a bank in excess of funds on deposit. House members accused in 1992 of bouncing checks in the **House Bank** preferred the term overdraft because the funds were covered by others' deposits.

override To annul or set aside a decision, such as a presidential veto. The sponsors of a vetoed bill must be able to muster a two-thirds majority of both houses to effect the override. Historically, the numbers have not favored Congress in challenging presidents. President Franklin D. Roosevelt had only 9 out of 631 vetoes overridden; Harry S. Truman had 12 out of 250; Dwight D. Eisenhower had 2 out of 181; and George Bush prevailed all but once in 38 challenges.

oversight

1 The systematic review by Congress of how the executive branch of government is carrying out the intent of the law.

2 The process by which Congress reviews laws it created to see if they are working properly. This is also known as *legislative oversight*. It has not escaped scholars that *oversight* may also be defined as unintentional or careless omission.

Bergan Evans wrote about this double meaning of this term in 1959 in his book *Comfortable Words,* when the public was still amused by the new congressional "Subcommittee on Legislative

Oversight," which sounded to most people like it was an entity created to cover Congress's own errors. Wrote Evans:

> But it was all a mistake. The word oversight has two meanings, almost diametrically opposed. The commonest meaning today is "a careless omission, an error due to inadvertence or a failure to see something that should have been noticed." However, the word can also mean "supervision, inspection, watchful care," and it is this, the older meaning, that is the committee's title.

pablum Writing and speaking that is soft, bland, and oversimplified, like the cereal.

ETYMOLOGY: Pablum was the trademarked name of a cereal for infants; the name derived from the Latin *pabulum,* for food or fodder. The cereal, which came on the market at the turn of the century, was bland and insipid, and the term made an easy jump to a new application as a label for childish political thinking.

PAC (pronounced "pack") Political action committee. Group that represents a point of view and parcels out campaign money to lawmakers or candidates sharing that point of view. PACs represent corporations, small business, labor, political philosophies, and single issues. The first was the CIO's (Congress of Industrial Organizations) Political Action Committee, which was formed on July 7, 1943, to represent labor. The number of PACs has proliferated since the mid-1970s; they now distribute more than $150 million per year. There were 113 of them in 1972 and 4,195 in 1993. The tremendous increase stems from post-**Watergate** restrictions on political contributions. The committees are allowed to make donations of up to $5,000 per election to a candidate. *See boxes,* "PACs Are...."; "PAC Men"; "Top PACs."

USAGE: The acronym is used much more commonly than the full name and has been since it first appeared in print in 1943. By November 1944 it was familiar enough that the *Reader's Digest* of that month was able to title a story "Is the PAC Beneficial to Labor and the Nation?"

PACS ARE...

...multiplying like rabbits, and they are doing their best to buy every senator, every congressman, and every issue in sight.
—*Sen. Edward Kennedy (D-Mass.), 1978*

...helping to substitute for weakening political parties in America and they are part of almost revolutionary changes that are transforming our system of government.
—*T. R. B. in his New Republic column of November 27, 1978*

PAC MEN

These are the top 10 Senate and House PAC recipients for 1991–92, according to the Federal Election Commission:

Member	PAC Donations Received	Member	PAC Donations Received
Senate		*House*	
Thomas Daschle (D-S.D.)	$1,285,772	Richard Gephardt (D-Mo.)	$1,157,306
John Seymour (R-Calif.)	1,274,103	Vic Fazio (D-Calif.)	960,358
John Breaux (D-La.)	1,253,450	Dan Rostenkowski (D-Ill.)	886,880
Christopher Bond (R-Mo.)	1,252,199	David Bonior (D-Mich.)	794,213
Arlen Specter (R-Pa.)	1,223,264	John Dingell (D-Mich.)	708,331
Christopher Dodd (D-Conn.)	1,218,464	Steny Hoyer (D-Md.)	661,517
Wendell Ford (D-Ky.)	1,208,122	Martin Frost (D-Tex.)	633,554
Richard Shelby (D-Ala.)	1,172,916	Thomas McMillan (D-Md.)	619,096
Robert Dole (R-Kans.)	1,137,278	Charles Wilson (D-Tex.)	557,125
Robert Packwood (R-Ore.)	1,116,995	Newt Gingrich (R-Ga.)	546,387

TOP PACS

Eleven PACs (political action committees) invested more than $3 million each, for a total of almost $50 million, in incumbent House members from 1981 to 1990, according to a study by Common Cause. The list follows.

PAC	Amount Donated
1. National Association of Realtors	$8,129,128
2. American Medical Association	5,970,606
3. National Education Association	5,397,061
4. International Brotherhood of Teamsters	4,505,860
5. United Auto Workers	4,424,327
6. National Association of Retired Federal Employees	4,050,140
7. National Association of Letter Carriers	3,805,171
8. National Association of Home Builders	3,738,685
9. International Association of Machinists and Aerospace Workers	3,533,725
10. Association of Trial Lawyers of America	3,341,483
11. National Automobile Dealers Association	3,056,398
Total	$49,952,584

package An assortment of bills or proposals with a common goal. President Bill Clinton's ill-fated 1993 economic stimulus program was a package of proposed taxes, deductions, credits, and expenditures. The package fell apart when opponents insisted on deeper spending cuts and fewer taxes.

packing In political **redistricting**, overconcentrating minorities in a district to minimize their impact on adjoining districts. *See also* **cracking** and **stacking.**

pack journalism The phenomenon of large numbers of reporters chasing after the same stories, using the same or similar leads and, by consensus, deciding what shall be the news of the day.

pacronym Blend word created ca. 1992 from **PAC** (political action committee) + **acronym,** in order to describe the motley assortment of acronyms, abbreviations, initialisms, and common names of the many groups whose aim is to effect political action at the federal level. Most of these groups have names ending with the initials PAC, ranging from SANE PAC (Political Action Committee for a Sane Nuclear Policy) to PAC PAC (the Progressive Action Coalition). A few, such as SPAD (the Seafarers Political Action Donation), do not have PAC in their pacronym.

padding *See* **payroll padding.**

page

1 Person between the ages of 16 and 18 who works on the **Hill** as a messenger, mail carrier, and all-purpose gofer. Pages

---

PAGE LIFE CIRCA 1939

A story on the life of pages in *Pathfinder* magazine, April 8, 1939, contained these lines.

A typical Senate page is between 12 and 16 years old, and small for his age. He wears blue serge knickers and coat, black stockings, a white shirt and dark tie. His voice is changing, and he is just beginning to take an interest in girls. He is probably the son of a politician—often of a member, for the page jobs are pure patronage—and he cherishes dreams of coming back to Washington some day as a congressman. Sometimes he does come back. Take Representative Donald H. McLean, New Jersey Republican. He used to be a page in 1897.

Each Senate stripling has five desks to tend. He must see that they are supplied with copies of new bills and the daily *Congressional Record*. One boy has to keep the Senate snuff box full. All new fellows go

through a lot of hazing, and the first assignment of every new page is to find "Senator Sorghum" at nonexistent Room 515, S.O.B.

Every Friday the pages gambol at the Y.M.C.A., box and wrestle and play basketball. Every spring the "House" plays the "Senate" at baseball. The "Senators" usually get licked. Pageboys have their favorites among the congressmen and argue volubly among themselves about their heroes. The late Huey Long was the pageboys' choice. He always gave them something for Christmas.

House pages are taller and older than the Senate boys and wear no special uniform. Altogether there are 50-odd pages, 22 of them in the Senate. If a midget should ever be elected to the Senate, the pages would be in a quandary. They are not supposed to be taller than the Senators.

Sen. George Wharton Pepper of Pennsylvania plays baseball with a group of Senate pages. *See* **page.**

are appointed by influential members and the position is eagerly sought. Their employment goes back as far as the First Congress in 1789, when they were called **runners.** *See box,* "Page Life Circa 1939."

ETYMOLOGY: The term comes directly from the Middle Ages, when a page was either a young man in training to be and in service to a knight or a youth attending a person of rank.

2 To send something by page, as in "Would you page this to the committee chairman."

pair Two members on opposite sides of an issue who agree to be absent when it comes to a vote so that their absence has no effect on its outcome. In a **live pair**, a member who has voted "in the affirmative," announces he is withdrawing his vote and pairing with Member X, who would have voted "in the negative." Thus, each member states a position. Their pair is listed after the vote as "paired for and against." In a *general pair*, members who expect to be absent notify the clerk that they wish to make a general pair with an opposing member who is also absent. Their names are listed in the *Record*, but not their positions. In a *specific pair*, their positions are identified and noted in the *Record*.

With questions requiring a two-thirds majority, such as an override attempt, members also can be paired, according to *Rules of the House of Representatives*, "two in the affirmative, one in the negative." Pairs are recorded in the *Record* immediately after those "not voting."

pander bear A candidate who panders to the interests of different constituencies. The term was used by former Senator Paul Tsongas (D-Mass.), a Democratic presidential candidate in 1992, to describe his party's eventual nominee, Bill Clinton.

panning the House Before May 10, 1984, **special-order** speeches, those often hour-long partisan harangues, appeared on C-SPAN to be given to a rapt House audience because only close-ups of the speech-maker could be shown. In fact, there was no one else in the chamber. But on that day, Speaker Thomas O'Neill (D-Mass.) was so angered at a speech by Minority Whip Newt Gingrich (R-Ga.) attacking his boyhood friend, Rep. Edward Boland (D-Mass.), that he ordered the clerk of the House to have the cameras pan the empty rows of seats. The minority was outraged, he said, but the precedent took, and it is now standard practice to show the full chamber during these speeches, with captions on the screen explaining that legislative business has been completed.

parliamentarian An acknowledged master of rules and precedents who advises the presiding officer of either house on matters of procedure. The parliamentarian, always on the floor and constantly murmuring advice to the presiding officer, is a powerful figure whose interpretations often shape legislation.

The parliamentarian is a virtual ventriloquist, sometimes whispering one sentence at a time so the presiding officer gets it right. "The parliamentarian always whispers because he doesn't know positively whether the senator knows the facts or not, and it's better to whisper and not let the presiding officer get embarrassed than it is not to whisper every time," former Senate Parliamentarian Floyd M. Riddick said in a 1978 oral history interview conducted by the Senate Historical Office.

The parliamentarian and his staff are experts in ways to route legislation to the most appropriate—and most sympathetic—committees, for finding precedents for rulings, and for setting strategy for floor debates. The House parliamentarian has virtual autonomy in referring bills to committees.

House Speaker Thomas S. Foley said the presiding officer bends over backward to avoid making partisan political rulings. "The parliamentarians are almost priestlike in their respect for the rules and for the precedents of the House and we follow those even when it hurts," Foley told the authors in an interview in late 1992.

parliamentary inquiry A question put to the presiding officer about the rules of debate.

party discipline The ability, much on the decline in recent years, of party elders to inspire obedience among their troops. As reporter R. W. Apple wrote in the *New York Times*, April 28, 1992, "It is every man or woman for himself or herself in American politics these days, and there are no real sanctions anyone can take against the nay-sayers."

party vote/party-line vote Vote that is taken along party lines. This occurs when a substantial majority of one party takes one side against a similar percentage in the other party. Occasionally, as in balloting for speaker of the House, the split is absolute on both sides. Some insist the definition applies to one-sided votes of 90 percent or better, while others say 75 percent; still, the main prerequisite is whether legislators are largely following—or toeing—the line of their party.

pass

1 To approve or **enact** legislation in the House or Senate and send it on to the president.

2 To abstain temporarily from voting in committee.

patronage The practice of appointing one's associates, party members, or friends to jobs. As government civil service jobs have grown, patronage has declined, but *political appointments,* as they are now called, or **plums**, are still substantial in number. Patronage jobs in the House, from the doorkeepers to elevator operators, will likely vanish with the recent appointment of a professional manager.

House Speaker Thomas Foley (D-Wash.) declared in late 1992, "I have no interest in continuing any hiring in the House that is not based on absolute qualification." He told a meeting of his leadership team, "The days of patronage are over."

Patronage jobs were a measure of a politician's power and a way of ensuring party loyalty in the days of big-city machines. They could also be a source of irritation for the patron, as onetime Arizona Sen. Harry Fountain Ashurst, a Democrat, lamented: "My chief occupation is going around with a forked stick picking up little fragments of patronage for my constituents."

pay *See* **congressional pay.**

pay as you go A requirement of the 1990 budget agreement that new programs involving direct spending or tax breaks that increase the deficit be offset either by spending cuts elsewhere or by additional taxes, or a sequester of funds in other accounts will occur. Also known as *PAYGO.*

pay equalization A euphemism used by legislators for **pay raise**, as in, "It's not a pay raise; it's pay equalization" (Sen. Ted Stevens, R-Alaska, in *USA Today*, July 19, 1991).

PAYGO *See* **pay as you go.**

payoff The act of settling one's debts to another with a speech, a vote, or a job.

Pay Raise Amendment Constitutional amendment drafted by James Madison in 1789 and finally approved by legislatures in Ohio and Michigan in 1992. They became the 38th and 39th states to ratify—one more than the three-fourths required. This 27th amendment prevents Congress from taking a pay raise until after an intervening election. Thus, if members vote themselves a raise, they do not get it unless they manage to get reelected.

pay raises Because the Constitution requires congressmen to decide how much to pay themselves, the subject of pay raises is always touchy. More than one incumbent has been defeated for participating in a **salary grab.** Congress tried to insulate itself by setting up a pay commission to recommend salary levels for top executives, judges, and congressmen, with the raises going into effect automatically unless Congress voted against them. It didn't work because opponents usually succeeded in forcing a vote and scuttling or deferring the raises. *See also* **congressional pay.**

payroll padding Putting **ghost employees** on the payroll or having employees who do no work. Congressional hiring rules require that members certify that their employees are correctly identified and that they do the work assigned.

pay your dues An expression of the political axiom that politicians may not advance to the upper rungs without having spent sufficient time on the lower. Congress is a perfect example of how this works, with newcomers expected to wait for years before advancing in the ranks. Indeed, running for Congress is supposedly a step taken only after years spent toiling in the political vineyards.

P.C. *See* **political correctness.**

peace dividend Term for the expected—but elusive—windfall that is supposed to result from a shift away from military expenditures in times of peace. The idea came into play at the end of the Vietnam War and again in 1990 as the Cold War came to a close and vast savings were expected in the defense budget. Benefits from the peace dividend of the 1990s have been limited, however, by the necessity of spending the savings for deficit reduction and savings and loan bailouts. At one optimistic moment in early 1990, a nonbinding **sense of the Senate** amendment was proposed in which the peace dividend would have been "returned to America's taxpayers in the form of tax cuts."

pecking order In Congress, the hierarchy of decision making based on rank, especially within committees.

ETYMOLOGY: This term has been a part of the language since 1928, when biologist W. C. Allee announced the results of a study showing that hens have a prestige system under which high-ranking

This is what Pennsylvania Avenue looked like in 1827 when John Quincy Adams was president. The cover for the Capitol rotunda, completed that same year, was a wooden canopy rather than the cast-iron dome that later replaced it. *See* **Pennsylvania Avenue.**

hens freely peck at those below them in status and that the lower-ranking hens readily submit to the treatment.

peel off To gain support for a measure by compromises that take away opposition votes one layer at a time.

Pennsylvania Avenue The historic and recently renovated boulevard connecting the legislative and executive branches. On November 16, 1992, after meeting with congressional leaders, President-elect Bill Clinton indicated that Congress and the White House would work together closely. "Pennsylvania Avenue will run both ways again," he said. *See also* **other end of Pennsylvania Avenue.**

East of the **Capitol**, the avenue has a small, college-town look, with several watering holes (including the Hawk & Dove), a bakery, a copy shop, and a bookstore packed with political publications.

Pentagon

1   The five-sided building in Arlington, Virginia, that houses the headquarters of the Department of Defense.

2   By extension the military establishment, regardless of location. Both a source of military **pork-barrel** spending and a target for budget cuts.

People's House, the   The House of Representatives—so called because its members, elected every two years from districts roughly equal in population, are supposedly closest to the electorate.

Pepper, Senator Claude   *See box*, "The Senator from Florida," p. 308.

perfecting amendment   *See* **amendment.**

perk   Short for *perquisite*. The extra bonuses of office or of employment on the **Hill** such as low-cost barbers and hairdressers, inexpensive medical services, taxpayer-funded trips both to one's district and abroad, private elevators, Capitol **hideaway offices**, gymnasiums, parking at National Airport, etc.

In the midst of controversy over its check overdrafts and lifestyle, Congress in 1992 curtailed several of its privileges. Members were charged higher annual dues for the House and Senate gyms, and for the first time they would pay for medical care and prescription drugs dispensed by a Navy physician stationed in the Capitol. Stationery stores would no longer stock heavily discounted gift items.

At the same time, congressional Democrats organized *perk patrols* to look into executive branch privileges. These include the White House swimming pool, tennis courts, putting green, bowling alley, movie theater, horseshoe pit, and a host of travel and entertainment privileges.

The term *perks* is loaded with negative implications and is a red flag to members. When *The Courier* (February 1990), a magazine published by the National Park Service, made an unflattering reference to Hill perks, a House and Senate conference committee withdrew all funding for the magazine, which then went out of business. The offending comment was this reference to the 1989 adjournment: "Having assured themselves a significant pay increase while retaining many of the 'perks' attendant to being a member of Congress, they made the nation safe again by recessing for the Christmas holidays in late December."

ETYMOLOGY: Though it has been stated that this verbal shorthand for *perquisite* dates from about the 1960s, it appears to be much older, as the editors of the *Merriam-Webster 10th Collegiate Dictionary* found it in use in 1824.

perk panic The scrambling for **perks** that are about to be cut off.

permanent appropriation Budget authority that is available as the result of previously enacted legislation and that does not need further action by Congress.

permanent authorization The authority to contract for services at any time—and often at any cost—unless changed by Congress.

permanent Congress Hyperbolic reference to the exceptionally high congressional reelection rate and what has been termed the fortress of incumbency. In response to the fact that challengers had won only 14 House races and lost 795 in the previous two elections, a group of failed challengers calling itself the Coalition to End the Permanent Congress was founded in 1989. One of its chief objectives was to establish term limits for members of Congress. *See also* **incumbent.**

petition A request by an individual or organization for a specific action from Congress. States frequently petition Congress to take certain actions, but Congress is under no obligation to listen.

petition in boots Allusion to the unemployed who marched on the Capitol in Coxey's Army in 1894, led by "General" Jacob S.

Coxey. The ragtag army was also referred to as a *living petition*. By extension, the term has come to mean any large group of people organized, usually around a specific issue, to seek redress from Congress.

pet project A favored program that a member or cabinet official seeks to insert in an appropriation or save from the budget ax. One of the most dramatic examples of pet project–saving climaxed in July 1992, when Defense Secretary Richard Cheney yielded to relentless pressure from members of Congress from Texas and Pennsylvania to spend $1.5 billion for six "Osprey" transport vehicles that the Pentagon did not want. The members were from districts where the short-takeoff-and-landing craft were being built.

Phillips curve A graphic illustration of a theory by British economist A. W. Phillips that rising employment causes wages and prices to increase.

photo finish *See* **horse race.**

photo opportunity Also *photo op*, or, as congressional press gallery television monitors advise reporters, *p.o.* This means that a politician, often with diplomat or other bigwig in tow, will emerge—or briefly invite cameras in to an otherwise closed meeting—for photos and television pictures only, not for comments. Reporters often pose or shout questions anyway.

Pickle's law Tenet laid down by Rep. Jake Pickle (D-Tex.) that "If Congress must do a painful thing, the thing must be done in an odd-numbered (nonelection) year."

Pig Book A publication by a group calling itself Citizens Against Government Waste listing projects it considers wasteful. Among the top **pork barrel** expenditures: $25 million for a supercomputer at the University of Alaska to try to devise a way to capture energy from the aurora borealis. The group's 1992 "pork king" was Sen. Robert Byrd (D-W. Va.), for landing $510 million in earmarked funds and projects for his state.

pigeonhole To kill a bill by keeping it in committee and not reporting it to the floor. The term comes from the small, side-by-side cubicles—or pigeonholes—in the old Congressional desks where bills were sent to die.

PL Public law. Used to identify and number laws: PL 11-100 refers to the 11th law passed by the 100th Congress.

place in the *Record* Put the text of articles or speeches into the *Congressional Record*.

plantation politics *See* **Starked.**

Plastic Palace A small restaurant in the basement of the Dirksen Senate Office Building, so-named because of its paper plates and plastic utensils. *See also* **restaurants.**

platform The principles on which a party runs during an election year. The extended metaphor of a wooden platform is an

"LET THE PUNISHMENT FIT THE CRIME."
15. For Politicians and Spell-Binders.

This 1906 postcard shows a politician forced to walk a rotten plank that was part of his platform. When this plank collapses, the politician will land in the deep pit of hell—a stiff penalty indeed. *See* **platform.**

almost pure one. The elements of a platform, *planks* and *splinter groups*, are forever trying to get their issues into the platform lest they fall between the cracks. Some planks, of course, are hard to nail down and platform builders have to hammer away at them. Once finished, the platform should be solid and sturdy enough that the party that created it can stand on it without collapsing it. If there is one place the metaphor is less than perfect, it is in regard to those who build the platform, who are invariably called *platform architects* rather than "carpenters," which would be more appropriate.

player A legislator, staffer, or lobbyist who operates effectively in Congress. Burdett Loomis, in *The New American Politician* (1988), describes players as "individuals who had to be taken into account, who could compete in the arena of National policymaking."

play or pay Catch-phrase for a national health-care system proposed in 1992. The plan called for employers to provide health insurance for their workers or pay a tax into a government fund for the uninsured.

play to the galleries Make speeches for the benefit of those watching from the public and press galleries—and now the television cameras. It is clearly a description that keeps bad company. Consider its context in this quotation from Donald R. Matthews, *U.S. Senators and Their World* (1960): "The words used to describe those senators who seem to slight their legislative duties are harsh—'grandstanders,' 'demagogues,' 'headline hunters,' 'publicity seekers,' 'messiahs.' They are said to 'play to the galleries,' to suffer from 'laziness' and 'verbal diarrhea,' and not to be 'team players.' "

pledge Campaign promise, usually broken only at one's peril.

plum A *political appointment;* a job given out by the president. Currently more than 5,000 jobs are in the president's gift bag. These jobs are outside the Civil Service system and include 145 ambassadorships and a number of top executive posts ranging from chief of the Forest Service to secretary of the Navy to director of the Centers for Disease Control. *See* **Plum Book**; *also box,* "A Plum by Any Other Name."

ETYMOLOGY: The political plum does not seem to come from the name of the fruit but rather from the slang use of *plum* for *money.* In *The Encyclopedia of Word and Phrase Origins*, Robert Hendrickson reports, "Plum in 17th century British slang meant one hundred thousand pounds, a fortune at the time. This use of the word *plum* probably gave birth to the expression of a political plum, a political job requiring little work that yields a lot of money." Several British slang books published in the late nineteenth century and cited in the Tamony collection of Americanisms at the University of Missouri insist that the plum of wealth and patronage does not come from English but from the Spanish word for feather—*pluma*—and that the person who had accumulated one hundred thousand pounds had feathered his nest.

> **A PLUM BY ANY OTHER NAME**
>
> Over time there have been many names for political patronage. Plum is the commonest term today but, according to *The American Thesaurus of Slang* (1953), by Lester V. Berry and Melvin Van Den Bark, the spoils of office have, over time, had many names in America, including: boodle, booty, melon, pap, pay-off, perk, pie, plum, pork, and rake-off. The source of political favors has been called the pear tree as well as the plum tree, and distributing political spoils has been called cutting the melon, cutting the pie, or shaking the plum tree.

Plum Book Informal name for *Policy and Supporting Positions*, the book that lists the jobs to which the president makes appointments. The Plum Book issued in April 1953 listed no fewer than 302,256 jobs, including a $9,320-a-year position as a coconut advisor in the Philippines. A columnist syndicated by King Features reported on April 13, 1953, that "Politicians are practically trampling each other to death to get a copy [of the book]." *See* **plum.**

pocketbook issue An issue that affects incomes, prices, or jobs in the home district. It is also known as a *bread-and-butter issue.*

pocket veto The ability of the president to veto a bill passed by Congress by simply not acting on it after Congress **adjourns.** This is possible for any bill passed within 10 days of adjournment. Conversely, if Congress remains in session a bill becomes a law automatically after 10 days on the president's desk, whether he signs it or not.

point man Member who is responsible for moving a specific piece of legislation through Congress.

ETYMOLOGY: The term stems from an Army designation for the lead man on a combat patrol or advance guard and implies a certain vulnerability. Earlier, point men in the cattle drives of the Old West were two cowboys who led the animals at the head of the herd.

point of order Objection raised by a lawmaker when a rule is being violated. It is also used to insist that the presiding officer restore quiet when there is noise and disorder in the chamber or hearing room. It became a catch-phrase during the televised Army–McCarthy Senate hearings in 1954, when it was intoned over and over in monotone by Sen. Joseph R. McCarthy (R-Wisc.). The phrase quickly became a point of ridicule for McCarthy's critics. As one nameless wag put it, "He [McCarthy] had no point and even less sense of order." On May 13, 1954, after two days of hearings during which McCarthy did not use the phrase, Scripps-Howard news service reporter Jack Steele slipped him a note asking him if he had quit raising points of order; McCarthy shot back a note reading: "I invoke the Fifth Amendment—Joe." McCarthy's note was photographed and appeared in papers across the nation.

point (question) of personal privilege A member may rise to state such a point if it involves matters touching on the member's reputation, through accounts impugning his character or motives. Former House Speaker Jim Wright (D-Tex.) utilized a question of personal privilege to respond to Rules Committee allegations against him and announced his resignation.

pointy head A derogatory characterization, usually of a liberal. The segregationist former governor of Alabama and onetime presidential candidate George Wallace contemptuously referred to civil rights advocates as "pointy-headed liberals." The term has also been applied to intellectuals.

poison pill A proposed improvement in a public program that would later come back to haunt the sponsors, or kill the program. Sen. John Heinz (R-Pa.), who died in a 1991 plane crash, called a 1990 proposal by Sen. Daniel Patrick Moynihan (D-N.Y.) to cut Social Security payroll taxes "a sugar-coated poison pill."

ETYMOLOGY: The term derives from a strategy to foil an unfriendly corporate takeover, such as a incurring huge debt to thwart an acquisition.

pol Short for politician, but with a negative connotation. Pols are usually older, comfortable with and perhaps beneficiaries of the **patronage** system, who hang on to office—or to those in office—longer than they should.

"What had he become?" James Carroll's character, Colman Brady, wonders about himself in *Mortal Friends*. "A two-bit pol, flashing about other people's corridors, waiting for his break?"

policy committee An informal organization of Republican or Democratic members who seek to define party positions. The **Republican Policy Committee** in the House is the GOP counterpart of the **Democratic Study Group (DSG).** But the **Democratic Steering and Policy Committee** is far more powerful. The Democratic and Republican policy committees in the Senate meet each week to discuss issues of the day.

policy lunches Simultaneous lunches held by each party in the Senate every Tuesday during a session. The private affairs, catered by the Senate dining room, are well attended, with the vice president making frequent appearances at the one held by his party. Reporters stake out the lunches in the hope of interviewing various attendees as they enter and leave.

Sen. Tim Wirth (D-Colo.), who resigned in 1992 rather than face a destructive reelection campaign, said that little of substance can be discussed at the meetings "because any controversial positions will be leaked to the press before we've finished digesting lunch."

political action committee *See* **PAC.**

political appointment *See* **patronage** and **plum.**

political correctness Since the mid-1980s, a code that holds that language and social customs should be revised to avoid any slight to the sensibilities of others. Often used as an initialism: *P.C.*

political football Any issue, bill, or nomination that is thrown and kicked around like a football.

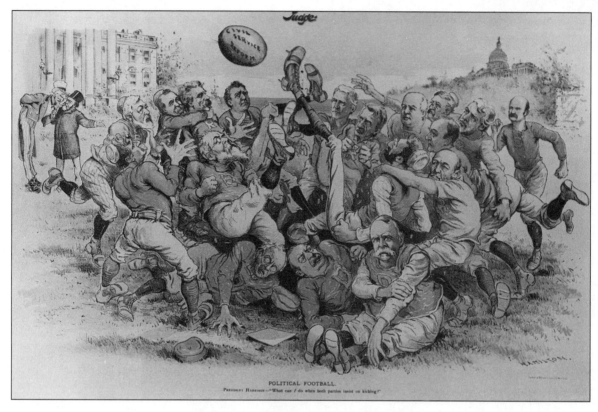

POLITICAL FOOTBALL.
Presdent Harrison—"What can I do when both parties insist on kicking?"

*"Political football.
President Harrison—'What can I do when both parties insist on kicking?'"*

The political football in this case is civil service reform; President Harrison is the puzzled gent in the foreground. *See* **political football.**

political infighting *See* **infighting.**

political plum *See* **plum.**

politicking Catchall term for **logrolling**, **lobbying**, **arm-twisting**, **electioneering**, and other political activities.

politico Politician.

USAGE: According to Howard Wentworth and Stuart Berg Flexner in their *Dictionary of American Slang* (1960), this term appeared around 1940 and was used in a derogatory fashion to refer to a power-hungry or unethical politician. It has since become a standard term for any politician.

ETYMOLOGY: *Politico* means politician in both Spanish and Italian.

politics The science and art of conducting political affairs, including the crafty or unprincipled methods used for political

Clay, Calhoun, and Webster adorn this early nineteenth-century cigar advertisement, which calls the three senators "statesmen" in English and "politicos" in Spanish. *See* **politico**.

advancement and to gain power. It is, said Prussian Chancellor Otto von Bismarck, "the art of the possible" (*"Die Politik ist die Lehre von Moglichen."*). Truman called it "the art of government."

Social critics have long held anyone who practices politics in low esteem: "An eel in the fundamental mud upon which the superstructure of organized society is reared," sniffed writer Ambrose Bierce. "When he wriggles he mistakes the agitation of his tail for the trembling of the edifice. As compared with the statesman, he suffers the disadvantage of being alive." Even Socrates took his swipe: "I was really too honest a man to be a politician and live." Robert Louis Stevenson called politics "perhaps the only profession for which no preparation is thought necessary."

polls Public opinion sampling by which politicians gauge the mood of the electorate. Most campaigns utilize polls to track how their candidates are faring. Also, the media and interest groups conduct or commission polls. *See box,* "Moving the Numbers."

MOVING THE NUMBERS

More and more sophisticated techniques are being used by campaigns to boost or lower a candidate's standing in the polls. Much of the language of modern campaigns is in the arcane language of polls. Dan Walter, vice president of The Media Team, a political consulting firm, offered these examples:

FAVORABLES/UNFAVORABLES The reactions that poll respondents have to candidates, measured in percentages. "What are his or her unfavorables?" a media consultant is likely to ask. TV ads are then designed to raise one's favorables at the expense of the other's—or as the consultants say, "move the numbers."

HEAD-TO-HEAD How a candidate does with respondents in a theoretical head-to-head contest with a specific opponent.

REELECT A question on just about every poll is, Do you think Candidate X deserves to be reelected? Or is it time for a:

NEW PERSON The percentage of respondents who would opt for this hypothetical fresh face. Consultants actually ask, "What's your new person?"

RIGHT TRACK/WRONG TRACK Is the candidate on it or off it?

BALLOT Regardless of the candidate, what percentage will simply vote the party line. If this percentage is high, no opponent has a prayer.

VERBATIMS The words respondents use when asked their feelings about a candidate.

---

pooh-bah A self-important official who holds several offices at once. *See also* **double dipper.** After a character in Gilbert and Sullivan's comic opera *The Mikado*.

populist A politician who appeals, frequently through rousing speeches, for votes on the basis of bread-and-butter issues like jobs and health care. Independent presidential candidate Ross Perot was a self-described populist. Originally the term denoted a member of the turn-of-the-century Populist party, which advocated free coinage of gold and silver, public ownership of utilities, an income tax, and support of labor and agriculture.

porcupine power The prickly power of blocking and obstructing legislation or policy changes.

pork

1 Funds from the **pork barrel**; and, by implication, fat in spending bills.

2 Traditionally, any gift or contribution to party funds.

3 **Patronage.** *See also* **academic pork.**

pork barrel Nickname for the Federal Treasury, into which legislators "dip" to finance projects for their home districts. The process of shoveling federal dollars into one's state and congressional districts for locally popular projects, such as special highway extensions, dams, and land reclamation, is known as *pork-barrel politics. See also* **bringing home the bacon** and **academic pork.**

ETYMOLOGY: There has been considerable speculation on the origin of this term, in use since before the Civil War. One theory holds that pork was the cheapest of meats and that the pork barrel was seen as a cheap way of currying constituent favor. Another theory is that pork is used for its association with fat (as in "salt pork") and that in this context it is a reference to abundant resources in expressions like "fat of the land."

A claim was made in the July 1948 issue of *American Notes and Queries* that the first bill to which the term *pork barrel* was specifically applied was the Rivers and Harbors Bill of 1916. But a reader responded that a member of the 51st Congress (1889–91) had said, "Don't adjourn until I've got my piece of pork." *See box*, "Pork and Champagne Music."

PORK AND CHAMPAGNE MUSIC

From time to time, a pork-barrel item is so outrageous that it becomes emblematic of what is wrong with the system and the profligacy of Congress. In 1980 a federal subsidy for a yacht marina raised hackles when a supporter claimed it was nothing more than "a lousy $300,000." The "lousy $300,000" comment from Rep. William Harsha (R-Ohio) became fodder for a number of newspaper columnists who knew full well that most of their readers saw nothing paltry about $300,000.

More recently there was the case of the $500,000 set aside by the 101st Congress to help the town of Strasburg, North Dakota, develop the birthplace of bandleader Lawrence Welk into a tourist attraction. Everybody ganged up on the idea of a Welk Museum, including President George Bush, who addressed the issue in New Hampshire in February 1992, a few months before Welk died: "I am all for Lawrence Welk. Lawrence Welk is a wonderful man. He used to be, or was, or whatever he is now, bless him. But you don't need $700,000 for a Lawrence Welk museum when we've got tough times and people in New Hampshire are hurting."

The appropriation was killed.

---

pork committee Any committee that deals with local public projects. The main example in the House is the Public Works and Transportation Committee.

pork meister A master of **pork,** a member of Congress who excels at **bringing home the bacon.**

pork panic Quick legislative response that ensues when **pork** is threatened. In 1978, when the Supreme Court sided with the snail darter fish over federal dam builders, a pork panic followed as legislators tried to rescue a project that was threatened by the Endangered Species Act of 1973. This term should not be confused with *perk panic*, which is the scrambling for **perks** that are about to be cut off.

positioning Taking stands on issues or lining up support so as to be able to run for higher office or a leadership position.

positives/negatives The relative good or bad qualities that a candidate inspires among voters, according to campaign gurus.

postal patron A category of mail delivered to all households and postal boxes in a congressional district or state.

postcard pressure Collective impact of large mailings from constituents, usually in the form of pre-printed postcards; often used by special-interest groups to support or oppose particular issues.

Postcard pressure is listed in the 1955 *Britannica Book of the Year* as one of the year's new words and phrases.

post-cloture filibuster A **delaying tactic** employed in the Senate after a **filibuster** is ended by **cloture** vote. Members of the losing team may still call up amendments and debate each one for an hour, request that they be read in full, and demand **quorum calls** or **roll-call** votes. The process can delay passage almost indefinitely.

Post Office Not a branch of the U.S. Postal Service, but an in-dependent House mail service with five locations staffed by 160

patronage employees. Allegations of theft, embezzlement, drug dealing, interest-free loans, and illegal check-cashing prompted congressional and federal investigations. Postmaster Robert V. Rota, who resigned in the midst of this scandal, had a reputation for going out of his way to be helpful to members. Charles Rose (D-N.C.), chairman of the committee looking into the matter, called him "Can't Say No Rota."

post up To get an item that is featured in a **press release** printed in a newspaper back home. The term is press-secretary lingo.

posture

1 To make an obvious bid for attention on an issue without really doing anything, such as coming out against "government corruption."

2 Military preparedness. Although the term goes back much farther than 1961, a book on the Soviet threat published that year by Maj. Alexander P. DeSeversky, *America: Too Young to Die*, contained a featured quote that helped give the term prominence: "Unless our military posture is changed radically and immediately, war is inevitable—and we will be the losers."

posture hearings Evaluations of military preparedness held by the Armed Services committees.

Potomac fervor A romantic relationship in Washington, possibly even between members of opposite parties. A *Chicago Tribune* headline on April 21, 1992, said that cross-party romances are possible, "but it helps to have similar politics, a reasonable ethics committee, and cable."

Potomac fever An addictive infatuation with Washington politics. Although it afflicts many, including reporters and columnists, it attains epidemic proportions on Capitol Hill and around the White House. In 1991 Rep. Patricia Schroeder (D-Colo.) noted George Bush's 25th year in Washington and said, "When it comes to Potomac fever, George Bush is a carrier." Schroeder said at the time that Bush, Vice President Dan Quayle, and the cabinet secretaries had piled up 230 years in Washington. *See box,* "Symptoms of Potomac Fever."

> **SYMPTOMS OF POTOMAC FEVER**
>
> ...a swelled head.
> —*Columnist Arthur Caylor, 1958*
>
> ...ambition to stay in office as long as one can.
> —*Sen. Edward C. Johnson (D-Colo), 1946*

Loretta Young is carried into the Capitol by Joseph Cotten in the 1947 film *The Farmer's Daughter.* Young won an Oscar for her performance as a woman who fights the man she loves for a congressional seat. *See* **Potomac fervor.**

ETYMOLOGY: Evidence indicates that the term was created in the Truman White House—and some strongly suggest by President Truman himself. From the September 1946 issue of *American Notes and Queries:*

> *Potomac fever:* Illusion of power and statesmanship fostered by a comfortable, padded existence in Washington, D.C.; coined by President Truman and applied by him to Senator Burton K. Wheeler.

The term gained popularity in 1951 when author Fletcher Knebel—who died in 1993—began a long-running nationally syndicated column, "Potomac Fever."

power Political force. This adjective gets much play in modern legislative talk: *power base* (the source of political support), *power breakfast* (an early morning pow-wow with other major **players**), **power broker** (anyone who controls a bloc of votes), *power play* (a display of one's political **clout**), *power politics* (politics based on strength rather than ethics or persuasion), *power tie* (serious neckwear, usually red or yellow), and *power trip* (pursuing power and control rather than solutions).

"The essence of government is power; and power, lodged as it must be in human hands, will ever be liable to abuse," said James Madison in words now inscribed in the Madison Memorial Hall of the Library of Congress. In a lighter vein, American writer Edgar Lee Masters in *Spoon River Anthology* advised, "Beware of the man who rises to power/ From one suspender."

power broker Politician or other agent who operates behind the scenes, usually with a bloc of votes, to nominate candidates or make political deals. Power brokers enjoy a mystique of shady effectiveness, but not always for the public good. In a *New York Times* article on May 1, 1992, Brown University political scientist Darrell West said, "In American politics, there's a tendency to be suspicious of power brokers no matter who they are."

power loop *See* **in the loop.**

power lunch Luncheon attended by two or more **power brokers**, with or without an agenda. They must, of course, wear *power suits* that are, needless to say, worn with *power ties.*

prayer breakfasts Weekly gatherings in the House and Senate for food, prayer, and reflection. From 40 to 60 House members gather every Thursday for the bipartisan breakfasts, a smaller group of senators on Wednesdays. Staff and families are excluded.

preamble In legislation, the language preceding the **enacting clause.**

prerogatives The exclusive rights or privileges of Congress. They include the power to advise and consent on nominations and treaties, to impeach high officials for misconduct, to declare war, to conduct investigations and, in the event that no candidate receives a majority, to select a president. In most cases they are jealously guarded. In urging colleagues to oppose a subpoena of House Bank records, Majority Leader Richard Gephardt (D-Mo.) suggested they vote as "custodians over our constitutional prerogatives." But the House, weakened by the scandal, chose to comply.

"This debate has gone on for a long time," Speaker Thomas F. Foley (D-Wash.) said in an August 25, 1992, interview, "but I don't think it's healthy for the system as a whole if any one of the branches starts to intrude dramatically on any other."

The House has a legal committee consisting of Democratic and Republican leaders, which meets periodically to decide whether Congress should appeal cases involving individual members or the institution itself.

present   A response during a committee vote indicating that a member abstained but was nevertheless present at the time.

presidential incubator   The Senate, from which many presidential candidates have emerged.

president of the Senate   The vice president of the United States, who is the official **presiding officer** of the Senate. The job is largely ceremonial. One event that brings the vice president to the Hill, along with a retinue of aides and Secret Service agents, is an expected close vote where he may be needed to break a tie.

president pro tempore   The **presiding officer** of the Senate "for the time being," usually the senior member of the majority party, who takes over in the absence of the **president of the Senate**, the vice president of the United States. The president pro tem—as the name is traditionally known—generally delegates the job of presiding to a succession of junior senators, who are addressed as "Mr. (or Madam) President." *See also* **pro tempore.**

President's Room   A small, ornate room near the Senate floor where presidents from Lincoln to modern times have conferred

The elegant President's Room in the U.S. Capitol features portraits and mural decorations by Constantino Brumidi.
See **President's Room.**

with congressional leaders and, although infrequently, signed bills. Reporters go there for off-the-floor interviews with senators.

presiding officer Any senator picked by the **president pro tempore** to preside during Senate sessions. In recent years, partisan rancor has been such that only members of the majority party preside. This is to avoid messy situations in which a potential troublemaker is recognized to speak over the majority leader when both are seeking recognition from the chair.

press conference An **on-the-record** question-and-answer session with the media. Ordinarily held in the ersatz library of the

House Radio and Television Gallery or the Senate Radio and Television Gallery, with its fake view of the Capitol in the background, these sessions are usually called to announce a position or a major bill, with questions to follow. *Impromptu press conferences* outside a committee room or policy lunch, or in just about any location on the Hill, can happen at any time.

press gallery Balcony above either House or Senate floor reserved for the working press.

press perks Perquisites enjoyed by the hundreds of reporters who cover Congress. These include government-paid staff help in the House and Senate **press galleries**, as well as government-

Sen. William Fulbright (D-Ark.) and Gen. Maxwell Taylor meet the press in front of the Senate Foreign Relations Committee Hearing Room. At the time this picture was taken, during the Vietnam era, Fulbright was chairman of the committee and Taylor was ambassador to South Vietnam. *See* **press conference.**

"The reporters' gallery."

This drawing dates from a time about the turn of the century, when reporters were gents with high collars who used ink pens. *See* **press gallery.**

paid local telephone service, fax and photocopy machines, work spaces, automobile parking spaces, rest rooms, and elevators shared with staff or members. A few news organizations contribute to the costs, but Congress has decided, in the interests of providing an outlet for news, not to charge for the services.

press release An announcement, usually on a single page, of a politician's or group's position or activity, intended to get the attention of the media.

press secretary A person whose job it is to deal with the media and, where possible, promote a favorable impression of a member through the media. Also called **flack**, *spin doctor, spokesman, spokeswoman.*

press the flesh To shake hands and otherwise mingle and move about a gathering of potential supporters or contributors; to gladhand.

prestige committee A committee like Appropriations, Finance, Armed Services, or Foreign Affairs with high visibility, but not necessarily any apparent benefits to one's constituents.

"Washington, D.C.—Press reporters at the telegraph office in the House of Representatives sending off dispatches on the opening day of the Forty-fourth Congress."

This illustration originally appeared in *Frank Leslie's Illustrated Newspaper* in 1875. *See* **press perks**.

previous question When any motion, like that for passage of a bill or resolution, is before a legislative body, a member may demand that the previous question be called. This is a privileged, nondebatable motion that calls for an immediate vote on the matter. The Senate in 1806 did away with the previous question, dooming its proceedings to unlimited debate except when a **cloture** motion prevails.

primaries Intraparty—as opposed to general—elections. In 1992, a post–World War II record of 19 House members were defeated in primary contests.

prime time Evening television hours during which a candidate can get the most **exposure.**

private bill A bill that provides for the relief—or the special treatment—of an individual or business. For instance, under special circumstances a person might be granted American citizenship through such a bill.

privilege

1 The personal rights of members of Congress. These are traditionally referred to as *questions of privilege.*

2 The relative priority of motions and amendments—a **privileged question** is a motion considered before other motions.

3 The right of Congress to withhold information sought by another **branch** of government. Although Congress normally grants requests from the judicial branch, it maintains the right to withhold material. As this right of refusal is shared by the other branches, it sometimes leads to controversy and drawn-out legal wrangling. The issue of **executive privilege** was a key one in both the **Watergate** and **Iran-Contra** cases, as the president invoked privilege over documents, memos, and tape recordings.

privileged class of rulers Phrase used by President George Bush in a harsh attack on the haughty and autocratic nature of certain members of Congress on October 24, 1991. His charges included the allegation that the Senate hearings to confirm the nomination of Clarence Thomas to the Supreme Court were a "circus and travesty." Bush maintained that Congress was out of control.

privileged question One that affects the rights of a house of Congress, its safety, dignity, and the integrity of its proceedings; or the rights, reputation, and conduct of members. A privileged motion goes to the floor directly rather than being referred to a committee, thereby giving it legislative priority.

probe An investigation by a congressional committee.

procedures The **rules** by which business is conducted in the House and Senate, vastly different in each body.

process, the The system, including the rules and procedures, by which Congress works. During the controversial 1991 hearings on the confirmation of Clarence Thomas to the Supreme Court, there were numerous cries for reforming "the process." Many complained about **leaks** of secret documents, a violation of Senate Judiciary Committee rules. President George Bush even got into the jargon. "The American people know fairness when they see it, and they know that this process is ridiculous and they know it's unfair."

proclamations Catch-all term for the various years, months, weeks, and days commemorated by Congress; for example, National Birds of Prey Month, National Digestive Diseases Awareness Week. *See also* **commemorative bill.**

pro forma amendments Amendments permitted in the House, such as motions to "strike the requisite number of words," which automatically give members—and their opponents—an extra five minutes to speak for or against legislation before the **Committee of the Whole**. Such motions are automatically withdrawn after the speeches and never put to a vote.

program, project, or activity (PPA) Under the **Gramm-Rudman-Hollings Act,** these are appropriated elements within each budget account. If a **sequester** occurs, equal percentages of funds must be taken from each PPA.

progressive One who advocates change. Distinct from a **liberal** in that *progressive* applies to action and *liberal* to an attitude of openness to change.

Progressive with a capital "P" refers to a movement in American politics, 1900–1917, that spurred reforms in employment, child labor, health care, and worker safety. The Progressives, originally Republican **insurgents**, helped kick out the big-city bosses and worked for direct election to the Senate and the graduated income tax.

In 1910, Progressives joined forces with House Democrats to strip the autocratic Speaker Joseph Cannon (R-Ill.) of most of his power. Progressive forces in the Senate were led by Robert M. ("Fighting Bob") LaFollette of Wisconsin. Spurred by a split with Republican conservatives, Theodore Roosevelt formed the Progressive (Bull Moose) party in 1912, thus splitting the Republican Party and handing Democrat Woodrow Wilson a landslide victory.

Noted editor William Allen White wrote that after 1916, when Roosevelt retired from presidential competition, the Progressive party was "all dressed up, with nowhere to go."

propose Suggest or offer legislation or submit a budget. The maxim that the president proposes and Congress disposes can be read to mean that White House proposals are acted upon responsibly or they are not. That is, they may be blocked for understandable partisan reasons or totally mangled after running the gauntlet of interaction with interest groups.

pro tempore/pro tem Latin term, literally meaning "for the time." The term is used to designate a temporary **presiding officer.** *See also* **president pro tempore.**

Proxmire, Senator William *See box,* "Fleecing the Public," p. 139.

proxy votes Those cast in one's absence by another. They are allowed in committees but not on the House or Senate floors. Senate committees permit proxies except when voting on whether to report—or approve—a bill. House committees permit proxies, but members must certify that they are "absent on official business or otherwise unable to attend." *See also* **ghost voting.**

prune A political appointee who has held his or her position (a **plum**) for a long time; whimsically, a plum with experience.

Prune Book A book of advice for incoming recipients of political appointments (**plums**) written by veteran political appointees (**prunes**) and published in 1988 by the Council for Excellence in Government.

public affairs ghetto Expression used by press secretaries for Sunday-morning talk shows. Getting one's boss on one of the programs is a plus, but the shows' ratings are low, hence the designation "ghetto."

public documents envelope A **franked** envelope, bearing the member's signature in place of a stamp. Intended to be used only for responses to letters from constituents, they have been used for publicity purposes.

public interest groups Associations that **lobby** Congress for changes in the law, usually—but not always—on public issues like consumer, environmental, clean government, and health matters.

public law *See* **PL.**

public trough Figurative place where consultants, corporations, and other members' constituents feed greedily. Sometimes called *the public teat*.

puff piece An article in a newspaper or magazine, or a story on radio or television, that contains little but praise or favorable treatment for an office holder.

pulse, taking the Oft-used expression describing would-be candidates who are trying to sample public opinion before deciding whether to run for public office.

pump priming The process of using federal funds to stimulate the economy, whether it be the national economy or a local one. It calls for spending money directly on projects or programs and is the opposite of **trickle-down** spending in the form of tax breaks, mostly for affluent citizens or corporations.

FIRST USE: The term's political meaning was listed as a new word for 1941 in the Encyclopedia Britannica's publication *10 Eventful Years:* "Temporary remedial action by the government designed to get the economic machine started." Lexicographer Peter Tamony recorded use of the term as early as April 1940.

punishment Disciplinary action taken against a member by party leaders. In its rawest form, it can mean removal of a member from a coveted committee assignment, relegation to undesirable offices, or refusal to recognize a motion. This sort of iron discipline is rare in this era of **young Turks** and divided power. One action, however, that never goes unpunished is desertion from party ranks by supporting the other party's presidential nominee.

purgatory The metaphoric place to which an erring member is consigned by the leadership by curtailing his or her **perks.** The term was made popular by House Speaker John W. McCormack (D-Mass.). In Lawrence F. O'Brien's *No Final Victories,* an incident is described in which McCormack, who served as speaker from 1962 to 1971, was asked what would happen if Adam Clayton Powell (D-N.Y.) refused to show up for a hearing:

> "I'll put him in purgatory," McCormack said firmly.
> "What does that mean?"
> "It means that I'll cut off all his prerogatives."
> "Have you ever put anyone in purgatory before?" [he was asked.]
> "Once."
> "Who?"
> "Carl Vinson, the distinguished member from Georgia," McCormack said....
> "Why?"
> "Because many years ago he pledged to vote for me for majority leader and then went back on his word."
> "How long did you keep him in purgatory?"
> "Twelve years," the Speaker said.

purse strings The power to control the flow of money in and out of the federal treasury. This power is held by Congress, particularly within its appropriations and taxation committees. The House has the tighter grip because of the constitutional requirement that all tax legislation originate there.

putting the question Calling for the **yeas** and **nays.**

puzzle palace

1 Nickname for the Pentagon.

2 Nickname for the Capitol. Here is how columnist Sandy Grady used the term in an October 10, 1990, column on Congress: "Inside the marble Puzzle Palace, the Honorables are dogged by frustration, fatigue, and self-loathing."

quagmire Soft, spongy ground in which it is difficult to move. Popularized during the Vietnam War and given new life amid the **gridlock** accusations of the 102nd Congress (1991-92).

qualifications The only requirements for congressional membership are constitutional minimums: A representative must be 25 years old and a U.S. citizen for 7 years; a senator must be 30 years old and a U.S. citizen for 9 years; both must be residents of the states from which elected with no stipulations on length of time. The Supreme Court has ruled that Congress may use no other qualifications in seating its duly elected members. *See* **expulsion**, however, for an explanation of how a member may be removed from office.

quasi-legislative Adjective for regulatory agencies, such as the Federal Trade Commission and the Food and Drug Administration, which act with power delegated to them by Congress.

quick fix A supposed quick and easy way to solve a problem. In the context of Congress, it is common to say that there is "no quick fix" for most problems. Ronald Reagan's 1982 plan to spur the sluggish economy with rapid infusions of money was widely berated as "no quick fix." Just as there is no quick fix, there is also no free lunch.

ETYMOLOGY: The term comes from the argot of the illegal drug culture, where a "quick fix" describes a hit of a narcotic that quickly satisfies one's addiction.

quickie, a $2,000 A brief speech, sometimes no more than a few remarks by a senator or representative, for which businesses or interest groups once paid the maximum $2,000 **honorarium**, plus travel expenses. Now the money must be given to charity or a nonprofit institution designated by the recipient.

quick study A legislator or aide who when thrown into the middle of a complex matter masters it quickly.

quid pro quo

1 Literally, "something for something." In former budget director David Stockman's *The Triumph of Politics* (1986), he refers to a "little gratuity" given to a Texas representative who wanted a $2,500-per-year tax credit for small oil companies. In return, the congressman agreed to an earlier effective date for President Ronald Reagan's tax cut. Wrote Stockman: "Naturally, there was a quid pro quo, but it seemed incredibly cheap."

2 An illegal campaign contribution: money given as reward for legislative support. In today's ethics-conscious Congress, even the hint of a quid pro quo must be avoided. As former Sen. Terry Sanford (D-N.C.), chairman of the Senate Ethics Committee, tells it, a company official said exactly the wrong thing in thanking him for his vote: "I don't know if we've ever made a contribution to you." "And you can't, now," Sanford replied.

quorum The number of members who must be present before official business may be conducted. The Constitution states that a congressional quorum shall constitute a majority of each house.

Obtaining a quorum has always been a problem in Congress. Meeting for the first time on March 4, 1789, neither house could muster enough members to conduct business. They had to repeatedly adjourn, sending letters to absentees to please show up. Finally, on April 1 in the House and April 6 in the Senate, quorums were mustered and the business of the new republic could begin.

quorum call A demand that the members present be counted to see if a quorum is present. Most quorum calls in the Senate are actually used to delay proceedings until a deal can be worked out or until a tardy speaker can get to the floor. Anyone may set a quorum call in motion, usually by saying—"I suggest the absence of a quorum."

A majority of senators present may direct the **sergeant-at-arms** to request and, when necessary, to compel the attendance of absent senators, an order determined without debate.

See box, "Feet First."

FEET FIRST

Although both houses of Congress have the power to demand the attendance of absentees in order to conduct business, cases where members have been "arrested" and brought to the chamber have been rare. Near midnight on February 24, 1988, Majority Leader Robert Byrd (D-W.Va.) decided the time had come.

The issue was campaign reform, and Republicans were blocking the bill by filibustering. Byrd's tactic was to wear them down by keeping the Senate in session and forcing the opponents to talk all night. The Republicans countered with a skillful parliamentary move: They forced a series of quorum calls and refused to come to the chamber to answer when their names were called. That made it necessary for the Democrats, late in the evening, to come up with 51 members required to stay in session.

Byrd, not about to be outmaneuvered, won approval to force the absentees to appear. The Senate sergeant-at-arms, with help from the Capitol Police, combed the halls and favorite haunts of senators. Tipped off by a cleaning woman that Sen. Robert Packwood (R-Ore.) was in his office, they pounded on his door, which had been blocked with a heavy chair. The police, with Sergeant-at-Arms Henry Guigni in the lead, forceably shoved their way in, slightly injuring Packwood, then marched him to the Capitol. When they reached the Senate chamber, Packwood refused to walk onto the floor and his escorts obliged by carrying him in feet first. "Here," he answered as he was deposited in the chamber.

---

quote   A sentence or two, or turn of phrase, by a congressman that appears in print. A reporter may use it as a noun in asking an official for "a quote," or as a verb in prompting a source: "May I quote you?"

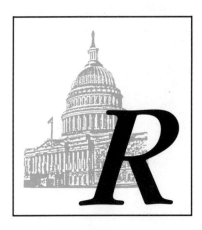

R Accepted abbreviation for Republican, as in R-Colo., meaning a Republican senator or representative from Colorado.

race card A candidate who stirs up racial prejudices by certain remarks or political ads is said to "play the race card." Sen. Bill Bradley (D-N.J.) wrote in the March 29, 1992, *Washington Post*, "Republicans have played the race card in a divisive way to get votes—remember Willie Horton—and Democrats have suffocated discussion of self-destructive behavior among the minority population in a cloak of silence and denial."

Rackets Committee The Select Committee to Investigate Improper Activities in Labor-Management Relations, headed by Sen. Estes Kefauver (D-Tenn.), made a name for itself as the Rackets Committee during the early 1950s. Kefauver, a potential presidential nominee, was on the losing ticket with Adlai Stevenson in 1956.

raid Term used by committee members who are protective about their prerogatives to describe an invasion of their turf by another committee. A raid might be signaled when a chairman asks the speaker to have a bill that normally falls under the jurisdiction of another committee to be sent to his or her committee instead. Raided committee members promptly send unfriendly letters to their counterparts and let the leadership know how outraged they are. Or the competing committee announces an investigation of a matter outside of its normal grazing area. In 1992, Judiciary Committee Chairman Jack Brooks (D-Tex.) decided to restrict the entry of telephone companies into the information services market on antitrust grounds while another committee, Energy and Commerce, was already considering legislation to do just the opposite. Brooks' raid succeeded in stopping the bill.

rail The barrier separating the House and Senate floor from passageways around the back of the chambers. Except during debate on bills, staff do not go beyond the rail. It is also a symbolic dividing line between elected officials and all others.

railroad To rush or ram a bill through Congress.

FIRST USED: Since about 1888 the term has been used as a verb for "to expedite." It was commonly used in reference to the trial and sentencing of a criminal who was convicted on weak evidence. An early use of the term in a legislative context appears in an 1889 issue of *Scientific American*: "The Alien Act that was railroaded through at the close of the last session."

rainmaker

1 Anyone with an ability to get things done legislatively.

2 A **lobbyist** capable of causing big money to flow into campaign chests. Lobbyist Bill Timmons was one of the first to attract the title, as explained in the 1982 book *Who Runs Congress?*— "…for his uncanny ability to change the weather on Capitol Hill." The Hill rainmaker has counterparts in the legal and investment banking fields who bring major clients or investors to the firm.

rainy-day war chest *See* **excess campaign funds.**

Ramseyer Rule A House requirement that committee reports show, by using different type such as italics, the changes that would be made in existing law. The **Cordon Rule** is the Senate parallel.

ranking member Member of the majority party on a committee who ranks first in seniority after the chairman.

ranking minority member   The senior minority party member on a committee. Should there be a change in party control, this person would probably become the chairman. In 1993, Republicans adopted a new party rule limiting the ranking Republican member of a committee to six consecutive years in that role.

ranks   Members of a party. Like rows of soldiers, these ranks may be held or broken under pressure from the opposition. A member who votes with the other party is said to **break ranks.** When things get rough, the party faithful **close ranks.**

ratification   The act of approving a treaty or approving a constitutional amendment. A vote of two-thirds of the Senate is required for the ratification of a treaty. Three-fourths of the states must ratify a change in the Constitution.

Rayburn's Rule   Sam Rayburn ruled the Democratic side of the House, most of the time as speaker, from 1937 to 1961. The tough Texas lawmaker may be best known for the expression, "To get along, go along," but many other Rayburnisms survive, including, "If you tell the truth the first time, you don't have to remember what you said."

reactionary   An extreme conservative who advocates a return to outdated principles. Reactionaries understandably dislike the label.

reading   Any of the three moments at which a bill must be "read" as part of the legislative process. The practice, common to most legislative bodies, was created so that bills could not be sneaked through without notice. The procedure is slightly different in the House and Senate, but in neither place are bills actually read in full. Usually the bills are announced by title only, with further reading "dispensed with" by unanimous consent. Occasionally, in order to stall for time, a lawmaker will object and the clerk will begin reading the bill in what can only be described as a mind-numbing drone—to which no one listens—until the objector mercifully relents.

Speaker of the House Rep. Sam Rayburn confers with Vice President Lyndon B. Johnson in this photograph taken in 1961. *See* **Rayburn's Rule.**

Reagan Democrats   Generally, white, blue-collar, socially conservative Democrats who voted for Ronald Reagan for president. Strategists constantly debate over how to keep them or win them back. Many returned to the fold in the 1992 elections.

Reaganomics   The policy of cutting programs and taxes, increasing defense spending, reducing government regulation, and encouraging private investment by the wealthy so that the benefits will **trickle down** through the economy. The most loyal subscribers to this theory were dubbed *Reaganauts.*

Reagan robot   Name given during the Reagan years to any legislator who voted with the president without question.

reapportionment The reallocation of congressional seats by state to reflect population changes after each census. *See also* **apportionment** and **redistricting.**

recess

1   To suspend business at the end of the day, instead of **adjourning,** so that the proceedings can begin at the same point the next day. This is common practice in the Senate.

2   Time off from legislative business, as in *Easter recess.*

recognition Permission to speak before the House or Senate. In the Senate, a member wishing to speak must seek recognition from the **president pro tempore** or **presiding officer.** This can get complicated and partisan when several senators are calling "Mr. President" at the same time, but the first to rise usually is recognized if no partisan advantage is to be gained.

recommit A motion to send a **bill** back to **committee,** effectively killing it. A frequent tactic in the House is to move to recommit a measure with instructions to add a specific **amendment.** This is a common parliamentary tactic, used most often in the House by the minority to fight for amendments that the **Rules Committee** did not allow to be considered.

Even so, the specific amendment to be included in the instructions must be preapproved by the Rules Committee—a matter of increasingly bitter contention in the House. Frequent appeals to the chair's ruling have been voted down by **party-line votes.**

reconciliation bill A massive piece of legislation passed near the end of a fiscal year in which Congress clears up and corrects details of the federal budget in order to bring projected spending and revenues into conformity with the policy-setting budget resolution.

reconciliation instructions Blunt orders given by the House Budget Committee to authorizing committees to trim the fat from the federal budget.

reconsider Take up a bill again. It has been the practice of Congress since its first days not only to consider legislation but to reconsider it. But the effect of a motion to reconsider is actually to prevent reconsideration at a later date. In both houses after a measure is passed it is customary for someone on the prevailing side to move to reconsider the vote. This is followed by a motion to **table** *that* motion which is agreed to by perfunctory voice vote.

Reconstruction The period from 1865 to about 1877 in which radical national leadership controlled Congress and pushed through punitive measures governing the post–Civil War South. Led by Republican firebrands like Thaddeus Stevens of Pennsylvania in the House and Charles Sumner of Massachusetts in the Senate, Congress passed laws immediately enfranchising former slaves, barring Confederate soldiers from public office, and sending an army of occupation and sundry **carpetbaggers** into the region. Many black congressmen from the South were elected in this era. After Republicans lost control of the House in 1874, an embittered post-Reconstruction era set in. *See* **unreconstructed.**

Record Short for *Congressional Record.*

redistricting Unlike **reapportionment**, which is the assigning of House seats to each state after the tenth-year census, redistricting is the actual carving up of new congressional districts within a state. This is usually done by state legislatures and is the subject of often fierce political fights that can only be settled by the courts. Districts must be contiguous, but not compact, leading to many creative shapes.

One Mississippi district, 500 miles long and 40 miles wide, was known as the "shoestring." Others have been described as dumbbells, saddle bags, turkey feet, and frying pans. *See* **gerrymander.**

reduction in force *See* **RIF.**

Reed Rules A set of rules adopted in the 1890s under Republican Speaker Thomas B. Reed of Maine, which helped streamline House procedures. Reed's motto was, "The object of a parliamentary body is action, not the stoppage of action." Among other things, he insisted that members who were present in the chamber answer when a **quorum** was called. *See also* **disappearing quorum.**

reestimates Revisions made in executive or congressional budget estimates due to changes in economic conditions. These may be entered into budget baseline projections and **scorekeeping** reports. In a slumping economy, reestimates can spell bad news for attempts to control the budget.

referral The assignment of bills to a committee by the **presiding officer.** When more than one committee has jurisdiction, as with an energy bill with environmental consequences, the bill may be referred to a series of committees, with each having a say— a *sequential referral.* Occasionally this results in overly complex legislation implemented by more than one agency. A *split referral* is the practice of dividing a bill and referring it to two or more committees.

reform To reshape in order to remove defects, a preoccupation in politics. There are reform movements, even reform tickets, which pledge to correct political systems.

regicide The killing of a king, but in the congressional context the overthrowing of a chairman by the party **caucus,** a rare and almost shocking occurrence on Capitol Hill.

regular order When the House is not proceeding according to the regular order of business, a member may protest at any time and make a demand for regular order. The presiding officer almost always upholds the demand.

remarks Virtually any words uttered by a congressman for public consumption. Members refer to *remarks* they made before a group. Although more casual than a speech or testimony, remarks may nevertheless be prepared in advance and distributed to the press or placed in the **Congressional Record.**

report

1 Action by a committee to send a bill to either house after holding hearings and voting on its provisions. It is often said that a bill has been *reported out* by a committee.

2 The actual printed proceedings or conclusions of a committee or subcommittee. It provides a summary of the bill, why it is needed, and the dissenting views of minority members. This written explanation, prepared by the committee reporting a measure, must accompany every bill.

repository This word, conventionally meaning a storehouse, is often used as a figure of speech in a negative sense, as in "Congress is not the sole repository of wisdom." Rep. Bill Schuette (R-Mich.) said this in a speech in October 1989, and both a Michigan newspaper and the *Washington Post* misquoted him as saying, "Congress is not the sole suppository of wisdom."

representative One of the 435 members of the **House of Representatives.** Every two years, voters in congressional districts throughout the United States elect a **congressman** or **congresswoman** to represent them in Congress. A representative must be at least 25 years old, a citizen of the United States for at least seven years, and an inhabitant of the state from which he or she is chosen.

reprimand A form of **punishment** for unethical or disorderly behavior. Members have been reprimanded for converting campaign contributions to personal use, testifying falsely under oath, trying to fix parking tickets for friends, and **ghost voting.** The punishment consists of the public humiliation of being formally scolded by a resolution passed by either the House or Senate. This can be a damaging—if not fatal—blow to a legislator's chances for re-election.

This punitive measure is milder than **censure**, because the member need not be present when the action is taken.

reprogramming Shifting funds from one purpose to another within the same **appropriation** account.

Republican Member of the Republican Party, which became a national political force after the 1854 collapse of the Whig Party. John C. Fremont was the party's first presidential candidate in 1856. The **GOP** ("Grand Old Party") surrendered the South to the Democrats following the Civil War, but still became the dominant national party until the Depression brought Democratic President Franklin D. Roosevelt to power in 1932. With some exceptions in recent years, the GOP has captured the White House but failed to control Congress.

The party is ideologicaly to the right of the **Democrats,** but it does harbor some **liberals.** It has long been seen as the party of the entrenched status quo. At a Republican congressional dinner on May 4, 1982, President Ronald Reagan said, "We're the party that wants to see an America in which people can still get rich!"

Republican big tent/Republican tent An inclusive Republican Party. When Sen. Everett Dirksen (R-Ill.) was asked if Sen. Joe McCarthy, a Wisconsin Republican, should be read out of the party, he was quoted as replying, "The Republican tent, as you know, is large enough to embrace a good many points of view."

Republican chairman Since 1990 the name for the ranking Republican of a committee or subcommittee, formerly known as a **vice chairman.**

Republican Conference A meeting of all House Republicans; comparable with the Democratic Caucus.

Republican leader Title preferred by longtime Minority Leader Robert Michel (R-Ill.), former leader John Rhodes (R-Ariz.), and others, to that of **minority leader.**

Republican majority coalition A group formed by current and former congressional Republicans seeking to move their party in a **moderate** direction. Outgoing Sen. Warren Rudman of New Hampshire, Sen. Nancy Kassebaum of Kansas, and outgoing Rep. Tom Campbell of California issued a joint statement on December 11, 1992, that said the group sought "to combat the religious right's efforts to seize control of the Republican Party."

Republican Policy Committee This group was originally formed by Republican **young Turks** in the House in the 1960s to define party positions and partisan opposition to the Johnson administration. It is now an official advisory group that discusses legislative proposals for House Republicans, and it now includes a cross-section of House Republicans.

rescission   A seldom-used but increasingly interesting part of the 1974 Budget and Impoundment Control Act that allows the president to propose that budget authority for specific projects be canceled. Both houses must approve a rescission proposal within 45 days, or the funds, if they are being withheld, become available for spending.

In March 1992 President George Bush sent Congress a total of $5.7 billion in rescission proposals, including $3 billion for two Seawolf nuclear-powered submarines, but also such **pork-barrel** projects as celery and asparagus research and manure disposal. Congress avoided the issue by proposing its own package of cuts.
See also **impoundment.**

resolution   A measure approved by a house of Congress that may or may not have the force of law and cannot be vetoed by the other body or the president. Resolutions usually deal with procedures of the house in question or express sentiments (such as a resolution of sadness over the death of a member). There are three distinct forms: **concurrent resolution, joint resolution,** and **simple resolution.**

restaurants   They do not rank among Washington's top 100 eateries, but the dining rooms, snack bars, and cafeterias honeycombing the Capitol and its numerous office buildings are reasonably agreeable spots for a fast snack or leisurely repast at affordable prices. Members of Congress, their staffs, the media, and tourists chow down in these facilities, which range from bland to elegant. *See also* **Plastic Palace.**

Hill restaurants largely escaped public notice until October 1991, when a House task force revealed that hundreds of lawmakers had stiffed the caterers. The unpaid tab for 250 members came to $250,000. The House Administration Committee cracked down. Deadbeats would be turned over to collection agencies and charged interest, and their names would be posted on restaurant walls. There'd be no more chits: members would pay with cash or credit card.

retail politics   A personal, face-to-face method of getting things done. As Christopher Matthews, author of *Hardball*, put it, Lyn-

The House restaurant as it appeared in 1892. Then as now, Hill restaurants are haunts of lobbyists eager to bend a legislator's ear. *See* **restaurants.**

don Johnson as Senate majority leader made his most important deals "at the retail level, one customer at a time." The *wholesale* approach is more broad-scale, usually issue-oriented, with an emphasis on media coverage.

retirement slump A drop-off in the percentage of votes for a party's candidate for an office when the party's long-incumbent holder of that office quits. *See also* **sophomore slump.**

revenue enhancement A euphemism for taxes. A similar expression cropped up in 1982 when a proposed tax increase was described as "updating the revenue mechanism." In 1992 it was "revenue raisers" like the sale of federal oil and gas rights. Still another: "closing loopholes."

"The refectory of the Senate, Washington, D.C.—Senators and their friends at luncheon."

This engraving appeared in *Frank Leslie's Illustrated Newspaper* in 1868. *See* **restaurants.**

revenue-neutral An action that has no apparent impact on the budget. Under the 1990 budget agreement, every change from the agreed-to budget must raise a dollar for each dollar it costs.

revenue shortfall One of several phrases that Congress has invented for not calling a deficit a deficit. If the word **deficit** is used, it is never "our deficit" but rather "the deficit."

revise and extend When House members are recognized to speak, most begin by asking for **unanimous consent** to revise and extend their remarks, allowing them to change what they actually said, or greatly expand it by later submitting speeches to be inserted. In fact, some speeches that appear in the ***Congressional Record*** are not made at all. Members get up, ask to revise and extend, and sit down. The next day an entire speech—a **ghost speech**—appears in the *Record*, as if they had commanded the floor and held their colleagues spellbound.

Since July 31, 1985, when the practice was modified, those parts of speeches not actually delivered in the House have been set off in the **"Extension of Remarks"** section of the *Record* in a distinctive typeface. Such speeches in the Senate are identified in the *Record* by small round "bullets."

revolving door Metaphoric term used to describe the movement between public office and private employment. It is often mentioned in discussing the short tenure of high government officials who take jobs in the private sector after a brief stint as a deputy undersecretary or whatever. The practice stirs up the most controversy when a Pentagon official leaves to take a job with a defense contractor. This turnover problem has been a longtime concern of Congress. The practice also comes into play when administrations change in Washington and executive branch officials, ambassadors, and other noncareer appointees leave for private jobs at companies doing business with the government or with foreign companies. At the same time, private officials then join the government in posts that may conflict with their past employment.

The revolving door also applies to former members of Congress who take jobs as lobbyists and consultants. The issue was one of those raised during Sen. John Tower's attempt to get confirmed as George Bush's secretary of defense. After leaving the Senate, Tower (R-Tex.) had taken consulting fees from defense contractors.

rhetoric The craft of using words effectively. But in criticisms of congressional politics and speech-making, rhetoric tends to be described as "artifical eloquence" or "posturing." The "usual rhetoric" is what is said to accompany half-thought-out proposals.

rich man's club The Senate, usually. Referring to the large number of wealthy people in the Senate, in the April 4, 1992, *Los Ange-*

les Times, Richard Reeves called it "our most comfortable country club." *See also* **Millionaires' Club.**

rider An often controversial measure, which might otherwise be defeated or vetoed, attached to a popular bill, or one, like a **continuing resolution,** that must pass if the government is to keep operating. Riders need not be **germane.** They are often tacked onto a bill on the assumption that they will ride along and become law, but riders can also be used simply to make a political point and in some cases put the brakes on the host bill.

Although attaching riders is most often a Senate ploy, House members have found ways to attach them to **appropriation** bills, restricting the use of funds for abortions, for instance.

The late columnist Charles McCabe had this to say on the subject in his *San Francisco Chronicle* column of October 23, 1975: "A paradox of our government is that some of our worst laws are enacted because bad laws are tacked onto good laws as riders." *See also* **clinker** and **joker** for interesting synonyms.

FIRST USED: The first recognition of this term for piggyback legislation was as a neologism from 1954 and was recorded as a new word of 1954–55 by lexicographer Peter Tamony.

RIF (pronounced "riff") Acronym for *reduction in force.* It is used to describe the cutting of personnel in a federal agency and is often stated as a percentage.

FIRST USED: This term first appeared in print in 1953. The earliest citation in the Tamony collection is from September 10, 1953, from George Dixon's syndicated column. In the column Dixon described the mock funeral held at Harold Stassen's Foreign Operations Administration after a cutback by the Eisenhower administration: "The indignant employees have put up...coffins at various places in the building with 'RIF' instead of 'RIP' over them. 'RIF' stands for 'reduction in force.' "

riffing Reducing in force, from the acronym **RIF.** The term applies to the federal work force and comes up as agency budgets are trimmed and riffing becomes rife.

right wing The **conservative** wing of either party, but most often the Republican. There's the *radical right,* the *far right,* and other gradations.

rise Get up to make a speech, as in, "Mr. Speaker, I rise in support of…"

road show A **field hearing**, usually conducted in the state or district of the committee or subcommittee chairman, with attendant local publicity.

Robo

1 An automated form letter that members use to answer some of their constituent mail. These letters, which are now created by computer, were formerly generated by a Robotype machine, which also affixed a facsimile signature. The old name lingers on.

2 The Robotype machine itself.

rocket scientist What you do not have to be to understand the obvious. Like so many other political cliches, this one has enjoyed a long run in Congress. As *Washington Post* reporter Guy Gugliotta wrote on July 4, 1991, it is as though members are attempting to say, modestly, "We may write and debate incredibly complex legislation, have lunch with the president, and get on national television all the time, but, hey, this isn't Rocket Science."

roll call A vote in which each member's name is called or electronically recorded. It is not the only opportunity for members to express themselves on bills, but as political scientist Nelson Polsby points out, it is "the public face that Congress wears." *See also* **call of the House.**

Roll Call The name of the only newspaper solely devoted to the goings-on in and around the U.S. Congress. It is published twice a week.

rolled Like a hapless street victim, an unprepared or arrogant leader or chairman is apt to be outvoted, if not jumped and mugged, by his or her colleagues.

roll over To yield to pressure and change positions.

roommates Several members of Congress stay in Washington during the week, sharing accommodations, and commute home on weekends. Four who lived together in a Capitol Hill townhouse were Representatives George Miller (D-Calif.), Leon Panetta (D-Calif.), Charles Schumer (D-N.Y.), and Marty Russo (D-Ill.). Russo was defeated in a 1992 primary election. Panetta became budget director in the Clinton administration.

root canal politics The politics of pain, of austerity budgets and deep program cuts.

Rosemary's baby Any monstrous piece of legislation. The name was given to the monster 1989 budget and the unwieldy 1,376-page budget reduction act by disgruntled legislators. The nickname comes from the novel by Ira Levin and the subsequent Roman Polanski movie in which a woman unwittingly bears Satan's baby.

Rosty watch Lobbyists' expression for the anxious waiting they do while **Ways and Means Committee** Chairman Dan Rostenkowski (D-Ill.) prepares new deficit reduction legislation, possibly involving tax changes their clients will not like.

Rotunda The circular hall under the Capitol **dome.**

rubber checks *See* **overdrafts.**

rubber-chicken circuit The often tedious round of political dinners, with their attendant after-dinner speeches, that politicians endure despite the mediocre catered meals served at these functions.

View from the top of the rotunda while the body of war hero Gen. Douglas MacArthur lies in state in April 1964. *See* **Rotunda.**

Rubbergate Name for the 1992 bounced-check scandal that embarrassed the House and focused attention on scores of individual members and on the **House Bank.** *See also* **-gate.**

rubber-stamp Congress Name given to Congresses dominated by the executive branch.

FIRST USED: Uncommon today, the term may have been created to describe Congress during the administration of Franklin D. Roosevelt. An early use appeared in the lead to a United Press dispatch in early 1938: " 'A "rubber stamp" Congress is a menace to constitutional government,' Sen. Edward R. Burke (D-Neb.) last night told the New York Bar Association."

rub elbows To be present at fund-raisers and cocktail parties and get close to important people.

"The interior of the dome of the Capitol at Washington."

The focal point of the Rotunda is this fresco, "The Apotheosis of George Washington" by Constantino Brumidi, in the interior of the dome. It was completed in 1865. *See* **Rotunda.**

Rule XIX Senate rule that prohibits a member from offending another state during debate. It tends to be invoked mirthfully, as on the eve of the World Series, Super Bowl, or NCAA basketball play-offs, when the senator from the state of one team takes a jab at the home state of the team's opponent.

rules In general, the vastly different **procedures** by which the House and Senate operate. But in the House, the term also applies to the rules for debating each bill approved by the House

---

RULES, RULES, RULES

Without strict rules of debate, the 435-member House would disintegrate like an off-course rocket. Order is maintained by the powerful Rules Committee, whose membership is controlled by the speaker. There are dozens of possible scenarios, but basically the choices for regulating debate are these:

OPEN RULE   Any germane amendment may be offered—an almost unheard-of condition these days—unless the open rule is accompanied by a limit, which would have the same effect as limiting amendments.

CLOSED RULE   No amendments. Often applied to tax bills.

MODIFIED CLOSED RULE   The most common debate situation. Amendments are restricted to those approved by the Rules Committee, and usually only upon the recommendation of the committee that reported the bill.

MODIFIED OPEN RULE   Much like the above, but slightly more open, allowing for consideration of some noncommittee amendments, as long as they are prepublished in the *Record*.

Rules Committee. Because the terms of the rules resolution are critical to a bill's survival, debate on the rule can be as intense as debate on the bill itself. These rules—**closed rule, open rule,** and **modified rule**—are not used by the Senate. *See box,* "Rules, Rules, Rules."

Rules Committee An all-important House committee that has the power to clear bills for floor action and recommend the rules of debate under which they may be considered. The chairmen of the committee, most notably Rep. Howard ("Judge") Smith (D-Va.), could block legislation on a whim. Speaker Thomas S. Foley (D-Wash.), who came to Congress near the end of the Smith era (1955–67), said Smith used to go off to his Virginia farm and refuse to answer President John F. Kennedy's telephone calls. In his *No Final Victories*, former presidential adviser Lawrence F. O'Brien said the committee was regarded as "the nation's last bulwark against socialism and civil rights legislation." Finally, in its reform measures of 1974, the House agreed to give the power to nominate the members of the committee to the speaker. Smith was not the first czar of the Rules Committee. Republican Philip Campbell of Kansas, who served as chairman in the 1920s, once told the House, "You can go to hell. It makes no difference what a majority of you decide. If it meets with my disapproval, it shall not be done. I am the committee."

rules of engagement Military term increasingly applied to strident political combat in Congress. It refers to what is generally considered to be within the bounds of fairness in mounting a political attack. Leaking a memo containing innuendos about the sexual peccadilloes of a nominee or member is a clear violation of the rules of engagement.

Rule XXII   Senate rule that established a mechanism for ending lengthy **filibusters.** It provides that a petition signed by 16 senators may force a vote, shutting off all debate on a matter. The rule was adopted in 1917 after a filibuster—conducted, in President Woodrow Wilson's phrase, by "a **little band of willful men**"—killed Wilson's bill to arm merchant ships.

run   To attempt to win a political contest.

ETYMOLOGY: In their *Dictionary of Word and Phrase Origins,* William and Mary Morris note that this a pure Americanism. "In England, one stands for Commons, while in America a candidate runs for office." It was in use in America, according to H. L. Mencken in *The American Language,* as early as 1789 and in universal American use by 1820.

run interference   Get "out front" on an issue and take whatever flak that provokes.

ETYMOLOGY: The term was borrowed directly from football, where it refers to a player who legally blocks opponents to allow the ballcarrier to move forward.

runners   The term for **pages** when first employed by Congress, as early as 1789. They were often orphans.

running room   An insider's term for the latitude given to a member for past favors or to a leader who shields members from unpopular votes. For instance, defending one's colleagues against an attack in the media can provide a certain amount of room to make internal changes that they might otherwise oppose.

S Abbreviation used before the number of a bill to indicate it originated in the Senate.

sacred cow Like the bovine creature that may not be harmed in some societies, this is an issue—like middle-class tax deductions or Social Security cuts—that is better left alone.

Sen. Kent Conrad (D-N.D.), who resigned over the failure of Congress to bring down the budget deficit, mixed metaphors when he said that everything from tax hikes to a freeze on domestic programs must be put on the table. "Every sacred cow has got to get gored," he told *USA Today*.

(Although Conrad gave up his Senate seat in April 1992, the death of fellow North Dakotan Quentin Burdick later that year left another vacancy and Conrad won a special December 4 election to that seat. He was thus able to keep his promise to resign *and* stay in the Senate.)

sacrificial lamb When the party has no one else to run against a popular **incumbent,** this hapless candidate makes the sacrifice. Even though the odds are long, the lamb gets praise from party bosses, name recognition, and maybe a chance to run next time. And there is always the chance that lightning will strike, the **front runner** will stumble, and the lamb will turn into a lion.

safe seat Incumbency that attracts no more than token opposition. Safe seats are also known as *safe incumbencies*. In the House, a safe seat is in a *safe district*.

safety net A minimum level of established financial support for individuals through Social Security, Medicare, welfare programs, and Veterans Assistance. The term is applied as a full-fledged circus metaphor and it is common to hear of a hole in the safety net large enough to let a given program fall through. In some cases, it is ripped to shreds.

Although most commonly associated with social programs, the term is also applied to other areas as well. This quote is from a July 21, 1979, Associated Press item slugged HOUSE OK'S SAFETY NET BILL FOR FED: "The House passed compromise legislation yesterday that would provide a 'safety net' for the Federal Reserve System without immediately imposing reserve requirements on all banks."

See also **social safety net.**

FIRST USED: In his language column of April 12, 1981, William Safire asked himself who first used the metaphor and he came up with this answer: "It may have begun with Jude Wanniski, an editorial writer for the *Wall Street Journal* in the 1970s. 'The safety net that I used,' he recalls, 'applied to the international banking system—that is, there would be an international lender of last resort that would serve as a safety net for Third World loans in the event of international turmoil. I always liked the idea of a safety net.' "

sagebrush rebels An informal but cohesive band of Western legislators—and certain business and political interests behind them—whose major concern since the late 1970s has been local control over the millions of acres of federal land in western states. They got a lot of attention during the Reagan era, but they failed to make major gains. They were and are regarded as a privileged minority whose rebel band includes tycoons of lumber, mining, business, and agriculture.

sail through To pass without opposition.

salaries *See* **congressional pay.**

salary grab Critics often attach this label to congressional **pay raises,** but the increase that occurred in the waning hours of the 42nd Congress in 1873 was the real thing. Congress that year voted

Comic depiction of the Salary Grab Bill of 1873 in which the high costs of living in Washington are underscored. *See* **salary grab.**

itself a 50 percent increase—from $5,000 to $7,500—and made it retroactive for each year of the 42nd, which meant everyone got a $5,000 bonus, even those who retired or lost their elections. The public outcry cost Republicans 96 of their 203 seats in the House—and their majority.

salt To mark a memo or document in such a way that if it is **leaked** to the press, the leaker will be identified. Commonly, a document is salted when one word is placed in one person's copy, a different in the next person's, and so forth. When it appears in print, the salter will know whose copy was leaked. This term and its meaning were brought to public attention by columnist William Safire when President-elect Reagan's team was preparing to take office and there were so many leaks that salting was threatened.

sanitize To edit out; to censor. Most probably a term borrowed from Pentagonese. The word describes the practice of deleting remarks made on the floor from the official record. A senator's office gets a transcribed copy of that day's floor speech and has several hours to make changes before the *Record* goes to press. Some, like Arizona Republican Barry Goldwater, scoffed at the practice. "Old timers stood on what they said," he wrote in *Goldwater*, his autobiography. "I knew of no senator who regularly sanitized the record."

sapless branch Pennsylvania's Democratic Sen. Joseph Clark's apt 1960s reading of the public's perception of Congress. Clark served from 1957 to 1969. Some think the description is still valid.

-scam Popular suffix used to denote political scandals, as in **Abscam,** Contrascam, and Debatescam. Abscam was the FBI code name for its foray into the realm of congressional ethics. It stood for AraB SCAM, a classic "sting" operation in which agents posed as Arab investors—under the bogus name of "Abdul Enterprises" to offer bribes to members of Congress and other public officials. Several members were bagged. *See also* **-gate.**

Scare Book Popular congressional nickname for the report issued regularly during the Cold War years by the Secretary of Defense entitled *Soviet Military Power*. It was so called because of its tendency to exaggerate the extent of Soviet military strength. Scare Books were usually released to coincide with the Pentagon budget request.

schedule The timetable for floor action.

scoop

1 Information obtained by or given to a single reporter, who thereby has an exclusive story and "scoops" his or her competitors.

2 Nickname for the late Sen. Henry M. Jackson (D-Wash.). A "Scoop Jackson" Democrat favors spending on both social programs and defense.

score A public relations coup by a **press secretary.** As one press secretary put it, a score is "when you get your guy on a newsmaker program."

scorekeeping Tracking legislative actions affecting budget authority, receipts, outlays, the surplus, or the deficit.

scuttle Literally, to sink by putting holes in the hull of a ship; in Congress, to defeat or set aside.

SDI

1 Strategic Defense Initiative, a multi-billion-dollar program, begun at the urging of President Ronald Reagan, to develop a space-based system that would detect and shoot down enemy missiles. Also known as **Star Wars**, it was canceled in 1993 by Defense Secretary Les Aspin, former chairman of the House Armed Services Committee.

2 Selective Dissemination of Information, a computerized system for getting selected information to a congressman.

3 State Department Intelligence, a spy apparatus in Nelson De-Mille's novel, *The Charm School* (1988).

search and destroy mission Characterization of an attempt to dig up and use derogatory information about a candidate or nominee. The expression was used frequently to describe Supreme Court Justice Clarence Thomas's 1991 confirmation ordeal.

seat The part of a legislative body that is held by a senator or representative. It has nothing to do with the chairs.

seatwarmer/seat-warmer Senator or representative who has been appointed by a governor to fill a vacancy with the understanding that he or she will *not* run in the next election. Occasionally seatwarmers have grown so fond of the job, and so popular back home, that they have disobeyed and run for the office they were appointed to. Seatwarmers are sometimes known as *caretakers*.

second Formal motion of support required in most parliamentary bodies to ensure consideration of a motion but not required for ordinary motions in Congress. *See also* **sufficient second.**

secondary items Noncritical items in the Pentagon budget that could easily be cut, saving billions of dollars, according to Sen. James Exon (D-Neb.), who tried unsuccessfully to do it. Exon said the Government Accounting Office in 1992 estimated that half of the items, from overstocked lightbulbs to 40 years' worth of spare parts for fax machines, are unnecessary.

second election That which takes place after someone is elected to Congress and is then judged by colleagues; an informal "election" by peers to committee or leadership positions. "In my view, that second election is much more important than the first," said former Rep. Dennis Eckart (D-Ohio).

secretary of the Senate The chief administrative officer of the Senate who oversees the operations of the parliamentarian, the bill, legislative, and journal clerks, the librarian, and the historian. The House counterpart is the **clerk of the House.**

secret session Meeting of the House or Senate in which the galleries are cleared, the doors are closed, and lips are sealed. The Senate Rules state that any senator who discloses the business of the session shall be liable "to suffer expulsion from the body." Also known as **executive session.**
   The injunction of secrecy applies to confidential communications by the president and the content of treaties until the Senate by resolution removes it.

section-by-section A staff-produced analysis of a bill, breaking it down one part at a time.

select committee Temporary committee formed for a special purpose; the opposite of a **standing committee**. Select committees tend to be investigative and do not have legislative powers. They are sometimes called *special committees*. The Select Committee on Presidential Campaign Activities was formed to investigate

*"Open the doors!
The secret session of the
Senate is the stronghold of
the spoils system—abolish
it!"*

Public Opinion is the name of the
figure knocking at the door. This
Joseph Keppler drawing originally appeared in *Puck* magazine.
See **secret session.**

Watergate. Some select committees became virtually permanent
until the House, as part of cost-cutting efforts in 1993, killed the
select committees on narcotics, aging, children, youth and families, and hunger. All told, they had 85 employees.

selective cuts Careful, item-by-item trims of **appropriation**
bills, rather than **meat ax** slashes.

Senate, the This exclusive club of 100 members, 2 from each
state, began as the distinctly inferior house of Congress. But because of the executive powers it shares with the president, such
as treaty ratifications and confirmations, the Senate has grown in
power. Until the 17th Amendment to the Constitution was ratified
in 1913 to provide for direct popular election of senators, they
were chosen by state legislatures.

Compared to the House, the Senate is a free-wheeling body without rules. Its procedures are based on a complex web of precedents intertwined with traditions of courtesy and informality. In keeping with its role as a restraining influence on the House, debates can and do stretch over several days, even weeks. Except for debate-limiting **cloture** votes, virtually everything on the floor is done through **unanimous consent** agreements. *See box,* "The Senate Is . . . "

> **THE SENATE IS . . .**
>
> . . . such a helpless body when efficient work for good is to be done.
> *—Theodore Roosevelt, March 23, 1905*

Senate bean soup   One of the traditions of the Senate, a dish that has remained on that body's luncheon agenda for decades. The official Senate recipe:

> Take two pounds of small Navy Pea Beans, wash, and run through hot water until Beans are white again. Put on the fire with four quarts of hot water. Then take one and one-half pounds of Smoked Ham Hocks, boil slowly approximately three hours in covered pot. Braise one onion chopped in a little butter, and, when light brown, put in Bean Soup. Season with salt and pepper, then serve. Do not add salt until ready to serve. (Eight persons.)

Senator Robert Dole (R-Kans.) explained the origin of the custom in a *Washington Post* interview. It seems that on one hot August day in 1904 House Speaker Joe Cannon (R-Ill.) wanted bean soup but could not find it on the menu. "Thunderation," he said, "I had my mouth set for bean soup. From now on, hot or cold, rain, snow, or shine. I want it on the menu every day." Some have questioned this story, wondering how a member of the House forced something onto the Senate menu. There are those who argue that the House Bean Soup is excellent—just as good as the Senate's—and that the famous Senate bean soup may have actually originated in the House.

senator   Member of the U.S. Senate, one of 100 so elected, 2 from each of the 50 states, to six-year terms. One-third of the Senate comes up for reelection every two years. A senator must be 30 years of age, a U.S. citizen for at least nine years, and a resident of the state from which he or she is elected.

ETYMOLOGY: The word *senator* derives from the Latin *senatus,* meaning "council of elders," and can be traced to the same source as the words *senior* and *senile*. *See box*, "The Senator from Florida."

The **Senator** All senators, to their aides and staff, as in, "The Senator likes extra cream in his coffee."

senatorial Adjective meaning "of the Senate" but with much more implied when used to describe an individual. For instance, many regard it as descriptive of a bigoted stereotype of "a senator": white, male, preferably tall. When she first ran for the Senate from Maryland, Democrat Barbara Mikulski, a compact, combative woman, said, "A lot of Americans, black or white or female, are always told they don't look the part [senatorial]. It's one of the oldest code words." Discussing Mikulski in their book *Momentum: Women in American Politics Now*, Ronna Romney and Beppie Harrison note Mikulski's height and working-class background: "It's a little difficult to come to the conclusion that looking 'senatorial' might refer to anything other than gender."

senatorial courtesy Custom under which the president solicits the approval of a state's senators before appointing a judge or other important official in that state. In case of a conflict between a senator and the president—most likely when they are from different parties—tradition dictates that the Senate side with the senator. In *On and Off the Floor*, Samuel Shaffer notes, "Senatorial courtesy is not to be underestimated, even though its rules are unwritten. Nominees sponsored by senators for federal positions in their own states are almost always approved unless there is great cause to the contrary."

The term also refers to the largely unwritten code of conduct and procedure that prevails in the Senate. *See box*, "Sinit Courtesy."

Pre–Civil War Mathew Brady collage of senators' portraits. The senator in the bottom left corner is Jefferson Davis, who left the Senate to become President of the Confederate States of America. This popular photographic image was sold directly to the public as a way of introducing them to the faces of their leaders. *See* **senator.**

309

"Senatorial courtesy."

In this sardonic cartoon, a big-mouth special-interest senator is given the floor for an indeterminate amount of time. This illustration originally appeared in *Puck* magazine in 1893. *See* **senatorial courtesy.**

Senator No Nickname of Sen. Jesse Helms (D-N.C.) for his many votes against the majority; also, any senator who routinely takes a position contrary to the prevailing one. The name is probably a play on the name of the title character in the Ian Fleming novel *Dr. No.*

sending a message Cliche for taking an action that will be noticed by the White House, the courts, the stock markets, or foreign countries.

send to the desk Introduce an amendment.

senility system Syndicated columnist Jack Anderson's description of the congressional **seniority** system, which rewards length of service rather than ability.

seniority

1 Number of sessions of unbroken service on a House or Senate committee.

2 System under which members with the longest tenure get preferential treatment. In *The Sweetest Little Club in the World*, by Louis Hurst (as told to Frances Spatz Leighton), Sen. Carl Levin (D-Mich.) joked: "I learned about seniority when Hill veteran Senator [Paul] Tsongas sent me to the end of the line in the men's room."

seniority rule Custom—not really a rule—generally observed in both houses, which have long conferred the chairmanship of committees to majority party members with the most continuous years on the committee. This situation caused former Sen. George Murphy (R-Calif.) to observe in the *San Francisco Chronicle* in 1971 that the Congress of the United States is the "only legislative body in the world whose members rise to power by merely surviving." When Murphy wrote that line the 91st Congress was in power and the ages of chairmen of the standing committees of the House were, in descending order, 84, 82, 80, 79, 77, 74, 72, 72, 71, 70, 68, 68, 65, 65, 64, 63, 61, 60, 58, 55, and 44.

In recent years, aging—and sometimes despotic—chairmen have been ousted by more able junior members. In January 1975, three long-term Southern committee chairmen were ousted by the Democratic Caucus and replaced by younger members, ending the practice in which seniority was the sole criterion for the job. Since then, House chairmanships have been determined by vote of the committees, assuring that sitting chairmen would have to remain attentive to their colleagues.

sense of Congress resolution Formal statement of a majority position with no force of law.

separation of powers The constitutional principle by which the three **branches** of government maintain their distinct roles and duties. Congress occasionally worries that this separation is being breached, as House Counsel Steven R. Ross indicated when he said on April 24, 1992, that the Justice Department's subpoena of members' **House Bank** records amounted to "the attorney general sitting as a general inquisitor on the financial affairs of the entire House of Representatives."

sequential referral *See* **referral.**

sequester

1 The withdrawal of funds from government programs in accordance with the **Gramm-Rudman-Hollings Act** of 1985. Under the act, a revenue shortfall had to be met by withdrawing spending authority from already funded programs, a politician's nightmare.

2 The period of sequestration, as in "everyone wants to avoid a sequester."

sergeant-at-arms An officer of the House and Senate charged with maintaining order. From what had been a largely ceremonial job of carting the **mace** into the chamber, the House sergeant-at-arms got his first challenge in 1789 when asked to rush onto the floor with the mace and quell what had been "extreme disorder." The job has grown to encompass a vast array of duties, from compelling attendance of members for votes and quorums (*see* **arrest**) to running the 1,124-member **Capitol Police** force and overseeing the **House Bank.** These duties can be problematic: In 1992, Jack Russ, the House sergeant-at-arms, resigned in the midst of the check-cashing scandal involving the House Bank, which was subsequently closed. Senate Sergeant-at-Arms Henry Giugni, who retired in 1990, pleaded guilty in January 1993 to a misdemeanor charge of accepting a free trip to Hawaii from the American Telegraph and Telephone Co. and was placed on probation for a year. *See also* **doorkeeper.**

Service Department The Senate equivalent of the **Folding Room** in the House.

session One legislative year, as opposed to a two-year **term.** A member of the House serves for a term of two sessions.

settle for a study Phrase used to describe what lawmakers and lobbyists must accept—a study instead of a law—if their bill is sidetracked.

setup A seemingly friendly question of a witness or legislator that leads to a damaging remark.

severe reprimand Condemnation by the Senate for improper conduct by a member. In 1991, Sen. Alan Cranston (D-Calif.) received a severe reprimand for "repugnant" actions in the **Keating Five** savings and loan scandal. *See also* **censure.**

sewer money *New York Times* characterization of **soft money,** the millions of dollars in campaign contributions, mostly by lobbies and wealthy donors, given for party building, thereby evading restrictions on contributions to individual candidates.

sew up To gain enough support to pass legislation or ensure a nomination.

sexual harassment Making unwanted advances to employees, strictly forbidden by Senate and House rules. On December 12, 1992, in his first public statement after revelations about his scandalous conduct toward female employees, Sen. Robert Packwood (R-Ore.) said, "I just didn't get it. I do now."

shadow chairman The ranking minority member of a committee, who has some power—to hire staff and influence decisions—but nothing like the power of the chairman.

shadow government The party out of power. Senate Republican Leader Robert Dole of Kansas, the highest-ranking elected Republican, was said to be the leader of this government-in-exile after the 1992 election.

shadow members Name for the delegation from Washington, D.C.—one representative and two senators—who would be seated as full-fledged members should the District of Columbia ever be granted statehood. At present they have no voting rights and are essentially official lobbyists for the D.C. statehood issue. The first shadow delegation was elected by D.C. voters in 1990.

shadow senator The District of Columbia, which has no formal representation in Congress, has two shadow senators with senatorial rights and no duties except to campaign for D.C. statehood. Former presidential candidate Jesse Jackson was the first elected shadow senator.

shimmying Speaker Sam Rayburn (D-Tex.) used this term to describe members whose support was wavering. Donald C. Bacon, in *Rayburn: A Biography*, says the speaker would phone such a member to "stiffen his backbone." The modern equivalent of shimmying is **waffling.**

shoestring district A long, slim **gerrymandered** congressional district. The term was originally applied to the 6th Mississippi district.

shootout Duel between government contractors for shrinking dollars.

shortfall A shortage or deficit; the amount by which expenditures exceed revenues; the amount by which expected revenues fall short of projections.

short titles Abbreviated names for sections of a bill that may be adopted later as popular names for laws. *See also* **title.**

showboat

1 A legislator who struts and carries on in the manner of actors who toured river towns in lavish floating theaters. A showboat is a showoff who has little standing among peers.

2 To show off. House Speaker Thomas Foley says a member known to showboat on an issue like pay raises would never be appointed to the Post Office and Civil Service Committee, which deals with pay.

showhorse Member who is known for the ability to garner attention and publicity; a **showboat.** There is a popular saying attributed to Lyndon Johnson (D-Tex.) among others that it is better to be a workhorse than a showhorse. More recently, Sen. Paul Wellstone (D-Minn.), a passionate public speaker, said he had successfully made the transition from the former to the latter.

James Gregory plays a high-profile legislator in *The Manchurian Candidate,* the 1962 movie about brainwashing and assassination. Directed by John Frankenheimer, this movie is regarded as a classic political thriller. *See* **showhorse.**

side-by-side A document that shows the provisions of House and Senate versions of bills alongside each other to show how they differ. These are used by **conference committees** in arriving at compromises.

signatory A signer of a letter, treaty, or agreement.

Silk Stocking District

1 A rich or well-heeled congressional district.

2 Specifically the district comprising New York's Upper East Side, which had been held by Republicans, including Republican John Lindsay, for decades before being won by Edward I. Koch, a Democrat, in 1968. Both Lindsay and Koch later became mayor of New York City.

The *New York Evening Post* of October 30, 1903, described the "silk stocking quarter" as "the middle reaches of Manhattan, between 14th Street and 96th Street."

ETYMOLOGY: The term dates back to the days when wool and cotton were commonplace for stockings and the rich wore silk. Since the early days of the Republic the term *silk stocking gentry* has been a stock political phrase. In his syndicated column "Words" for May 20, 1984, Michael Gartner noted that it was a term used on at least one occasion by Thomas Jefferson.

At first the term was mostly derogatory, but today it is mainly one of description.

silver bullet

1 A tax break or loophole that benefits a particular interest group, such as a silver bullet for the oil industry. In late 1989, the *Washington Post* carried a guide to what tax lobbyists really meant when they presented their case. The original "taxspeak" reads "We have an idea that will benefit all the people," which translates as, "What we're looking for is a silver bullet that would exempt us entirely from the 1986 reform."

2 Any dramatic solution or major new technology; a single thing that can solve a complex problem. In this context it is often seen as something like a **quick fix** or a panacea that does not exist.

3 Money. As early as 1952 this term was heard in a Senate committee room when a witness advocated military intervention in China and urged "the judicious use of money—silver bullets."

simple conference See **conference committee.**

simple majority A majority of those present and voting, as opposed to a majority of the entire membership.

simple resolution A statement passed by one house of Congress expressing an opinion or regarding its internal affairs. It lacks the force of law, as does a **concurrent resolution**, which is a statement approved by both houses. *Compare* **joint resolution.**

sine die, adjournment *See* **adjourn sine die.**

sitting committee What a **standing committee** is when it actually convenes.

six characters in search of a standard Name applied to the members of the Committee on Standards of Official Conduct assigned to investigate the **House Bank** scandal.

six o'clock The time of day, according to Speaker Thomas P. ("Tip") O'Neill (D-Mass.) when adversaries turn into friends. O'Neill is said to have told President Ronald Reagan, "After six o'clock we can be friends, but before six, it's politics."

SIXPAC The short-lived name for the National Beer Wholesalers Association's political action committee (**PAC**). The name suffered from ridicule in the early 1980s and was changed.

Six-Pack Republican/Joe Six-Pack Republican Populist **GOP** member or candidate, described by Mark Shields in 1985 in the *Washington Post* as "a shot-and-a-beer kind of guy with the guts to take on liberal elitists on such issues as busing and school prayer, and to take on those country-club conservatives who were forever looking down their Ivy League noses at ordinary working people." *See also* **Joe Six-Pack.**

skin the cat Any clever method used to attach unpopular or controversial amendments to popular bills. In trying to append his massive energy bill to **appropriations** measures in late 1992, Sen. J. Bennett Johnston (D-La.) said, "This is just another way to skin the cat, and we have got to get this cat skinned this year."

slash and burn Tactics used without consideration of the possible harm to others. Sen. John Danforth (R-Mo.) used this phrase in 1991 while describing what he called deliberate attempts to find dirt on Supreme Court nominee Clarence Thomas.

sleaze factor Any corrupt, unethical, scandal-prone, or otherwise shady component of an administration, political party, or similar institution. In the 1980s, Democrats used the term to describe certain elements of the Reagan administration, but according to William Safire, it seems to have originated as a chapter title in Laurence Barrett's 1983 book, *Gambling with History*.

slip law First official version of a bill after it has become a law. It appears as a single sheet or unbound pamphlet.

slippery slope What nominees find themselves on when a committee finds, and perhaps leaks, damaging information, and support begins to erode.

slop-over Pejorative description of the items found in the back of the **Congressional Record.**

slush fund

1 Any political fund used for personal purposes or any tainted source of campaign money.

2 Money raised legally for a political campaign but used by the candidate for personal or other expenses. Such funds frequently end up embarrassing the candidate or triggering a scandal. When Richard Nixon was running on the 1952 Republican presidential ticket with Dwight Eisenhower, it was learned that Nixon had an $18,000 slush fund to cover unofficial expenses relating to his Senate duties. The disclosure stirred a furor and led to Nixon delivering his famous "Checkers" speech, in which he said that the only gift he had ever accepted was a dog named Checkers—which he would never give back. In 1968 the mingling of personal expenses with campaign funds led to the **censure** of the late Sen. Thomas Dodd (D-Conn.).

Under modern ethics rules, members of Congress are prohibited from mingling campaign, personal, and office expenses. The House Committee on Standards of Official Conduct said in 1992 that it had condemned the practice so often that members were clearly on notice that they may not dip into their campaign accounts for anything but political purposes.

ETYMOLOGY: In the nineteenth century slush was the surplus fat or grease from a sailing ship's salt pork. The slush was sold in port and the profits were put into the crew's general fund, which was used to buy luxury items. In his magnificent *Encyclopedia of Word and Phrase Origins*, Robert Hendrickson points out, "By 1866 the nautical term had been applied to a contingency fund set aside from an operating budget by Congress, and in later years it took on its current meaning of a secret fund used for bribes or other corrupt practices."

smoke and mirrors Popular **Hill/Pentagon** metaphor for anything deceptive or illusory, such as attempts to make an out-of-control federal deficit look like it is under control. The smoke is what clouds the issue and the mirrors give it a favorable image. In trying to expose the "wonderland budgeting" that arose in the wake of the **Gramm-Rudman-Hollings** budget law, Rep. Lee Hamilton (D-Ind.) blamed both the Bush administration and the Democratic-controlled Congress: "They provide the smoke, and we provide the mirrors." In his book *Assignment Pentagon*, Major General Perry M. Smith notes, "One of the reasons that many weapons systems do not live up to expectations is that they have been sold using smoke and mirrors rather than substance and objectivity." The term was popularized by former Rep. John Anderson (R-Ill.) in his independent 1980 presidential campaign. *See also* **blue smoke and mirrors** and **gimmick.**

smoke-filled room A place where secret and shady deals supposedly are made.

ETYMOLOGY: The term was popularized at the 1920 Republican Convention in Chicago when the leading contenders deadlocked over the nomination, and Warren G. Harding emerged from a smoke-filled room at the Blackstone Hotel as the party's nominee. In his memoirs, Harry S. Truman said that the term was not new at the time, "but Harding's nomination dramatized the tag and made it stick."

smoking gun Metaphor used at either end of Pennsylvania Avenue for the unequivocal proof of guilt, as if police found a killer with a smoking gun in his hand standing over a bullet-riddled body. Just before the Senate report on the **Iran-Contra** affair was released in 1987, Senator David Boren (D-Okla.) was quoted as saying, "There's no smoking gun."

The metaphor was popularized during the Senate **Watergate** hearings in 1974 when investigators sought a "smoking gun" linking President Nixon to the scandal and its cover-up. As it turned out, the "smoking gun" was in the audio tapes Nixon had made of Oval Office conversations. For some the gun metaphor was not strong enough for the Nixon tapes. Conservative columnist

George Will called the tape of June 23, 1972 (on which Nixon called for a limit to the FBI investigation of the Watergate incident) a "smoking howitzer."

Although it was once seen as a nonce expression of the Nixon years and was expected to fade away, the phrase has become part of the language of politics. There have been many situations since Watergate in which a smoking gun (or lack thereof) has been the central theme. The *San Francisco Chronicle* editorialized on October 4, 1980: "The special Senate investigating subcommittee has failed to find 'the smoking gun' in its nine-week study of Billy Carter's unsavory relationship with the disreputable Libyan government of Colonel Moammar Khadafy."

ETYMOLOGY: The term smoking gun or smoking postol had a long and lurid past, which began years before Watergate in non-metaphoric use in detective fiction. One researcher, Peter Blau of Washington, D.C., was able to track it back a far as April 1893, and a Sherlock Holmes story, "The Gloria Scott," in the *Strand Magazine*. Holmes's creator, Arthur Conan Doyle, describes a mutiny on a convict ship: "Then we rushed on into the captain's cabin, but as we opened the door there was an explosion from within, and there he lay with his brains smeared over the chart of the Atlantic which was pinned upon the table, while the chaplain stood with a smoking pistol in his hand at his elbow."

snakeoil/snake oil Information that is slanted, shaded, or misleading. One who purveys such information is a *snake-oil salesman*, as would be someone trying to sell political opinion as fact. This political meaning differs from the general meaning of the term, which refers to a phony panacea. The term in both meanings alludes to the bogus cure-alls peddled by members of traveling medicine shows.

snaps The traditional call for a Senate **page** defined in the April 8, 1939, issue of *The Pathfinder:* "a sound frequently heard on the floor of the Senate in legislative season, produced by a senator's drawing his thumb forcibly over his second finger, and indicating that the gentleman wants a glass of water or has thought of something he has left in his office."

sniff test Unscientific method of testing whether an idea will fly or a bill will pass. Talking about support for the Strategic Defense Initiative (SDI) in Congress, Sen. Sam Nunn (D-Ga.) said, "Those are the kind of things you don't measure by votes—you put your nose in the air and smell. If you give it the old sniff test, there's an awful lot of uneasy feelings about SDI."

snollygoster A politician who is all talk and no action. Former Doorkeeper William "Fishbait" Miller said that is what President Eisenhower was called on the Hill. The term goes back at least to October 28, 1895, when the *Columbus* (Ohio) *Dispatch* said it was "a fellow who wants office regardless of party, platform, or principles, and who, whenever he wins, gets there by sheer force of monumental talknophical assumnacy," apparently meaning "wordy hocus-pocus." The editors of the *Merriam-Webster Collegiate Dictionary*, 10th Edition, opine that it is probably an alternative form of *snallygaster*, a "mythical creature that preys on poultry and children."

soap box A portable platform once used by candidates and others for making improvised street orations, usually impassioned. Still applied to expressing an opinion: getting on one's soap box.

SOB Senate Office Building. After the second building went up, it was the OSOB for Old Senate Office Building and NSOB for New Senate Office Building. They got new names in 1972: the Russell Building and the Dirksen Building. A third structure, the Hart Building, adjoining Dirksen, has since been added.

SOB has long been beloved by headline writers and columnists for its similarity to a profane acronym in common usage. When the name was abolished on October 11, 1972, the next day's headline in the *San Francisco Chronicle* read NO MORE SOBS FOR THE SENATE. For the same reason, visitors to senators' offices were often taken aback by the large, oblong, canvas mail trucks running up and down the halls emblazoned with the initials.

social safety net In the Reagan administration, Budget Director David Stockman defined it as the minimum level of benefits for the poor, sick, elderly, and disabled. He said: "A social safety net encompasses the long-range programs of basic Social Security and Medicare; unemployment compensation; the two components of what we call welfare (Aid for Families with Dependent Children, and Supplemental Social Security Income), and basic veterans' benefits." *See also* **safety net.**

softball An easy question, which an experienced politician can easily belt out of the ballpark.

soft landing A nice career after Congress with good pay, perks, and power.

soft money Donations to state political parties for phone banks, campaign literature, and voter registration drives that do not count against federal limits on campaign donations. The Center for Responsive Politics estimated that $28.5 million in soft money went to nine presidential battleground states in 1992, with the typical contribution being $100,000. President Clinton said in March

A young Sen. John F. Kennedy prepares to catch a strike being signaled by Sen. Mike Mansfield. The game is softball (the real game, not the metaphorical softball), the batter is Sen. Scoop Jackson, and the time is the late 1950s. *See* **softball.**

1993 that he wanted to do away with soft money in presidential campaigns.

soldier A loyal worker who does not seek personal attention.

solon Synonym for lawmaker, courtesy of an Athenian statesman of that name. The term is rarely used except by headline writers.

sons of the wild jackass Midwesterners who came to Congress in the 1920s with a platform combining leftist economics and isolationism. In his 1975 book *Conservative Votes, Liberal Victories*, Patrick Buchanan resurrected the phrase in describing one of Sen. George McGovern's speeches. Buchanan, a tough-talking conservative who ran for president in 1992, occupies the opposite end of the political spectrum.

sophomore A member serving his or her second term. *See also* **freshman.**

sophomore surge Gain in percentage of votes for a member between his or her first and second elections. *See also* **retirement slump.**

sound bite A quotation or statement carried by the electronic media. It has become a valuable tool in election and reelection campaigns because a few words summing up a candidate's position can serve as an unfiltered, spot commercial. By contrast, statements that show up in the print media may not have the same effect and run the risk of ending up in editorials opposing the candidate. The term first appeared in 1972.

soup kitchen This is what is figuratively thrown open when there are not enough votes and it is time to lure **fence-sitters** from their perches with funds for a new highway or dam back home.

Southern Manifesto A defiant stand by Southern conservatives in 1956 against the Supreme Court's ruling on school desegregation. Those who did not sign it were thought to be in deep political jeopardy.

Movie stars Mary Pickford and Charlie Chaplin are among those selling Liberty Bonds on the Capitol steps during World War I. *See* **sparklies.**

space race When senior members retire or suffer defeat, this is the ritual contest to claim that person's larger, closer-to-the-Capitol suite, in the House or Senate office buildings.

sparklies Celebrities, especially movie stars, who take part in campaigns.

sparrowhawk Species defined by the *New York Times* in 1985 as "liberal Democrats posing as hawks by shrilly attacking small prey." An example given by the *Times* was liberal support of the death penalty for members of the Armed Forces found guilty of spying.

Thomas P. "Tip" O'Neill in his role as speaker. *See* **speaker.**

speaker The leader of the majority party in the House who, through powers of appointment and persuasion, controls the party's legislative agenda. The speaker, third in succession to the presidency after the vice president, is often called the second

---

MR. SPEAKER

Former speaker Tip O'Neill had an abstract definition of power as something you have if people think you do. In fact, the power of the speakership is as blunt as it is subtle.

There are highly prized committee assignments in the House that the speaker either controls or greatly influences. He settles jurisdictional disputes between committees, and he largely sets the House agenda. Members do not always have to go along to get along, but it does not hurt.

"If I call a member and ask him to think about voting on a bill in support of our position, very few members are going to want to give the impression that they don't give a damn about my call and I can go peddle my papers," House Speaker Thomas S. Foley said in an interview.

It was August 25, 1992, five days after the Republican National Convention. August is normally quiet in the Capitol, but Foley had been busy answering President George Bush's charges about Congress (*see* gridlock). He had a headache, which he soothed with a container of milk and a waferlike cracker.

The age of the czar speakers like Joe Cannon is long gone, but Foley has more real power than some others, even the legendary Sam Rayburn, who had little control, for instance, over the Rules Committee. Foley, in fact, helped rewrite the rules in 1974, adding to the speaker's power.

"The more powerful one is, the less you need it," he said. "The weaker one is, the less use it is. If you don't have much influence to begin with, strutting around demanding things is ludicrous as well as ineffective. If you really are very powerful, you can also speak with courtesy just as effectively."

CHOSEN TO PRESIDE

Speakers of the House	Period(s) served as speaker	Speakers of the House	Period(s) served as speaker
Frederick A. C. Muhlenberg (Pa.)	Apr. 1, 1789–Mar. 3, 1791 Dec. 2, 1793–Mar. 3, 1795	Howell Cobb (D-Ga.)	Dec. 22, 1849–Mar. 3, 1851
Jonathan Trumbull (Conn.)	Oct. 24, 1791–Mar. 3, 1793	Linn Boyd (D-Ky.)	Dec. 1, 1851–Mar. 3, 1855
Jonathan Dayton (N.J.)	Dec. 7, 1795–Mar. 3, 1797	Nathanial P. Banks (American-Mass.)	Feb. 2, 1856–Mar. 3, 1857
Theodore Sedgwick (Mass.)	Dec. 2, 1799–Mar. 3, 1801	James L. Orr (D-S.C.)	Dec. 7, 1857–Mar. 3, 1859
Nathanial Macon (N.C.)	Dec. 7, 1801–Mar. 3, 1807	William Pennington (R-N.J.)	Feb. 1, 1860–Mar. 3, 1861
Joseph B. Varnum (Mass.)	Oct. 26, 1807–Mar. 3, 1811	Galusha A. Grow (R-Pa.)	July 4, 1861–Mar. 3, 1863
Henry Clay (R-Ky.)	Nov. 4, 1811–Jan. 19, 1814 Dec. 4, 1815–Oct. 28, 1820 Dec. 3, 1823–Mar, 6, 1825	Schuyler Colfax (R-Ind.)	Dec. 7, 1863–Mar. 3, 1869
		Theodore Pomeroy (R-N.Y.)	Mar. 3, 1869 (Served 1 day)
Langdon Cheves (R-S.C.)	Jan. 19, 1814–Mar. 3, 1815	James G. Blaine (R-Me.)	Mar. 4, 1869–Mar. 3, 1875
John W. Taylor (R-N.Y.)	Nov. 15, 1820–Mar. 3, 1821 Dec. 5, 1825–Mar. 3, 1827	Michael C. Kerr (D-Ind.)	Dec. 6, 1875–Aug. 19, 1876 (Died in office)
Philip Barbour (R-Va.)	Dec. 4, 1821–Mar. 3, 1823	Samuel J. Randall (D-Pa.)	Dec. 4, 1876–Mar. 3, 1881
Andrew Stevenson (Jacksonian-Va.)	Dec. 3, 1827–Mar. 3, 1829 Dec. 7, 1829–June 2, 1834	J. Warren Keifer (R-Ohio)	Dec. 5, 1881–Mar. 3, 1883
		John G. Carlisle (D-Ky.)	Dec. 3, 1883–Mar. 3, 1889
John Bell (Tenn.)	June 2, 1834–Mar. 3, 1839	Thomas B. Reed (R-Me.)	Dec. 2, 1889–Mar. 3, 1891 Dec. 2, 1895–Mar. 3, 1899
James K. Polk (Jacksonian-Tenn.)	Dec. 7, 1835–Mar. 3, 1841		
Robert M. T. Hunter (Whig-Va.)	Dec. 16, 1839–Mar. 3, 1841	Charles F. Crisp (D-Ga.)	Dec. 7, 1891–Mar. 3, 1895
John White (Whig-Ky.)	May 31, 1841–Mar. 3, 1843	David B. Henderson (R-La.)	Dec. 4, 1899–Mar. 3, 1903
John W. Jones (D-Va.)	Dec. 4, 1843–Mar. 3, 1845	Joseph G. Cannon (R-Ill.)	Nov. 9, 1903–Mar. 3, 1911
John W. Davis (D-Ind.)	Dec. 1, 1845–Mar. 3, 1847	James B. (Champ) Clark (D-Mo.)	Apr. 4, 1911–Mar. 3, 1919
Robert C. Winthrop (Whig-Mass.)	Dec. 6, 1847–Mar. 3, 1849	Federick H. Gillet (R-Me.)	May 19, 1919–Mar. 3, 1925
		Nicholas Longworth (R-Ohio)	Dec. 7, 1925–Mar. 3, 1931
		John N. Garner (D-Tex.)	Dec. 7, 1931–Mar. 3, 1933

CHOSEN TO PRESIDE *(continued)*

Speakers of the House	Period(s) served as speaker	Speakers of the House	Period(s) served as speaker
Henry R. Rainey (D-Ill.)	Mar. 9, 1933– Aug. 19, 1934 (Died in office)	Joseph W. Martin, Jr. (R-Mass.)	Jan. 3, 1947– Jan. 3, 1949 Jan. 3, 1953– Jan. 3, 1955
Joseph W. Byrns (D-Tenn.)	Jan. 3, 1935– June 4, 1936 (Died in office)	John W. McCormack (D-Mass.)	Jan. 10, 1962– Jan. 3, 1971
William B. Bankhead (D-Ala.)	June 4, 1936– Sept. 15, 1940 (Died in office)	Carl Albert (D-Okla.)	Jan. 21, 1971– Jan. 3, 1977
Sam T. Rayburn (D-Tex.)	Sept. 16, 1940– Jan. 3, 1947 Jan. 3, 1949– Jan. 3, 1953 Jan. 5, 1955– Nov. 16, 1961 (Died in office)	Thomas P. O'Neill, Jr. (D-Mass.)	Jan. 4, 1977– Jan. 3, 1987
		James C. Wright, Jr. (D-Tex.)	Jan. 6, 1987– June 6, 1989 (Resigned)
		Thomas S. Foley (D-Wash.)	June 6, 1989–

most powerful public figure in the United States. The speaker is selected by a **caucus** of the majority party and elected by the House. The position was created and is guaranteed by the Constitution: "The House of Representatives shall chuse their Speaker and other Officers...." *See boxes*, "Mr. Speaker"; "Chosen to Preside"; *and* "Speaker: Mr. Misnomer."

SPEAKER: MR. MISNOMER

In 1963 Arthur Edson of the Associated Press created his own *Congressional Glossary of Terms,* which included this entry:

SPEAKER This is a humorous term used to describe Rep. John W. McCormack, D-Mass.

Speaking is what a speaker doesn't do. He rarely comes down on to the floor to take part in the purported debate. And when he presides over the House he usually mumbles expertly so no one will be sure exactly what is said.

Sam Rayburn, greatest of speakers, turned mumbling into a science. Rayburn could sneak a passel of legislation through the House before the snoopiest legislator could cry, "Hey, what's going on here?" Once he mumbled so wonderfully that he even fooled the official reporters and the *Congressional Record* came out next day saying the House had zigged when it really had zagged.

Speaker's Lobby A long, narrow corridor at the back of the House chamber, decorated with paintings of past speakers, with comfortably furnished waiting rooms stocked with newspapers and an old wire-service ticker. Directly off the House floor and open to the press, it is a popular place on Capitol Hill for on-the-spot interviews.

special committee *See* **select committee.**

special function A party or reception in the Capitol or a congressional office building. Here is the description of the special function from *The Sweetest Little Club in the World* by former Senate employee Louis Hurst as told to writer Frances Spatz Leighton: "Most people who testify in hearing rooms, or sit there as observers, do not realize that when the solemn proceedings are over, the joint may soon be jumping. Yes, it's true! Committee hearing rooms are also used for special functions. The words *partying* or *party* are never used. They are called *special functions* to give them dignity." Hurst goes on: "We were never allowed to write on a bill the word *liquor* or designate the alcoholic beverage, such as bourbon or scotch. We were only permitted to indicate the drink as *special beverage*, a term that covered everything from alcohol to lemonade."

special interests The lobbies that influence legislation partly by contributing to election campaigns through their political action committees (**PACs**). Woodrow Wilson's comment that the government "is a foster child of special interests" may well be applicable today. Some say that in America every citizen belongs to one or another special interest.

On the other hand, Opus the penguin in "Outland," Berkeley Breathed's Sunday cartoon, after demanding "responsible" spending for things like "breath insurance for herring-chewers," says, "We have met the special interests...and they is *us!*"

special order A long-winded—lasting in the House up to 60 minutes—speech on any subject. In the House these speeches are given after the end of legislative business, usually to an otherwise empty chamber. They are called special orders because members reserve a block of time to give them. In the Senate they are given at the beginning of a day's session. Since television made them so popular, they have been restricted to 15 minutes but only in the Senate. *See also* **panning the House.**

special session A legislative session, usually called for a specific purpose, and held after **adjournment sine die** and before the next Congress takes office, if called after Election Day. *See also* **lame duck.**

specific pair *See* **pair.**

spin Partisan interpretation, such as that given by a press secretary to the press. Those who specialize in political spin are known as *spin doctors* and the art itself has been called *spin control*. It is practiced at either end of **Pennsylvania Avenue** and is epidemic during election campaigns.

According to the *Economist* journal, the term was coined in the Reagan White House during his first term and was first practiced after the first 1984 Reagan–Mondale presidential debate in Louisville. By the time of the 1988 Bush–Dukakis debate at Wake Forest University, there were so many *spinners* working for each candidate that the *Washington Post* declared a postdebate state of "spinlock." The *London Telegraph* says the idea of spin comes from pool players' ability to artfully direct their shots.

spin club Informal name for the Senate Press Secretaries' Association.

spittoons Brass cuspidors were a common sight in the Senate chamber, but historians are uncertain when they were last put to use. Two of them are still at the ready, next to the rolltop desks of the two party secretaries.

Spittoons have been less prominent in the House, although James H. Hutson, in his book *To Make All Laws*, writes that a federal **filibuster** against a declaration of war against Great Britain in 1812 was disrupted "by the warhawks throwing spittoons around the House chamber."

TONGS AND TOBACCO JUICE

One of the nastiest fights ever to take place on the House floor was prompted by a grave insult: Roger Griswold of Connecticut charged that Matthew Lyon of Vermont had been forced during the Revolutionary War to wear a wooden sword as punishment for cowardice. On January 30, 1798, Lyon approached Griswold with a mouth full of tobacco juice and spat in his face. Griswold retaliated 15 days later by flailing Lyon, as he sat at his desk, with a stout hickory stick. Lyon got to his feet and defended himself with a pair of fire tongs before the two wrestled each other to the floor. Neither was seriously hurt and no discipline was taken. Lyon was called the "spitting hero" by his fellow Federalists.

Spitting, along with hissing, coughing, and whispering during speeches, is disapproved of in *Jefferson's Manual*, the basis for House rules. *See box*, "Tongs and Tobacco Juice."

split referral *See* **referral.**

spoils system From the phrase, "To the victor belong the spoils of the enemy." The term was coined in a January 5, 1825, speech by Sen. William Learned Marcy (Jacksonian-N.Y.) for the disreputable practice of awarding government jobs to friends of the party that wins the election.

Marcy's description of the practice, which President Jackson had embraced, was a "colossal blunder," says historian Robert Remini in his book *Henry Clay, Statesman for the Union*. "It was a shocking admission and gave the National Republicans a telling quotation with which to bludgeon the administration during the election campaign."

The spoils system once extended to a relatively large number of federal jobs, including low-ranking ones. But it has been narrowed to a smaller number of **political appointments** since Congress in 1883 set up the civil service system based on merit. *See also* **plum.**

sponsor Legislator who introduces a bill or an amendment.

squaring off Like prizefighters preparing to throw punches, members of both Houses have had recent chest-to-chest confrontations just shy of fisticuffs. Daniel Patrick Moynihan (D-N.Y.) and Christopher S. Bond (R-Mo.) were said to have struck this posture in the heat of a Senate debate. After Bond criticized the **earmarking** of $500 million in the transportation bill for a new Brooklyn courthouse, Moynihan approached him and, according to *CongressDaily*, shoved Bond with an open palm to the shoulder. Colleagues later said the two men merely "squared off."

squawk box A listening device that allowed legislators to hear the debate **on the floor** while they were elsewhere in the Capital. It was replaced by television monitors.

squeaky clean Describing a person or committee without any real or implied conflicts of interest. This term was applied to the panel created in 1991 to investigate the check-bouncing scandal at the **House Bank.**

squish Nickname for an uncommitted conservative.

stacking In **redistricting**, a tactic combining a political or racial group with a larger, more dominant opposition group. *See also* **cracking** and **packing.**

staff The veritable army of Capitol Hill workers that has accompanied the mushrooming growth of subcommittees. Staff size was just over 15,000 in the FY 1993 legislative branch appropriation. Rep. Christopher Cox (R-Calif.) urged President Bush to veto the 1993 legislative appropriations bill because "this huge, wasteful and bloated morass of congressional staff must be cut."

staffer Congressional jargon for anyone on the staff of a member or committee. In the press, staffers are almost always anonymous because members do not want staff aides who speak for them to be identified by name.

staff oversight A mistake, often a whopper; the Hill equivalent of "pilot error." For example, in 1986 Sen. Jesse Helms (R.-N.C.) accidentally had an X-rated dial-a-porn message read into and published by the *Congressional Record*. It was blamed on staff oversight.

This evocative image from the summer of 1929 shows two congressional staffers proving that the day was a scorcher by frying eggs on a marble railing on the Capitol grounds. *See* **staffer.**

stake out

1   In a political sense, to take an early position on an issue or lay claim early to a committee assignment.

2   In a journalistic sense, to wait, often for hours, outside a closed meeting to find out what went on inside. In **press gallery** shorthand, these are *SO's.*

Both definitions arise from the action of a miner who sets out stakes to establish a claim.

stalking horse A politician whose candidacy is advanced temporarily to fool the opposition while the actual choice prepares to run. The strategy involved is akin to that of a baseball manager who trots out a left-handed pinch hitter, then switches to a righty after the opposing team brings in a left-handed pitcher.

stall Any of dozens of ways to halt or slow down the legislative process. *See* **delaying tactics.**

stalwart One who steadfastly supports a cause or party.

standing committee One of 22 House and 15 Senate committees organized around a specific subject area, such as armed services, commerce, and agriculture. *Compare* **sitting committee.**

Standing Committee of Correspondents The committee of journalists who govern the operations of the House and Senate **press galleries**. They oversee credentialing of "reputable" reporters—some 2,100 are accredited to cover Congress—to the galleries.

standing vote A nonrecorded vote—that is, one in which those taking part are counted when they stand but no record is made of whether a given individual voted for or against.

stand pat To hold one's position.

ETYMOLOGY: It was first stated as Republican policy by Senator Mark Hanna, the most powerful political boss of the McKinley era. Its significance was described in Mark Sullivan's *Our Times*, Volume I:

> To Hanna, with McKinley in the Presidency, God was in His Heaven, and the world was good. On the eve of McKinley's second campaign, in 1899, Hanna expressed not only his party's policy, but his own contentment in the words: "All we need to do is 'stand pat.'" (Hanna was proud of the phrase, and by repeating it often and proudly, gave the Republican party a name that became a permanent symbol.) The Republicans had stood pat, and McKinley had been re-elected; but death had taken a hand in the game.

standpatter Time-honored name for a conservative who will sanction no radical changes in the party or the government.

standupper Television term for a report in which the correspondent stands, with microphone in hand, and delivers a segment of the news, with a prop like the Capitol in the background.

Starked When a black leader is attacked by a white politician for not espousing the liberal ideological line, he or she has been "Starked." Not to be confused with **Borked,** which is what happens to a conservative Supreme Court nominee. The verb *to Stark* was born in August 1990 when Rep. Fortney "Pete" Stark (D-Calif.) called Secretary of Health and Human Services Louis Sullivan, an African-American, a "disgrace to his race" for opposing federal health insurance and other programs that would benefit the poor. Sullivan did not get an apology, but he got the last word: "I don't live on Pete Stark's plantation."

star print A reprint of a bill or committee report correcting a mistake in the previous printing, distinguished by a small black star on the cover.

Star Wars The notion, sold to President Ronald Reagan by nuclear scientists, that enemy missiles could be tracked and shot down from space-borne laser guns. It became the Strategic Defense Initiative (**SDI**) or, as Sen. Edward Kennedy (D-Mass.) dubbed it, "Star Wars," after the George Lucas classic movie.

State of the Union Message The Constitution requires that the president "from time to time" give Congress information about the condition of the union and recommend changes, if needed. This requirement was satisfied by an annual address until 1801, when Thomas Jefferson sent a message in writing instead and began a tradition that lasted until April 8, 1913, when President Woodrow Wilson revived the practice by delivering his message in person before a **joint session** of Congress. Most presidents since, with the exception of Herbert Hoover, have taken their message to the **Capitol.** It is delivered, with House and Senate in joint session—and hundreds of diplomats, the Supreme Court,

President John F. Kennedy delivers one of his three State of the Union messages to a joint session of Congress. *See* **State of the Union message.**

the President's cabinet, and other dignitaries present—in a packed House of Representatives.

BEYOND THE HILL: Variations have been created to fit this idea to other levels of government: there are mayors who deliver "state of the city" reports and governors who make "state of the state" speeches.

Statuary Hall The hall of the House of Representatives from 1816 to 1857. It replaced the first hall, which was destroyed when British soldiers burned the Capitol in 1814. The hall is a Greek-style amphitheater with curved acoustical ceilings, which tour guides use to show how near-whispers can be heard from one

Clio, the muse of history, in her chariot in Statuary Hall. When Congress met in Statuary hall, Clio's clock was the official timepiece of the House. *See* **Statuary Hall.**

side of the chamber to the other. One of the most elegant legislative halls in the world, it is now the abode of brooding statues of American notables.

Visiting dignitaries like former Soviet President Mikhail Gorbachev have made speeches there. And once a year, after the **State of the Union Message**, the hall is turned into a media mob scene as members of Congress line up to react to the presidential message. It is also the site of a luncheon for the president following a presidential inauguration.

Statue of Freedom The bronze statue on top of the Capitol dome. The $19\frac{1}{2}$-foot figure is that of a robed woman wearing an eagle helmet encircled by stars. She is clutching a laurel wreath in one hand and a sheathed sword in the other. Her draperies are held in place by a brooch bearing the inscription "U.S. Freedom." Early documents refer to the statue as "Freedom Triumphant in Peace and War." It was designed by American sculptor Thomas Crawford and mounted on the dome in 1863.

One hundred and thirty years later, on May 9, 1993, the statue was removed for a four-month program of restoration and cleaning. As thousands looked on, a Skycrane helicopter plucked the 14,985-pound figure, trussed around its shoulders and waist with nylon straps and fitted in a protective cage, from its base and lowered it to a platform on the East Plaza.

Many tourists, and even longtime Washington residents, believe that the statue depicts an American Indian because of its "headdress." But the statue is actually crowned by a helmet encircled by stars and surmounted by an eagle's head and feathers.

The Statue of Freedom during its installation atop the U.S. Capitol, circa 1915. *See* **Statue of Freedom**.

statute A law enacted by Congress.

steamroller Tactics used in getting something accomplished by crushing the opposition. Supporters of Theodore Roosevelt at the 1912 Republican convention accused backers of William Howard Taft of using a steamroller to obtain the presidential nomination.

steer To guide legislation through the process, from **committee** to the **floor.**

steering committee An informal group, made up of top party leadership, that recommends committee assignments and legislative priorities. Each party has a steering committee in each house.

stemwinder A speech that commands attention; an old-fashioned oration that galvanizes a crowd. It is often preceded by the redundant adjective "real." The term "stems" from the portable clock, which became a watch wound by a stem. The *National Review* (May 14, 1990) contended that one "cannot give a stem-winding speech, nor can an audience be stem-wound by it."

sticker shock Term borrowed from the auto showroom that has been facetiously used on Capitol Hill to describe the reaction to the unit cost of new weapons. On the June 23, 1989, *Meet the Press*, Senate Armed Services Committee Chairman Sam Nunn (D-Ga.) said of the $530-million-per-plane price tag for the B-2 Stealth bomber, "All of us are going through sticker shock with the cost of the B-2."

stiff A politician with a wooden speaking style.

stipend Compensation for a continuing activity like teaching or column writing is treated by the House and Senate as a stipend and is not subject to the ban on **honoraria.**

stonewall To refuse to comment, or to reply in such an unhelpful manner as to be unresponsive. It is sometimes a tactic to conceal wrongdoing. The expression was made famous by Attorney General John Mitchell in his advice to Nixon aides during the **Watergate** scandal. During Mitchell's testimony in the Watergate hearings on July 10, 1974, Rep. George Danielson (D-Calif.) said trying to get information from him was "[l]ike trying to nail a drop of water to the wall."

ETYMOLOGY: The word appears to have entered the language of politics in 1880 as a borrowing from cricket, where it describes a player who has decided to keep his play defensive by just blocking balls without trying to score runs. Contributing to the metaphoric use of the term in America was the fact that it was the nickname of Gen. Thomas Jonathan Jackson, who earned it by standing firm and refusing to retreat.

During the Watergate hearings the term was stained as it took on a new meaning: to obstruct justice.

strange bedfellow *See* **bedfellow.**

stranger Any unknown outsider. From ***Jefferson's Manual***: "[Thus] any member has the right to have the House or gallery cleared of strangers...." In theory, this right still exists, but the power to clear the **gallery** has been given by rule to the speaker and the chairman of the Committee of the Whole. British novelist Jeffrey Archer, in *First Among Equals*, refers to the "strangers' dining room" in Parliament.

The labeling of all outsiders as strangers is a practice mired in history on both sides of the Atlantic. In their *Parliamentary Dictionary,* L. A. Abraham and S. C. Hawtry say, "In the parliamentary vocabulary all persons who are not either members or officers of the House of Lords or House of Commons, as the case may be, are termed strangers."

straw man Like the scarecrow for which it is named, this is a false or flimsy opposing argument that can be easily knocked down, but with pleasing fanfare and all the while ducking the real issue. In floor debate on January 28, 1992, Sen. Paul Wellstone (D-Minn.) said his opponents were "critiquing an amendment which does not exist. This is the age-old debate tactic of lifting up a straw man or straw woman and then tearing it down."

ETYMOLOGY: Logic would suggest that the term refers to an entity without conscience able to serve any purpose. Another possibility: A straw man is also useful as a target or decoy to draw enemy fire away from real men. There may be a much less obvious explanation, however. In his *Encyclopedia of Word and Phrase Origins,* Robert Hendrickson suggests that the term comes from real "straw men" who in the past loitered near English courts with a straw in one of their shoes—indicating that they would be willing to give false testimony or swear to anything in court if given enough money.

straw vote An unofficial vote or poll taken to gauge sentiment on a particular issue or candidate. A House member is not permitted to conduct a straw vote **on the floor**, such as asking for a show of hands, before a vote. Straw votes are carried out by **whip counts**, off the floor.

stretch race *See* **horse race.**

strike force A team of lawmakers, either Republican or Democratic, that goes into action at the call of party leaders, usually to counter the other side's latest strategy, with floor speeches, press releases, and press conferences. A *rapid deployment strike force* goes to work immediately.

strike from the *Record* To have an offensive or controversial statement removed from the official record—that is, the *Congressional Record*—after it has been uttered.

strike out the last word A meaningless motion allowed in the House to give opponents of an amendment a few extra minutes to speak after time has expired, but without any requirement to vote on the motion.

strip, the Commercial area on the House side of the **Hill** that runs for several blocks along **Pennsylvania Avenue.** The strip harbors a number of restaurants, a bookstore, and a bakery.

stroke To flatter a colleague or member of the press. One strokes or gives strokes. "I don't think a day went by when I didn't say, 'Everett, we can't pass this bill without you,' " Sen. Hubert Humphrey (D-Minn.) said of his relationship with Republican leader Everett Dirksen of Illinois. "Oh, I was shameless."

study

1 A minor investigation; the only possibility left when a member cannot get a bill passed. Getting the leadership to go along with funding a study is a weak substitute for action.

2 To put off a decision or opinion on a matter, perhaps indefinitely, by *studying* it.

stuffed bird What diplomatic personnel have dubbed a government airplane used to ferry back loot from congressional shopping sprees, according to *Newsweek*.

stump

1 To travel around giving political speeches. It derives from the *stump speech*, which is one given on the road, usually in a small town. The term dates back to the nineteenth century, when campaigning candidates often stood on tree stumps or chopping blocks to address rural crowds.

2 Where stump speeches are delivered. After the 1988 election, Senator Lloyd Bentsen (D-Tex.) told a *Philadelphia Inquirer* re-

Rep. Robert M. "Fighting Bob" LaFollette, Sr., on the stump in Cumberland, Wisconsin, in 1897. The stump in this case is actually a wagon. *See* **stump**.

porter, "In Congress you get into relatively technical subjects. It's much more fun on the stump when you can simplify stuff."

ETYMOLOGY: The true origin of both meanings of the word was suggested in the 1716 book *Memoirs of a Huguenot Family*, by Ann Maury: "I went down to the Sapony Indian town. There is in the center of the circle a great stump of a tree. I asked the reason they left it standing, and they informed me that it was for one of their head men to stand upon when he had anything of consequence to relate to them, so that being raised he might better be heard."

The American term has a long history of use in a political context as the pulpit for a candidate seeking office. Citations in the Peter Tamony collection of colloquial Americanisms at the University of Missouri dating back to 1835 show that a candidate moving from point to point was said to be "stumping" the district, and when he was actually delivering a speech he was said to be "on the stump."

A Studebaker subway car in operation in the Capitol, circa 1905.
See **subway.**

Subcommittee Bill of Rights In 1973, to counterbalance the power of committee chairman, House Democrats gave the power to name subcommittee chairmen to a minicaucus of Democratic members of the committee. This spread the power once concentrated in the hands of a few chairmen among younger, often more aggressive, subcommittee chairmen.

substitute A **bill**, **amendment**, or **motion** introduced in place of a **measure** being considered. If adopted, a substitute kills the original measure.

subway Senators and at least some representatives are carried from their offices to the Capitol and back by subway cars. In the House, only the Rayburn Building, completed in 1965, is connected by subway. There is a separate tunnel for walkers to the Longworth and Cannon buildings. The Senate has subways to all three of its office buildings. Subway service began on March 9, 1909, with a pair of lemon-yellow, battery-powered buses made by Studebaker. They were so tall that senators were in danger of crushing their hats on the ceiling.

ALL ABOARD FOR THE CAPITOL! CAR LEAVES AT ONCE! THROUGH EXPRESS, head-lined the *Washington Evening Star*, according to Sen. Robert Dole in his *Historic Almanac of the United States Senate*. The *New York Evening Journal* added a little rhyme:

A subway for our Senators is running every day;
There's no "Step Lively! Hurry Up!" and best of all, no pay.

sufficent second   Parliamentary term for an adequate number—one-fifth of those present—to require a **roll call** vote. *See also* **second.**

suffrage   The right to vote. The 15th Amendment, ratified on March 30, 1870, prohibited states from denying or abridging this right on the basis of "race, color, or previous condition of servitude." The 19th Amendment, approved on August 26, 1920, guaranteed the vote to women.

Alice A. Paul, head of the National Woman's Party, raising the suffrage flag over the balcony of suffrage headquarters in Washington in 1920. The flag bears a star for each of the 36 states that gave the vote to women. The occasion for this celebration was Tennesee's ratification of the Susan B. Anthony Amendment to the Constitution, which gave women the right to vote. *See* **suffrage.**

suits *See* **lobbyists.**

sunset The close of an agency or bureau, such as the sunset of the Civil Aviation Administration that took place during the Reagan administration; also, to close something under a sunset law. In early April 1979 Congress closed the U.S. Renegotiation Board, occasioning a press release from Sen. Alan Cranston (D-Calif.) with this comment, "If ever a government agency deserved to be sunsetted out of existence, the Renegotiation Board was it."

sunset law Legislation that specifies the periodic review and reenactment of programs or agencies so that they are not permitted to continue indefinitely without positive action by Congress.

sunshine rule Rule that opens a previously closed proceeding to public scrutiny, or as columnist Neal Pierce put it in his column of early June 1976, an idea "to force government agencies and programs to justify their own existence or face extinction." *See also* **secret session.**

In May 1993 a group of 48 Republican freshman proposed a sunshine rule that would open all House hearings to the public except where national security or defamatory matters were being considered.

supermajority More than a normal majority of 51 senators or 218 representatives in the House. Certain congressional functions, such as impeachment votes in the Senate, veto overrides in both houses, treaty ratifications, and constitutional amendments, require a two-thirds majority. Sixty votes are needed in the Senate to end a **filibuster.**

supplemental The extra funds granted to an agency by Congress during the **fiscal year.** A supplemental **appropriation** bill is designed to respond to unforeseen emergencies or to fund new activities.

supply-side economics Theory, advanced by President Reagan, that lower taxes on businesses cause fresh capital to flow into

PUCK.

"They hate the light, but they can't escape it."

In this Joseph Keppler cartoon from *Puck* magazine, the press is shining the light of publicity on a secret session of the U.S. Senate. *See* **sunshine rule.**

the economy, in turn creating new jobs, economic growth, and new tax revenue. Unlike most orthodox conservative economists, supply-siders are not particularly concerned about large government budget deficits. *See also* **trickle down.**

support A vote or the announcement of intention to vote for a bill or amendment of a colleague. Also, that which interest groups give candidates when they back them.

Supreme Court The highest court in the United States and the only one provided for in the Constitution. The Supreme Court has the power to review laws passed by Congress as well as state and local legislative bodies. The court's nine justices are nominated by the president, and are subject to **confirmation** by the Senate. *See box,* "Supreme Court Nominations Rejected or Dropped."

SUPREME COURT NOMINATIONS REJECTED OR DROPPED			
Nominee	Year	President	Action
John Rutledge	1795	Washington	Rejected
Alexander Wolcott	1811	Madison	Rejected
John C. Spencer	1844	Tyler	Rejected
Reuben H. Walworth	1844	Tyler	Withdrawn
Edward King	1844	Tyler	Withdrawn
John M. Read	1845	Tyler	No action
George W. Woodward	1845	Polk	Rejected
Edward A. Bradford	1852	Fillmore	No action
William C. Micou	1853	Fillmore	No action
Jeremiah S. Black	1861	Buchanan	Rejected
Henry Stanbery	1866	Johnson	No action
Ebenezer R. Hoar	1869	Grant	Rejected
George H. Williams	1873	Grant	Withdrawn
Caleb Cushing	1874	Grant	Withdrawn
William Hornblower	1893	Cleveland	Rejected
Wheeler H. Peckham	1894	Cleveland	Rejected
John J. Parker	1930	Hoover	Rejected
Abe Fortas	1968	Johnson	Withdrawn
Homer Thornberry	1968	Johnson	No action
Clement F. Haynsworth	1969	Nixon	Rejected
G. Harold Carswell	1970	Nixon	Rejected
Robert H. Bork	1987	Reagan	Rejected
Douglas Ginsburg	1987	Reagan	Withdrawn

Source: **Congressional Research Service.**

SUSPENDED IN SONG

Rules of the House do not permit singing or other performances—other than public speaking—on the floor. But that did not stop Minority Leader Robert Michel (R-Ill.). On May 29, 1978, he had a special reason. Comedian Bob Hope was in the gallery on the occasion of his 75th birthday. Michel asked for unanimous consent to suspend the rules—which he, of course, was granted—and in a rich baritone turned to Hope and sang his theme song, "Thanks for the Memories."

suspend the rules Procedure used to save time and bring an issue to a vote. It is used primarily in the House, where a two-thirds vote is required "to suspend the rules and pass the bill." In the Senate it requires unanimous consent.

The rules are usually suspended only for minor or noncontroversial issues, but some members, for example, Veterans Affairs Chairman G. V. "Sonny" Montgomery (D-Miss.), have been able to use the *suspension calendar* to bring up major legislation and get it passed. Veterans' matters, traditionally considered noncontroversial, have been automatically placed there and thus cannot be amended. Noncontroversial House bills are placed on the calendar and set aside for action once a week when the body is in session. *See box,* "Suspended in Song."

suspension days Days in the House when rules are suspended and noncontroversial bills are considered.

sweetener Additions and modifications that legislators add to their bills to attract support from colleagues or to avoid White House opposition. These changes may include major concessions. In 1992 energy appropriations bill negotiators threw in $517 million for the Texas-based superconducting supercollider—which had been previously rejected—to ensure President Bush's signature.

sweetening Money contributed to a **pork barrel** bill or fund. *See* **pork barrel.**

Sweetest Little Club in the World Title of a book by Senate employee Louis Hurst and writer Frances Spatz Leighton describing the Senate: "The sweetest little club in the world, known as the Senate, made its own rules and the club broke its rules."

swing district A congressional district that can go, or swing, either way—Republican or Democrat—in an election.

swing voter Legislator who changes his or her vote on an issue, or one who frequently switches from one side to the other.

switch To change a vote.

system, the The political structure. William Safire says "the system" is now "the process."

table A motion to remove a bill from consideration on the floor or in committee. If successful, it postpones or shelves the matter indefinitely. Some legislators prefer voting on the motion to table instead of being recorded as voting against what might be seen as a popular bill or amendment. Tabling is also an efficient way to dispose of unwanted amendments.

The motion is also routinely used to prevent a later motion to reconsider from being offered. After a vote is taken in the Senate, there is a quick, perfunctory exchange: one senator moves to reconsider the vote; a second moves to lay that motion on the table; and, with hardly anyone saying yea or nay, the presiding officer declares that the motion is tabled. That cements the action. In the House, the speaker routinely states that, without objection, the motion to reconsider is tabled.

Winston Churchill quipped that, unlike the British meaning of putting an urgent matter on the table for immediate action, the American meaning was "putting it away in a drawer and forgetting it."

tag team Like a team of wrestlers, these are **filibustering** senators who trade off holding the **floor** with long-winded speeches.

take, the Corruption. Writing in *Business Week* in 1990, economics columnist Robert Kuttner wrote about the Savings and Loan debacle and the deregulation that led to it and concluded: "Republicans at least embraced deregulation out of ideological principle; Democrats did it mainly because they were on the take."

take a walk To fail to show up for a vote, thereby giving opponents one vote less to contend with or proponents one less to count on. The phrase has an unsavory connotation, implying under-the-table deals.

When former Speaker Thomas P. O'Neill (D-Mass.) ran for speaker of the Massachusetts House in January 1949, he said Republicans, who stood to lose control of the state House of Representatives for the first time in history, were determined to buy the election. "They were offering $5,000 for walks and $10,000 for votes." It didn't work, partly because Democrats made counteroffers. O'Neill and his allies promised to appoint Republicans—who would, if necessary, vote for him—judges or department heads.

Former Rep. Toby Moffett of Connecticut said **PAC** money paralyzes recipients. "It makes 'em take a walk on a lot of issues," he explained.

take up To consider.

talking heads Politicians or analysts talking on and on, on television—a sure channel-switcher for viewers, television producers feel. On February 21, 1992, under fire for a slumping economy, President Bush said, "Let's not listen to the gloom and doom from all those intense talking heads who are happy only when they say something negative."

talking points Staff-prepared notes for speeches, or committee hearings.

Tammany One of the most notorious big-city political machines in U.S. history. The powerful Democratic organization, incorporated in 1789, was run in its heyday by William Marcy "Boss" Tweed. *Tammany Hall* (New York), as it was also known, is synonymous with bossism. *See* **machine politics.**

tap To choose for a position or as a source of money.

tap dance

1 A briefing or testimony that is slick and pleasant but says little.

2 An adroit avoidance of coming to grips with tough issues or pointed questions from the press.

task force A group with a specific, temporary assignment on the Hill or off. President Clinton's task force on health care, headed by Hillary Rodham Clinton, is an example.

tax-and-spend Democrat Label applied by conservative Republicans to "liberals" who want to spend more on social programs. At the Democratic Convention in 1992, speakers acknowledged that the label had stuck and argued that not all problems could be solved by more taxes and programs. Liberal critics of the White House in turn noted the propensity of conservative Republicans to engage in **deficit spending** and called them "borrow-and-spend Republicans."

taxpayers' friend Title bestowed on legislators who, in the opinion of the National Taxpayers Union, are tightfisted about spending public money. At the opposite end of the scale, the NTU deems others to be *big spenders*. In 1992, 64 "taxpayers' friends" were identified in the House and Senate and 182 were labeled "big spenders."

Tea-Bag Revolution Name given to a movement initiated and spurred on by radio talk-shows, to demonstrate one's opposition to the proposed 1989 Congressional **pay raise** by mailing tea bags to member's offices. On February 6, 1989, *Newsweek* reporter Eleanor Clift wrote, "Angry voters stirred up by radio talk-show hosts are sending tea bags by the thousands to Capitol Hill in a modern-day version of the Boston Tea Party."

Teapot Dome An epic scandal related to a government-owned oil reserve in Wyoming, buried in a reservoir shaped like a dome under a sandstone formation resembling a teapot. Like **Watergate**, it became the generic term for government corruption and triggered congressional investigations.

The chief culprit was Interior Secretary Albert B. Fall, who in 1922 secretly leased the reserve to Mammoth Oil Co. for about $400,000, including a $100,000 cash kickback delivered in a "black bag." Fall was accused of using the money to improve his ranch. He served 11 months in prison for taking a bribe. The hearings were not held until 1928, but the investigation stretched over three administrations, from Warren Harding's to Herbert Hoover's.

tedious Verbose and wearisome. A bit of friendly advice from *Jefferson's Manual* is that if members find they are being drowned out by other conversations or unruly noises, they should take the hint and sit down, "for it scarcely ever happens that they are guilty of this piece of ill manners without sufficient reason, or inattention to a Member who says anything worth their hearing."

The *House Rule Book* observes that, since House procedures limiting debate and calling the question are deterrents to lengthy speeches, "the parliamentary method of suppressing a tedious Member has never been imported into the practice."

Teflon Trade name for a nonstick commercial coating; when applied to politics, the term describes a person or idea that can't go wrong—Teflon president (Ronald Reagan), Teflon factor, Teflon Congress, etc.

The term apparently was first used by Rep. Patricia Schroeder (D-Colo.), who labeled Ronald Reagan the *Teflon candidate* in 1984 because bad news did not seem to stick to him. Tim Carrington cited the *Teflon factor* as an explanation for Reagan's uncanny ability to deflect embarrassment.

See also **Velcro** and **inoculated candidate.**

ETYMOLOGY: Teflon is the trade name for polytetrafluoroethylene, which was first produced in 1938 and patented in 1945. The trademark and patent were issued to the E. I. DuPont de Nemours and Company; the name Teflon was created by the company. The substance was invented by DuPont chemist Dr. Roy J. Plunkett. It has many applications, among which is a nonstick coating for cookware.

television Once considered an invitation to political **grandstanding**, television cameras were not permitted in the House until 1979 and the Senate until 1986. The first television coverage was of the House's opening session in 1947, but Speaker Sam Rayburn's adamant opposition, adopted by successors, delayed full-scale coverage for three more decades.

The Senate allowed television at several early hearings, including the riveting 1954 Army–McCarthy hearings (*see box,* "The Army vs. the Senator," p. 213). In 1977 Speaker Tip O'Neill (D-Mass.) permitted a 90-day trial of a House-run, intraoffice system. The first live coverage on C-SPAN (Cable Satellite Public

W. A. Rogers.

An aide shuffles through on-the-air identification cards for those regularly appearing on the congressional television facilities. The photo was taken in 1955 when Richard M. Nixon was vice president. Then as now, these facilities represent an important political perk. *See* **television.**

Sen. William Peffer (1891–97) of Kansas, known as a droning and tedious speaker, on the Senate floor preparing for what the original caption describes as "an oratorical eruption." *See* **tedious.**

LIGHTS! CAMERA! QUORUM CALL?

Quorum calls are nearly always perplexing to outside observers. For example, the viewer who switched to C-Span at midday, on July 30, 1992, would have seen a large blue-bordered message that said, "The Dodd Amendment to the Wellstone Amendment to the Committee Substitute Amendment to H.R. 776, the Energy Efficiency Act, is the pending question."

But nothing was happening. Four men in suits sat at the clerk's table, with a dozen white-shirted pages sitting on the steps, and Sen. Joseph Lieberman (D-Conn.) presided. Instead of debate, the viewer heard only a soothing string octet by Schubert (Opus 66, according to C-SPAN's control room). This lasted for nearly an hour, with the only activity being the entrance of Sen. Harris Wofford of Pennsylvania to take Lieberman's place.

One reason the Senate was initially so reluctant to allow broadcasts of its proceedings was its fear that viewers would not understand the long periods in which nothing seems to be going on. As C-SPAN often explains to viewers, once the absence of a quorum has been noticed, the clerk is ordered to call the roll, and "all action stops." The reason quorum calls can go on so long is that the Senate's real business is being conducted off the floor as leaders jockey to reach agreement. A quorum call is simply a tactic to fill time until agreements are reached.

On June 2, 1986, the day the C-SPAN coverage began, *USA Today*'s Bob Minzesheimer led his story with, "Lights! Camera! Quorum Call?"

Affairs Network) was on March 19, 1979. *See box,* "Lights! Camera! Quorum Call?"

teller vote A method of voting anonymously in the House, virtually ended by the **electronic vote**, in which *tellers,* or counters, are assigned to count members as they file past them in the aisles.

tell our story The reason most likely cited by private or special-interest groups after gaining what is usually described as "timely access" to members of Congress. Such access is commonly accomplished by first contributing to members through political action committees (**PACs**).

temperature The inclination or disposition of a member or key aide toward a proposal, as in "What's so-and-so's temperature?"

tending the store President Lyndon Johnson's phrase for staying in Washington—and enhancing his reputation—while other presidential contenders battled it out in primaries.

term As opposed to a **session**, which lasts for one year, a congressional term runs for two, as does the term that each House member serves. A **Congress** lasts two years; the 103rd, for example, which began in 1993, lasts until the first week of January

1995. Bills brought up may be considered at any time during a term, but they die when it ends. Senators serve six-year terms, with roughly one-third coming up for reelection every two years. Unlike the House, the Senate is a **continuing body**, with **rules** carried over from one Congress to the next.

Until the **lame-duck** 20th Amendment of 1933, members elected in November were not sworn in until the following March, even though Congress was required to meet every December. There was a lengthy lame-duck session every two years, often characterized by **filibusters** and other delaying tactics. All terms now begin on January 3 in odd-numbered years, and second sessions begin on the same day unless Congress deems otherwise.

term limitation The theory that restricting members to a set number of terms, from three to six, would make them more accountable. A national term-limit movement appeared to fizzle in 1990, but gathered renewed momentum two years later as Congress plunged in public esteem. Term-limit advocates played a major part in the 1992 congressional elections, winning pledges from many **outsider** candidates to support a constitutional amendment on term limits. Fourteen states approved term-limit referenda.

In an October 26, 1992, speech, President George Bush said, "I'd like to try it out on some of these old geezers in Congress. It wouldn't hurt them a darn bit."

testimonial A fund-raising event to which supporters bring praise and cash. The proceeds must be reported as campaign contributions and may not be treated as personal gifts.

testimony As in court, sworn statements given to a congressional committee under oath. "Witnesses" are called to testify before congressional committees.

testing the waters Hackneyed phrase for a candidate trying to decide whether to run. The decision often is based not so much on popular approval as on the availability of campaign money.

therefore The operative conjunction often found at the beginning of the last paragraph of a proclamation or resolution, preceded by **whereas.**

third house of Congress The House **Rules Committee** during the nearly 30 years when it was in the grip of staunch conservatives who refused to let progressive legislation reach the floor. Its back was finally broken in the 1960s with the passage of the civil rights legislation bill and the defeat of powerful committee chairman "Judge" Howard Smith (D-Va.).

third reading The last **reading** of a bill before final passage. It is a formality, neither debated nor contested.

third senator Senate **aide** with considerable prominence and power within a state delegation. A longtime administrative assistant (**AA**) to Senator Mark O. Hatfield (R-Ore.) was given this title in a headline in the September 22, 1990, *Washington Post*: QUESTIONS ABOUT S&L CONNECTIONS, TRAVEL EMBROIL "OREGON'S THIRD SENATOR."

three I's/Three I's League Three countries with large naturalized constituencies in the United States: Ireland, Israel, and Italy. In many places, no election or reelection campaign can be successful unless a candidate pays homage to the three I's. A whirlwind fact-finding trip to the three nations is also regarded as essential for a presidential candidate. "The first thing we ask," says a character in a Russell Baker column for December 24, 1967, spoofing candidate travel, "is whether they've toured the Three-I-League—which contains Ireland, Italy, and Israel. Touring it is considered basic to every candidacy and, in fact, most men will have put all three countries under their belts long before they start thinking of the White House."

THRO Throw the Hypocritical Rascals Out is a Tampa, Florida–based group that sought to defeat every incumbent member in 1992. One of the more whimsical offshoots of the THRO campaign was a round adhesive sticker, found on various restroom hot-air hand dryers, that read: PRESS HERE FOR A MESSAGE FROM CONGRESS. The group was emblematic of the anger aimed at Congress in the early 1990s.

throw To give one's support to help nominate candidates.

throwaway vote

1 A vote with no political repercussions.

2 A vote cast on one side of an issue with the understanding that it will not affect the outcome, while the member privately works on the opposite side.

throw the bums out/throw the rascals out *See* **bums.**

tie breaker A vote cast by the vice president in the Senate or by the speaker of the House in the event of a tie.

tie the president's hands Words commonly used when a legislator decides not to challenge the White House, as in "I won't tie the president's hands on this one." The phrase is most often invoked during foreign policy debates.

TIGR A "topographically integrated geographic referencing and coding system" (or "Tiger"): an electronic map developed by the U.S. Geological Survey that breaks down the population to city block-sized units. It was used in 1992 **redistricting** to help remap congressional boundaries.

time agreement In the Senate, it is the amount of time allotted to each side in a floor debate, agreed to by **unanimous consent.** It is similar to a **rule** handed down for floor debate in the House. Without time agreements the Senate would be paralyzed. Such agreements are struck between the majority and minority parties for every important bill. When Democrats moved on July 29, 1992, to restrict the taxpayer-financed travel of presidential surrogates campaigning for George Bush, Republican Leader Bob Dole of Kansas threatened to bring the Senate to a standstill by refusing all time agreements.

tinhorn politician One who pretends to have influence and ability but has neither. *Webster's New World Dictionary, Second College Edition,* says the term stems from the metal dice shaker in chuck-a-luck gambling games. William Allen White applied it to two-bit political hacks in his *Emporia Gazette* as early as October 25, 1901.

tiny jewels A term popularized by Sen. Daniel Patrick Moynihan (D-N.Y.) for **pet projects** that are **earmarked** during the appropriations process by legislators. In 1992 Moynihan created his own jewel by earmarking $500 million for the remodeling of a Brooklyn post office into a courthouse. Once the public got wind of it, the jewel was removed from the bill.

title The descriptive caption summarizing the purpose of each section of a bill. Titles are normally all that is read when a bill is considered. Some titles, like those in civil rights and education measures, are as famous as the acts themselves.

title creep The process by which the job titles of Hill **staffers** become inflated. Administrative assistants have become *chiefs of staff;* press secretaries are *directors of communication*. The person who answers the phones in the House Democratic Cloak Room is the *master of phones*.

titular leader Traditional title given to the retired or defeated president or presidential candidate in the prior election, which gives that person the leadership of the party in name only. The term is still used, but it lost much of its luster after many refused to grant Richard Nixon the honor when he lost the election for governor of California two years after losing the 1960 presidential election.

"Throw 'em out!"

In this cartoon from *Puck* magazine, Joseph Keppler shows how he would deal with senators who filibustered against repeal of the Sherman Silver Purchase Act in 1893. *See* **throw the bums out.**

token opposition Insignificant, probably underfunded, election challenge of little or no concern to the favorite, usually an incumbent.

to the right of Attila the Hun Ultraconservative. *To the right of Genghis Kahn* is also popular.

Tower rules Phrase that arose in 1989 during the controversial confirmation hearings and bitter Senate debate over the nomination of former Sen. John Tower (R-Tex.) as defense secretary. It referred to the stringent standards applied to aspects of Tower's personal behavior—drinking, womanizing, and alleged conflicts of interest—that had been overlooked in previous nominations.

town meeting notice A type of congressional mass mailing in which a member of the House or Senate announces upcoming public meetings in the home district or appearances in his or her home state. Under a 1989 limit imposed on mass mailings of newsletters, restricting them to a maximum of three per year, town meeting notices were excluded. The result, as reported in the *Washington Post* in June 1990, was that town meetings became a new reason to circumvent the rules against mass-mailing abuses. One member of the House had already sent "town meeting notices to every person in his district four times" within the first five months of the year.

track Legislative pathway. Legislation can be on a slow or fast track, depending on its urgency. **Fast track** refers to a specific method of considering trade bills without amendments.

trade group representative *See* **lobbyist.**

trading Also *vote trading*. The nearly universal practice of legislators voting for another member's bill in exchange for similar support. Said former Sen. Terry Sanford (D-N.C.), "I've made it clear that I don't trade votes." Maybe so, but Sanford admitted that when he wanted Sen. Bennett Johnston (D-La.), chairman of the Energy and Natural Resources Committee, to help with a Corps of Engineers project in North Carolina, Sanford told himself that when a bill of Johnston's was **on the floor**, "I believe I'll vote with old Bennett on that."

traffic cop The House **Rules Committee**, so called because it controls the flow of legislation to the floor.

treatment, the What President Lyndon Johnson, with his overwhelming personality, applied to disobedient Democrats: scorn, tears, rage, threats, cajolery. Said Roland Evans and Robert Novak in an essay "The Johnson System," in the anthology *Readings on Congress*: "He moved in close, his face a scant millimeter from his target, his eyes widening and narrowing, his eyebrows rising and falling. From his pockets poured clippings, memos, statistics. Mimicry, humor and the genius of analogy made The Treatment an almost hypnotic experience and rendered the target stunned and helpless." Also known as *treatment A. See also* **Lyndonology.**

treaty Agreement or compact between two or more sovereign nations. The Senate has the duty under the Constitution to advise and consent on the signing of treaties, with approval requiring a two-thirds majority of those present. Most proposed treaties have been approved, although hundreds have been amended. The most famous one to be rejected was the Treaty of Versailles, which formally ended World War I and established the League of Nations.

tree-huggers Derogatory term for environmentalists who come to Congress to lobby their cause. They are sometimes called *enviros* or *the nuts and berries crowd. See also* **greenies** *and* **nature-fakers.**

trickle down To benefit from a law or a program after it first has benefitted and filtered through its prime target. This is a politically loaded term that suggests an arrogant attitude by wealthy and corporate taxpayers—who leave only a few drops for the have-nots after first getting their fill of tax or other benefits. Some conservatives have embraced the idea, believing that the downward trickle of money from wealthy investors would create jobs at the bottom.

A similar concept, popular in the Eisenhower administration during the 1950s, held that if you fed the horses you would see the sparrows thrive.

An opposing concept is **pump priming**, in which government money is spent directly on a program or project to stimulate economic activity and create more jobs.

See also **supply-side economics.**

ETYMOLOGY: Lexicographer and columnist William Safire says "trickle down" was used by William Jennings Bryan in his June 10, 1896 "Cross of Gold" speech opposing the Gold Standard, though the orator did not use the specific phrase (December 27, 1981). A subsequent letter to Safire from a reader in Boston points to page 946 of Samuel Eliot Morrison's *Oxford History of the American People* and a humorous but trenchant attack on Herbert Hoover's Reconstruction Finance Corporation by Oklahoma wit Will Rogers: "The money was all appropriated for the top, in the hopes it would trickle down to the needy."

Lexicographer Peter Tamony left notes in the Tamony Collection on the possible origin of the trickle-down metaphor for public spending. He points to a moment at which the concept was, if nothing else, given new metaphoric vividness. The occasion was a speech given by Andrew Furuseth, head of the sailor's union in the 1930s, in a speech at the Lyceum Theater in San Francisco advocating the Democratic candidacy of William Gibbs McAdoo for U.S. senator from California. Tamony wrote that Furuseth said, "That capitalist stood at the top of the tree, pissing on it, and proclaiming that the benefits of the watering would eventually reach the lower classes—the workers—at the bottom of the scale."

trimmer A colleague who promises support but never follows through. Christopher Matthews, a former aide to Speaker Tip O'Neill (D-Mass.), says the oath "you trimming bastard" is frequently heard in Congress.

triple alliances The interaction among congressional subcommittees, the federal agencies they oversee, and interest groups trying to influence what is being regulated or changed. Also called *subgovernments. See also* **iron triangle.**

trophy/Trophy City What Washington, D.C., is to successful congressional candidates and their families.

truth squad Members of a campaign staff assigned to follow an opponent and deal with any accusations on the spot, hoping to flood the press with contrary information.

Try A bogus promise a member makes about an item in a schedule or an event that the member will never have time for. The scheduler, with an eye to making everybody happy for the moment, always promises the member will try.

tub thumping Adjective describing a speech that booms with partisan or ideological rhetoric. The minority and majority have certain members they can call on for tub-thumping speeches to drive home their partisan points.

Tuesday–Thursday Club Collective nickname for members who spend long weekends in their home state or district. Little is accomplished in Congress on Monday or Friday until the end of a session, when the calendar is crowded. In their book *Washington: Magnificent Capital*, Robert A. Smith and Eric Sevareid wrote, "This so-called Tuesday-through-Thursday Club accounts for the practice in the House of scheduling votes on major legislation in midweek." In one of his columns, Drew Pearson alleged that the members of the club frequently spent Friday through Monday "taking care of law clients at home."

tumbleweeds Humorous description of nonvoting citizens. According to author Douglas Coupland in a *New York Times* column on August 15, 1992, these are "citizens who don't vote because they move too often and don't know where they're registered."

turf/turf battle/turf war The area of responsibility of a committee or subcommittee, jealously guarded by its **chairman.** Jurisdictional battles are usually fought in memos back and forth among **chairmen,** the **presiding officer** or speaker, and the **steering committees.**

Turnip Session When he accepted the Democratic nomination for president in 1948, President Harry S Truman said that on July 26, "which out in Missouri we call 'Turnip Day'," he would call

Congress back into **special session** to pass several laws. The term was applied to this session, which, however, accomplished little, and prompted Truman to characterize the 80th Congress as the **Do-Nothing Congress.**

20-minute vote What the 15-minute limit on Senate votes becomes when senators are given extra time to get to the chamber. In 1993 Majority Leader George Mitchell (D-Me.) ended what had become open-ended vote periods, saying that 20 minutes was long enough except for **extraordinary circumstances**, which he did not define.

27th Amendment Provision ratified in 1992 prohibiting any Congressional pay raise that Congress grants itself from taking effect until after the next general election.

twins Democratic senators Hubert Humphrey and Walter Mondale were the *Minnesota Twins*, as were Supreme Court Justices Warren Burger and Harry Blackmun, both from St. Paul. Ed Koch said that he and Barry Goldwater were the *Gold Dust Twins*.

twisting slowly in the wind Left in a state of political limbo. This is how the White House left FBI Director L. Patrick Gray after he told the truth to **Watergate** investigators. The phrase was revived by Sen. Bob Dole (R-Kan.) during the 1991 hearings on Clarence Thomas's nomination for the Supreme Court. He said the Senate had left the nominee "twisting in the wind" for 105 days.

two-door system Formerly, how members of Congress got around prohibitions against their law firms representing clients with claims before the federal government. One door of a law firm in Washington or in the member's district had the congressman's name on it; the other did not. It was the latter that interested parties entered. Political journalist Robert Sherill wrote that former Democratic New York Rep. Emanuel Celler's double doors were "one of the longest-standing and most notorious embarrassments to Congress."

two-fer A position that allows a president or member of Congress to appear to stand up to something without really doing anything. For example, Christopher Hitchens, in the January 1992 *Harper's*, noted President George Bush's criticism of the Israeli lobby while assuring a lobby official that nothing would upset their friendship. "In vulgar politics," wrote Hitchens, "this is known as a two-fer."

two percent Before 1993, this was the percentage of women in the U.S. Senate. In her campaign for one of two open California Senate seats, former San Francisco Mayor Dianne Feinstein, a Democrat, used the slogan "Two Percent Is Not Enough."

two-thirds The improbable majority needed to overturn a presidential veto. As the late Rep. Claude Pepper (D-Fla.), a onetime Senator, wrote in his autobiography, "It would be impossible to get two-thirds of the Senate to agree that the sun rises in the east."

two-track system Devised by former Senate Majority Leader Mike Mansfield (D-Mont.) to prevent marathon, around-the-clock **filibusters** from halting all Senate activity. This system let other, less controversial legislation go forward while disputed bills were put on a separate track with scheduled **cloture** votes.

ultras Liberals or conservatives who are so far beyond right or left that they defy further categorization; near the extremes of the American political continuum.

unanimous consent A timesaving agreement allowing uncontested matters to pass, developed to an art form by one-time Senate Majority Leader Lyndon Johnson (D-Tex.).

In the House, unanimous consent is always asked to interrupt the regular order of business or to **revise and extend** one's remarks. When so requested, the chair replies, "Without objection, so ordered," and the matter is disposed of without a vote. The Senate, which has almost no limits on debate, could not operate without unanimous consent. Every time the majority and minority leaders propose time schedules for debate, for adjournment, and for reconvening, they must get unanimous consent. A single senator can—and not infrequently does—bring business to a halt by objecting.

uncontrollable categories Budget items over which Congress has almost no control, such as Social Security, civil service pensions, unemployment assistance, Medicare, food stamps, and other **entitlements.**

undecideds People who tell pollsters that they have not yet made up their minds as to their preferences in an upcoming election.

underdog A candidate who is expected to lose in an election.

undertow Term for the negative effect that one candidate is having on another; as when an unpopular presidential candidate threatens to pull a congressional candidate down with him. It is the opposite of **coattails.**

undue influence Situation in which **conflicts of interest**— due to financial considerations or other self-interest—create a powerful temptation to act unethically.

unholy alliance In politics, a coalition between such unlikely allies as business and labor, or Republicans and Democrats.

United States Capitol Historical Society Since 1962, a private organization that celebrates, publishes, and preserves congressional history.

In August 1992, still hearty at age 86, Fred Schwengel, the society's director, spoke of the Capitol as "a place of resounding deeds." In a rhetorical flourish that hinted of countless special tours, he added, "More has happened in the shadow of the dome through the elected representatives of the people to bring the biblical promise of an abundant life to all people and to share it with the world than has happened in all of time."

(Schwengel, an Iowa Republican who served in the House in 1954–64 and again in 1966–72, had just returned to his office near the Capitol when he spoke to the authors of this book. As he rounded the corner he playfully sounded a toy horn that was attached to his cane.)

United States Code The sum total of the general and permanent laws of the nation arranged by subject under 50 separate titles. It is revised every six years and a supplement is issued after each session of Congress. The 1988 edition of the *Code,* the one in use in 1993, was contained in 19 volumes including 5 supplements.

unity When combined with *campaign, slate,* or *ticket,* the term denotes a coordinated effort to elect candidates at all levels, to share resources and, perhaps, to develop a common theme. Sometimes *unity* is more a slogan than a reality.

unlimited debate A senator's right to talk as long as he or she wishes when a bill is being debated. It is the source of the Senate **filibuster** and one of the principal procedural distinctions between the Senate and the House, where debate is always limited.

unofficial caucus Temporary group of members, often bipartisan, formed around a single issue such as rescuing an endangered defense program. Same as *bipartisan task force*.

unofficial office accounts Set up with private contributions, these accounts once enabled House members to pay their unreimbursed expenses. Once in widespread use, they were banned in 1977.

unreconstructed Describing those who cling to outmoded or discredited views, such as Southerners who did not change their views about slavery despite—or possibly because of—the post–Civil War Reconstruction laws. Some say it would be impossible to be an unreconstructed liberal, who by definition is always changing views.

Unwritten Constitution, the The body of customs and practices *not* specified in the Constitution but essential to the operations of the government. Some elements of the Unwritten Constitution include cabinet meetings, the congressional committee system, political parties, and political conventions.

up or down Yes or no; not a test vote, not a substitute or amendment, but the real thing.

up or down vote Resolution of an issue; what is called for when the debate on a subject has gone on too long and it is time to vote directly on the subject at hand—rather than on a procedural motion such as a motion to **table** or **recommit.**

upper house   The Senate. As House historians point out, this is a misnomer, because the framers of the Constitution intended the House as the preeminent body. The mistake came in comparing the Senate with the upper-crust House of Lords in England. Long-established lore of Congress has it that "upper" is a reference to the tendency of the Senate to "up" the **appropriations** made in the House.

veep The vice president.

ETYMOLOGY AND FIRST USE: This short item from *Time*, May 23, 1949, entitled "The Veep," is most definitive:

> How do you correctly address the Vice President of the U.S., a reporter wanted to know. Well, said Alben Barkley in a relaxed moment last week, at work some called him Mr. President (because he is president of the Senate). Some called him Mr. Vice President, which is correct according to Emily Post, but a mouthful, and some still call him Senator. "But my children call me 'Veep,'" he confided.
>
> At week's end, Barkley discovered that he had added a new word to the language. "Darned if it hasn't gone all over the country now," he said. "Every time I pick up a paper I find I'm 'The Veep.'"

By the summer of 1949 every newspaper in the country was referring to Barkley as "The Veep." When he mentioned he was contemplating remarriage, the *San Francisco News* carried this headline: THE VEEP MAKES AN IMPORTANT DECISION. It was also quickly transferred to others who might be interested in the number two job: Walter Winchell's column for September 9, 1949, was titled SEN. MARGARET SMITH TO BID FOR "VEEP?"

vehicle A bill that is moving through Congress and may be loaded down with other measures. Since the Senate has no **germaneness** rule, any bill that is likely to pass can serve as a vehicle for other legislation. Especially accommodating are **continuing resolutions** passed at the end of the year.

Velcro Trade name for a hook-and-loop fastener. A Velcro candidate is one to whom everything sticks. The opposite is **Teflon.**

velvet steamroller Former Speaker Thomas P. O'Neill's description of President Reagan's smooth but powerful legislative tactics. *See also* **steamroller.**

veto To reject legislation. In the context of Congress, this term refers to the right of the president to reject a bill that has been passed by both the House and Senate. When this happens, the president returns the unsigned bill to the house in which it originated with a message explaining his veto. The only option left to the supporters of the bill is to muster enough votes—two-thirds of those present in each house—to **override** the veto.

A variant of the veto is the **pocket veto,** by which the president takes no action on a bill for 10 days. He thus "pockets" it. Normally his refusal to sign a bill simply delays it from becoming law, since any bill passed by Congress automatically goes into effect after 10 days—if Congress remains in session. But if Congress adjourns during the 10-day period and the president has not signed the bill, it is vetoed by default. Because Congress often passes a number of

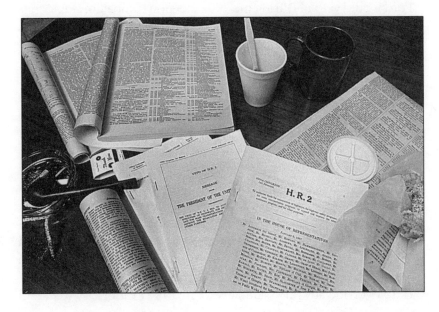

Paperwork associated with President Reagan's veto of the 1987 Transportation Bill. *See* **veto.**

bills at the end of sessions, presidents have relied on the pocket veto as a way of killing them without having to explain why. The first pocket veto was employed by Andrew Jackson.

President George Bush was so successful at stopping legislation with vetoes that could not be overridden—the final score was 37 to 1—that critics called his administration "government by veto." Indeed, during fights with Congress over extended unemployment compensation benefits, Bush miffed Democratic leaders by saying they were "sending me a bunch of garbage I will not sign. I'll continue to veto the bad stuff until we get good bills." In a June 13, 1991, Senate speech, Sen. Howard Metzenbaum (D-Ohio) said of Bush, "He sleeps at night and dreams about the veto. He breathes the veto. The veto is his constant companion."

ETYMOLOGY: *Veto* is Latin for "I forbid."

veto bait Legislation certain to be vetoed by the president. A veto-bait bill can offer an opportunity for a member to go on the record in favor of something without having to live with its consequences. A 1975 energy bill that would have forbidden the busing of children to any school other than the one closest to their home was a classic example of a veto-bait bill. House members passed it 255 to 148 with the full knowledge that President Gerald Ford would veto it. During the 1992 election campaign, Democrats sent bills to the White House that they knew Bush would not sign in an effort to score political points. This was called *veto-dare strategy.*

veto-proof Since a two-thirds majority is needed to override a veto, legislation that passes by at least that much is considered veto-proof.

veto-proof Congress A Congress in which both houses have a two-thirds majority in the party opposing the president—a virtual impossibility. It was a goal of the AFL-CIO (American Federation of Labor and Congress of Industrial Organizations), which spearheaded a campaign to take power away from President Richard Nixon by helping Democrats win two-thirds control of both the House and Senate in 1974, which would have ensured their ability to override any presidential veto. In a 1974 Labor Day weekend interview, AFL-CIO President George Meany, then age 80, told a reporter from the *San Francisco Examiner* that the union had scaled back its campaign for a veto-proof Congress when President Gerald Ford took over after Nixon's resignation in August. "Our campaign for a veto-proof Congress was directed at Nixon," Meany said. "Ford is open, he's very easy to talk to . . . we'll have no trouble communicating with the president."

vice chairman The subject of a title war in the House. In 1988, House Republicans decided to call the ranking **GOP** member of a committee or subcommittee a vice chairman. But in 1990, Democrats countered by claiming the title for their second-ranking member. The GOP retreated and the senior Republican is now **Republican chairman.**

view with alarm . . . point with pride Tiresome cliches used in typical congressional speeches.

virtucrats Conservative columnist George Will's nickname for liberals who put bumper stickers on their Volvos with slogans such as "You can't hug a kid with nuclear arms."

visibility
1 Exposure in the media needed by politicians to get elected. It can be dangerous to have too much visibility or get out front on controversial matters.
2 The art of getting free exposure for your candidate at political rallies, especially in the line of sight of TV cameras. A campaign worker is often put in charge of visibility at campaign stops.

viva voce vote (pronounced "vee-vah voh-chay") A method of voting individually by voice, rather than by **electronic device.** In the speaker's election in the House—since it is not a "yea" or "nay" question—the vote is always taken thus, by "live voice."

voice vote Vote cast in unison, without individual votes being recorded. Many actions are taken in this matter to save time. In such cases, the presiding officer determines the outcome based on the auditory volume of responses. If there is a dispute, the "yeas" and "nays" can be demanded, and if one-fifth of those present provide a "**sufficient second**," a recorded **roll call** is ordered.

voodoo economics   George Bush's phrase for Ronald Reagan's plan to cut marginal tax rates when the two were opponents for the Republican presidential nomination in 1980.

vote

1   To formally express one's opinion or position legislatively by accepting or rejecting a proposal in the form of a bill, amendment, nomination, or other vehicle.

2   The result of balloting expressed numerically, as in "the vote was three to two against."

3   **Suffrage** or the right of political participation, especially in reference to women gaining the right to vote.

4   To express onself, as in "voting one's conscience" or, by extension, "voting with one's feet," as a political refugee is said to do when escaping oppression.

5   To pick a candidate for public office; to be a voter.

ETYMOLOGY: Directly derived from the Latin word *votum,* for "vow" or "wish," the word originally appeared in English in the fifteenth century.

voter   One who participates in elections or, at a miniumum, has the legal right to do so.

vote trading *See* **trading.**

vulnerability study   A brief, preferably one-page analysis of an opponent's weak points distilled from **opposition research.** It is a "road map" for developing the issues to defeat one's opponent.

waffle To waver or equivocate. A politician may be known to waffle under pressure. The term also enjoyed temporary usage in descriptions of Washington bureaucratese that seems portentous but actually says little or nothing. *See also* **wiggle room.**

walk *See* **take a walk.**

walls up/walls down Separate budget plans offered by Budget Committee Chairman Leon Panetta (D-Calif.) in March 1992, with a choice of leaving the walls between military and domestic spending in place or taking them down. Until 1993, budget-makers were prohibited from moving funds from one category to another. The term **fire walls**, which originally applied to only Medicaid and appears to be the forerunner for the use of "walls" in this sense. The concept was later used to prevent the transfer of defense dollars to domestic programs.

walruses, old Members of the **old guard.**

war chest Campaign **kitty**; funds held in reserve by an incumbent to fend off future challengers. *See also* **cash on hand.**

   In early 1989, Congress Watch, an arm of the public-interest group Public Citizen, reported that members of the House collectively had a war chest of $67 million—an average of $154,000 each. The biggest kitty at the time belonged to Rep. David Dreier (R-Calif.): $1,244,729.

war Democrat Term given to Democrats who supported Lincoln's Civil War policies. "As a prominent 'war Democrat,' his standing with the administration was very high," Bruce Catton says of Gen. John A. McClernand in *The American Heritage Short History of the Civil War*. In a May 13, 1992, editorial, the *New York Times* referred to congressional Democrats who were "spending billions to build unneeded weapons" as "war Democrats, 1992 style."

war gaming Examining all possible responses to a challenger's moves or potential moves; applicable to either defense strategy or political campaigns. Thus, if one candidate makes his or her tax return public, should the opponent do the same, call it a lame stunt, or up the ante with a more comprehensive release?

war powers The Constitution says Congress has the power to declare war, but it is the president's job to conduct it. Vietnam illustrated how headstrong presidents could commit hundreds of thousands of troops to an undeclared war. Sen. George McGovern (D-S.D.) said in a September 1, 1970, Senate speech, "If we don't end this damnable war, those young men will some day curse us for our pitiful willingness to let the Executive carry the burden that the Constitution places on us."

In 1973, Congress sought to shift the balance. Over President Richard Nixon's veto, it passed the War Powers Act. This act requires the president to consult with Congress before committing troops unless the United States comes under attack. To send troops into combat, the president must report to Congress within 48 hours and the forces be withdrawn within 90 days unless Congress declares war, extends the deadline, or cannot convene because of an ensuing attack.

In 1990, President George Bush threatened to commit troops to the Persian Gulf without approval, but Congress asserted its right to vote on whether to give him that option—and voted to authorize the use of force. Some members said if Bush had committed troops without approval, it would have been an impeachable offense.

war wimp Insult by Rep. Andrew Jacobs (D-Ind.), a Marine veteran, in an April 25, 1985, speech that made fun of the war-prone

Protestors on the Capitol steps in May 1971 opposing U.S. involvement in Southeast Asia. *See* **war powers.**

hawk who never spent any time in military service. Jacobs' definition: "one who is all too willing to send others to war but never gets around to going to war himself."

Washington representative *See* **lobbyist.**

Washington ways Customs and practices that define the folkways of the Capitol; that which upsets the public. A 1992 *Washington Post* article hit on the subject when it asked the question, "Should the president's staff include five calligraphers who write invitations and thank-you notes?"

377

watchdog A person or agency that investigates government programs; most notably the General Accounting Office, the investigative arm of Congress. The term is also applied to budget-conscious congressmen, as in "watchdog of the Treasury." Sen. Bob Dole of Kansas, the senior elected Republican after the defeat of President George Bush, assumed the watchdog title for himself in keeping an eye on the Clinton Administration.

FIRST USED: The term *watchdog commission* (for a government unit set up to carefully observe some trouble spot) appears in the 1948 *Britannica Book of the Year* under the heading "New Words and Their Meanings."

Watergate

1 The hotel-apartment-office complex in Washington where the 1972 burglary of the Democratic National Committee headquarters, later tied to the Committee for the Re-election of the President, took place. The subsequent investigation of the burglary and the White House **cover-up** led to televised Senate and House hearings. On August 8, 1974, President Richard Nixon resigned rather than face almost certain impeachment. *See* **smoking gun** and **twisting slowly in the wind.**

2 Benchmark in American political history; found in such constructions as *post-Watergate morality,* implying that politicians would be held to higher ethical standards after the Watergate incident and its aftermath. *See* **-gate.**

Watergate babies The group of 70 new Democratic congressmen and 6 other former Democratic members elected in 1974 by

Sen. Sam Ervin, chairman of the Senate Watergate Committee, and Counsel Sam Dash confer during the 1973 Watergate hearings. *See* **Watergate.**

voters disgusted with the corruption turned up in the **Watergate** scandal.

watermelon bill Term popularized in 1975 by Senator J. Bennett Johnson (D-La.), who termed a railroad bill a watermelon bill in that it was "sweet and juicy with a slice in it for everyone." Thus, the term refers to any bill with lots of goodies for a particular industry or a particular state or region.

water's edge According to speaker Sam Rayburn (D-Tex.), where politics stops—meaning, support the president on foreign policy even if you hound him on his domestic programs. This policy was rigorously tested and violated by many during the Vietnam War.

wax To grow in size or volume as a speech-maker does in becoming eloquent, poetic, or angry.

Ways and Means Committee Powerful House committee that originates *all* bills having to do with raising money.

wedge issue An issue used by campaign strategists to separate voting constituencies from a candidate or their traditional party, as in driving a wedge between voting blocs. An example: civil rights legislation and racial quotas. In an October 23, 1991, floor speech, Sen. William Cohen (R-Me.) criticized those who used civil rights issues to "drive middle-class voters into the arms of the Republican party, leaving blacks, feminists, labor unions, and vacuous liberals in the backwash of the Democratic party."

Wednesday group An informal organization of about 40 Republican House members of generally moderate leanings that meets on Wednesdays for late-afternoon snacks and discussions. The group also conducts seminars and retreats.

weeks and days Periods of time set aside to commemorate products, concepts, maladies, and noncontroversial issues, for instance, National Hosiery Week. *See* **commemorative bill.**

One moment of truth in this matter occurred in 1973 when Rep. Ken Heckler (D-W. Va.) concluded that if one were to observe the days and weeks proclaimed for that year by Congress and the executive branch, it would take more than 35 years—until 1 A.M. on March 12, 2008—to observe them all. Heckler was one of a number of crusaders who periodically declared war on "weeks and days." At the time of his crusade he noted that National Next Door Neighbor Day made nobody more neighborly and that Clean Water Week made no water cleaner. Another member of the 93rd Congress, Bertram Podell (D-N.Y.), underscored the absurdity of the practice on March 6, 1973: "Mr. Speaker, yesterday was the start of National Procrastination Week, and for that reason I would like to put off my remarks on the subject until a later time."

well Semicircular area just in front of the member's seats in the Senate and House, just below the podium. *See also* **go to the well.**

West Front The side of the Capitol that today faces the Mall, the Washington Monument, and the White House. At one point in history it overlooked marshland, a railroad station, and a canal. It has been the site of recent presidential inaugurals, including Bill Clinton's in 1993. In 1983 work began to strengthen, renovate, and preserve the West Front; the project was completed in 1987.

What do you hear?/Whaddaya hear? Insider's query about the tenor of political/legislative currents on the **Hill.**

wheeler-dealer A high-powered, but not always successful, person in business or politics who makes deals.

whereas The word used at the beginning of what can be several introductory clauses in proclamations and resolutions explaining why they are important. It is often followed eventually by the word **therefore.**

whip

1 Member of each party in each house charged with keeping advance tallies of how members are leaning and with rallying the party to pass or defeat a piece of legislation. The position amounts

The Western Terrace, which abuts the West Front of the Capitol, circa 1890. *See* **West Front.**

to that of assistant party leader. Whips preside over a "whip organization" comprising state or regional deputy whips, who keep tabs and turn out the vote in their areas. *See also* **assistant majority leader/assistant minority leader.**

2   To act as a whip. The term is used in phrases such as "whipping the Ohio delegation." If a legislator needs a friendly shove, the whip provides it. The member is whipped.

ETYMOLOGY: The term derives from the "whipper-in" in foxhunting. This servant to the hunt keeps the dogs from following false scents and keeps them in a pack. First in the British Parliament and later in the U.S. Congress, the "whipper-in" became the whip, a member of the party who tries to keep his members from straying.

whip count   An attempt by the whip to get an accurate estimate of his party's alignment behind a bill. In practice, the whip relies on **zone whips**, who individually poll a segment of the membership. *See also* **head count.**

whistleblower   Federal employee or an employee of a federal contractor who reveals—blows the whistle on—government waste, fraud, or abuse. Whistleblowers traditionally tell their stories to congressional committees, the press, or both. Some members of Congress have taken the lead in protecting whistleblowers by law from the wrath of the bureaucracy; others have extolled them with little more than rhetoric. Whistleblowing has often borne a price. In 1969, A. Ernest Fitzgerald was fired from his civilian job with the Air Force after disclosing massive cost overruns in the building of C-5A cargo planes. He got his job back but only after 14 years of court battles. Whistleblowers who "go public" are those most likely to run into trouble. K. William O'Conner, a special counsel appointed to defend whistleblowers from harassment, was quoted in *Congressional Quarterly* in November 1984: "Unless you're in a position to retire or are independently wealthy, don't do it [go public]. Don't put your head up, because it will get blown off."

ETYMOLOGY: This term first showed up in print in 1970 to describe one who reveals covert wrongdoing, but it was already in the air as a basketball term for referee. For instance, the 1949 *Clair Bee Basketball Annual* includes an article entitled "A Whistle Blower Talks."

whistle stop   A political tour of small towns, places where trains do not stop unless requested by a whistled signal.

White House

1 The official residence of the president of the United States, encompassing family living quarters, the Oval Office, and the offices of key staff members.

2 The office of the president figuratively. The term is used in constructions like "the White House position on the issue...," in the same sense that a statement by the British prime minister is alluded to as word from 10 Downing Street (his or her residence). It is this figurative White House that may be at odds with or in agreement with Congress.

widows' club Women elected to Congress upon the death of their congressmen husbands.

wiggle room A public statement that sounds authoritative but is really so vague that the speaker can later change positions and still use essentially the same words. Writing in the *Washington Post*, journalist Susan Trausch noted, "The phrase 'cautious optimism' has about a mile of wiggle room on either side. So does 'tentative acceptance' and 'he is leaning in that direction.'" One tends to give political allies as much wiggle room as possible and enemies as little as possible. *See also* **waffle.**

There is usually a lot of wiggle room in foreign policy. In August 1990, Sen. John Kerry (D-Mass.) said President George Bush should give Saddam Hussein "diplomatic wiggle room" to withdraw from Kuwait.

However, the *ritual of wiggle*, as defined by writer James Boyd in the *Washington Monthly*, has a different meaning. For instance, when asked to comment on an uncomfortable issue, a congressman may ignore it and leave for a trip, or simply say "no comment."

FIRST USED: Lexicographer/columnist William Safire concluded in his September 23, 1984, column that wiggle room is an "evidently new" term, with the earliest use he could find in the September 11, 1978, *Business Week*: "Congress has drafted regulatory legislation in such a way that gives legislation as little wiggle room as possible." Safire referred to that column: "Wiggle room has become the Star Chamber in the tax legislators' boarding house."

windbag One who speaks self-importantly but says little or nothing of substance.

window dressing A speech or release of information that makes something seem more important than it is.

wing A faction of a political party that tends to be out of the mainstream; for example, left-wing Democrats.

winger A person of the extreme, whether right or left; shorthand for left- or right-winger. Syndicated columnist Joseph Kraft, writing on wingers on January 8, 1976, concentrated on Alabama's Democratic Gov. George Wallace (right) and Oklahoma's Democratic Sen. Fred Harris (left). Kraft concluded, "My strong sense is that the 'winger' candidates cannot possibly get the nomination this year."

wing-spreader Term first used around 1976 for Democrats interested in rebuilding their old coalition of liberals, labor, ethnic groups, and the South. Sen. Hubert Humphrey of Minnesota and Gov. Jimmy Carter of Georgia were two early examples of wing-spreaders.

wired The condition of legislative deals or nominations when enough votes for approval are assured, or when the appropriate chairmen have signed off on them. The term is similar to the expression *precooked*.

wire-puller An individual who uses behind-the-scenes manipulation to achieve objectives.

WISH Acronym for Women in the Senate and House, a group formed in December 1991 to support Republican candidates who favor abortion rights. *See also* **EMILY's list.**

wish list A list of programs or projects particularly desired by the President or by congressional leaders; legislative priorities.

witches and goblins Rep. Andrew Jacobs' characterization of members of the ultra-right.

witch hunt An investigation supposedly directed at uncovering wrongdoing or subversive activity but really aimed at intimidating and silencing political opponents. On June 13, 1992, Republican President George Bush accused congressional Democrats of conducting a "witch hunt" by investigating his actions leading up to the Persian Gulf War. In a July 22, 1992, press release, Rep. Dan Rostenkowski (D-Ill.) called the investigation of his alleged exchange of stamps for cash a "political witch hunt." He also labeled it a **fishing expedition.**

without objection The way in which a noncontroversial bill is passed or a **unanimous consent** is agreed to.

wizard of ooze A humorous sobriquet for the throatily mellifluous Everett Dirksen, the late Senate Republican leader from Illinois.

women in Congress The first woman elected to Congress was Rep. Jeanette Rankin (R-Mont.) in 1916. Since then, 158 women have taken their seats in the U.S. Congress. With the exception of Rankin and a few other pioneers, it would be decades before significant numbers of women were elected to the House or

---

THE COURAGE OF HER CONVICTIONS

In 1916, when Montana's Jeanette Rankin launched her campaign for election to the House of Representatives, only a handful of states allowed women to vote. But Rankin, a women's rights advocate, pacifist, and prohibitionist, was not daunted by such obstacles. The 28-year-old Republican ran and won, becoming the first woman to serve in Congress.

As playwright Kate Walbert wrote, Rankin

received a standing ovation as she entered the House carrying a bouquet of yellow and purple flowers given to her that morning at a suffrage rally. It was reported she wore a dark blue suit and that she walked well and unselfconsciously. Everyone

seemed to breathe a collective sigh of relief that the new representative, born on a ranch, had not ridden in on a horse.

Rankin was one of 49 members to vote against U.S. entry into World War I. She ran for the Senate in 1920 and was defeated, but in 1940 was reelected to the House. When war sentiment again swept through Congress Rankin stood alone. "I want to stand by my country, but I cannot vote for war," she said, locking herself in a phone booth to escape from angry crowds. In 1968, in her late eighties, Rankin led the Jeanette Rankin Brigade to the Capitol to protest against the Vietnam War. She continued to work as a peace activist until her death in 1973.

Rep. Jeanette Rankin, the first woman *elected* to Congress. *See* **women in Congress.**

THEIR GROWING RANKS: WOMEN IN THE U.S. CONGRESS		
	Number of Female Members	
Congress	House	Senate
65th (1917)	1	
66th (1919)		
67th (1921)	3	1
68th (1923)	1	
69th (1925)	3	
70th (1927)	5	
71st (1929)	9	
72nd (1931)	7	1
73rd (1933)	7	1
74th (1935)	6	2
75th (1937)	6	3
76th (1939)	8	1
77th (1941)	9	1
78th (1943)	8	1
79th (1945)	11	
80th (1947)	7	1
81st (1949)	9	1
82nd (1951)	10	1
83rd (1953)	12	3
84th (1955)	17	1
85th (1957)	15	1
86th (1959)	17	1
87th (1961)	18	2
88th (1963)	12	2
89th (1965)	11	2
90th (1967)	11	1
91st (1969)	10	1
92nd (1971)	13	2
93rd (1973)	16	
94th (1975)	19	
95th (1977)	18	2
96th (1979)	16	1
97th (1981)	21	2
98th (1983)	22	2
99th (1985)	23	2
100th (1987)	23	2
101st (1989)	29	2
102nd (1991)	29	2
103rd (1993)	47	7*

Source: Women in the United States Congress, Congressional Research Service, and the *Washington Post.*
*Six were elected in the general election of 1993; a seventh was sworn in in June 1993 as the result of a special election.

Sen. Rebecca Felton of Georgia, seen here after being appointed to the Senate on October 3, 1922. She was the first woman ever to serve in that body. She served for one day, which was the unexpired portion of the term she was appointed to fill. *See* **women in Congress.**

Senate without first being appointed to fill a vacancy. In 1948 Margaret Chase Smith (R-Me.) became the first woman elected to the Senate in her own right. Barbara Mikulski (D-Md.), elected to the Senate in 1986, was the first Democrat. It wasn't until 1981 that the number of women in the House reached 20. The largest single jump in history occurred in 1992, the Year of the Woman, when 47 women were elected to the House and 6 to the Senate. *See boxes,* "The Courage of Her Convictions" *and* "Their Growing Ranks: Women in the U.S. Congress."

wonk   A bureaucrat or politician who understands and thrives on discussions about government policies. President Bill Clinton is said to be a policy wonk.

Etymology: There are those who insist that the term was created by spelling the word *know* backwards.

woodshed   Figurative place to which underlings who leak damaging or embarrassing items to the press are taken by their bosses for punishment.

woodwork theory   This supposition holds that if the right liberal or conservative is nominated, voters will somehow "crawl out of the woodwork" to support that candidate. This theory turned out to be wrong when Barry Goldwater, a conservative Republican, and George McGovern, a liberal Democrat, each considered by his supporters to be that "right" candidate, were nominated for president in 1964 and 1972, respectively. Both men were defeated in landslides.

words taken down   A procedure in the House for calling to order members who use unparliamentary language during debate. This has been interpreted to mean unseemly language but also words that malign or call into question the motives of another member, the Senate, or the president. A member who objects to the language may demand that the words be "taken down." The clerk is asked to read the offending language from a transcript, and the presiding officer rules on whether the language is offensive. If it is ruled offensive and the offender refuses to retract or modify the statement, the House may be asked to vote on striking it from the *Record*. Even so, the clerk's reading of the slur and the altercation surrounding it survive. The Congressional Research Service found 31 instances of words taken down between 1979 and 1989. *See box*, "Unparliamentary Language."

UNPARLIAMENTARY LANGUAGE

In a floor debate on March 19, 1985, Harry Reid (D-Nev.) accused a fellow representative, Vin Weber (R-Minn.) of "speaking out of both sides of his mouth."

In Weber's mind, Reid had committed the cardinal sin of impugning his motives and he demanded "that the gentleman's words be taken down."

Reid did not back down. When asked to withdraw his words, he replied, "What if I do not want to?"

The chair had no choice but to rule and, after having the clerk read the transcribed remarks, declared that the words had "an unparliamentary connotation, and shall be stricken."

Because Weber's objection was upheld, and others objected, Reid was not permitted to address the House again on that legislative day.

On May 15, 1984, Speaker Tip O'Neill was rebuked for his choice of words. Rep. Newton Gingrich, (R-Ga.) had criticized O'Neill's friend, Rep. Edward Boland (D-Mass.), during an "extension of remarks" floor speech to an empty chamber. Angered that the fixed TV camera made it appear that Gingrich was speaking to a packed House, O'Neill phoned the clerk and ordered that the cameras pan the House, showing the orator and the sea of empty seats. Faced with a chorus of disapproval from Republicans, O'Neill took to the floor.

"My personal opinion is that you deliberately stood in that well before an empty House and challenged these people and you challenged their Americanism and it is the lowest thing that I have ever seen in my 32 years in Congress," O'Neill said.

After Rep. Trent Lott (R-Miss.) demanded that O'Neill's words be taken down, the chair ruled against O'Neill and he became only the second speaker in history to have his words erased from the record.

If words spoken on the floor are not immediately challenged, however, they cannot be removed. For instance, on October 17, 1989, one member used the phrase "her goddamn alcoholic father," but was not called to order and the language remained as spoken.

---

workhorse   Member known for effectiveness and for getting the job done. Compare with **showhorse.**

working the chairs The process of advancing in Congress, particularly in the House of Representatives, by moving from one leadership post to the next, arriving ultimately at the pinnacle, the speakership.

working the crowd Currying political goodwill at a gathering. Any politician worthy of the title will work the crowd at a county fair, funeral, or Memorial Day parade.

working the doors Lobbying expression for the thankless job of standing outside entrances to the House and Senate chambers and waving—sometimes slipping in a word of encouragement— to members as they go in to vote. It does not accomplish anything, but the lobbyists' clients expect them to do it.

world's greatest deliberative body Name often applied to the U.S. Senate by its members. In a 1987 *Glossary of Senate Terms*, Sen. William S. Armstrong (R-Colo.) wrote: "The Founding Fathers envisioned an upper chamber of thoughtful and experienced legislators lending a cool and detached perspective to the sometimes turbulent national policy debate. Well, sometimes it is and sometimes it isn't."

A more admiring view was expressed in *A Senate Journal: 1943–1945*, by author Allen Drury, who wrote of "the greatest deliberative body on earth." "That is what they [the senators] call it, and after twenty years' close acquaintance, that is what I call it too."

write To **author** legislation.

written testimony Witnesses appearing before committees are frequently required to make their points in writing and, according to House Rule XI, Clause 2, to "limit oral presentation in such appearance to a brief summary." The brief summary requirement is often violated by long-winded witnesses.

Year of the Woman Slogan referring to the record number of women running for Congress in 1992, including eleven Senate nominees. Four new female members were elected to the Senate and 24 to the House. A fifth new female Senator, Kay Bailey Hutchison, was seated in June 1993 after a special election in Texas.

yeas and nays This antique phrase for **roll-call** vote in the House and Senate comes straight from the Constitution, including the requirement that it be "at the desire of one-fifth of those present." The response is never "yea" or "nay," however, but "aye" or "no."

yellow-dog Democrat A Southern expression for a Democrat who will vote for whomever the party fields, even if the candidate is a yellow dog. Also known as "yallah dog," which the *Oxford English Dictionary* defines as a mongrel "of no particular breed but its own" or "a person or thing of no account or of a low type."

yield/yield time To allow another legislator time to speak on an issue without surrendering the floor. In the classic book *In Congress Assembled*, Daniel M. Berman noted:

> The word *yield*, which is used in the House as well as the Senate, lends itself to some fairly obvious punning. There are many variations on this tale told about Congressman Joseph Cannon (R-Ill.), the former Speaker of the House. Cannon was in his eighties when he asked a

woman member of the House if she would be good enough to yield. She replied with apparent ardor, "The lady will be delighted to yield to the gentleman from Illinois." Cannon then demanded of one of his colleagues, in a stage whisper that could be heard in every corner of the chamber: "My God! Now that she has yielded, what can I do about it?"

The story is undoubtedly apocryphal but has been repeated many times, using the names of many other aging male members and unnamed female legislators.

you Seldom used in debate in either house. One never says, "You can have the floor," but rather, "I yield to the gentleman from Arizona." In the late hours of the 1989 Senate debate that resulted in the rejection of John Tower as defense secretary, senators began calling each other "you." It was immediately seen as a barometer of the bitter turn that the debate had taken.

young Turk A relatively young, recently elected congressman who demands a prominent voice in party affairs and legislative strategy, and threatens to unseat the **old bulls** who control the committees if they don't get more respect. *See also* **old Turk.**

ETYMOLOGY: Borrowed from reformers of the Ottoman Empire who seized power from the aging sultans in 1908, it was first applied to a group of Republican senators who in 1929 defied their leaders over tariff legislation.

zero-based budgeting Disregarding the previous year's budget and starting from scratch. A process for evaluating the worth of specific programs and projects and determining whether they should be continued or abolished.

zero-fund An action by Congress or the Office of Management and Budget to kill a program by cutting off its money.

zero-sum game In politics, as in game theory, a situation in which a gain for one must produce a loss for another. In a three-way race, if one candidate attacks another, a third candidate is the likely beneficiary. Writing in the June 7, 1992, *Washington Post*, political consultant Doug Bailey said the two-party spilt between Congress and the White House "has brought the zero-sum game to governing—if the White House wins, Congress loses, and vice versa."

zone whips Assistants to the **whip** who provide information about the sentiment for or against bills among members from specific regions and try to whip them into line.

Bibliography

In preparing this book we have used hundreds of books, pamphlets, and magazine and newspaper articles. The following is a listing of the most important sources. To conserve space, we have not listed the major general-purpose dictionaries which, of course, were invaluable.

Abraham, L. A. and S. C. Hawtry, *Parliamentry Dictionary.* London: Butterworth & Co., 1956.

Asbell, Bernard. *The Senate Nobody Knows.* New York: Doubleday, 1978.

Bacon, Kenneth H. "When the Navy Says ABRACADABRA It Isn't Really Magic." *Wall Street Journal* (August 31, 1977), pp. 1, 33.

Barnhart, Clarence L., Sol Steinmetz, and Robert K. Barnhart. *The Barnhart Dictionary of New English Since 1963.* New York: Harper & Row, 1980.

——. *The Second Barnhart Dictionary of New English.* New York: Harper & Row, 1980.

Bazelon, David T. *Point of Order.* New York: W. W. Norton, 1964.

Bendiner, Robert. *Obstacle Course on Capitol Hill.* New York: McGraw-Hill, 1964.

Berg, Paul C. *A Dictionary of New Words in English.* New York: Crowell, 1953.

Berrey, Lester V., and Melvin Van Den Bark. *The American Thesaurus of Slang.* New York: Corwell, 1952.

Binkley, Wilfred E., and Malcolm C. Moos. *A Grammar of American Politics.* New York: Alfred A. Knopf, 1958.

——. *President and Congress.* New York: Vintage, 1962.

Bolling, Richard. *House Out of Order.* New York: Dutton, 1965.

——. *Power in the House.* New York: Dutton, 1968.

Bowles, Chester. *The Coming Political Breakthrough.* New York: Ballantine, 1959.

Breslin, Jimmy. *How the Good Guys Finally Won: Notes from an Impeachment Summer.* New York: Viking, 1975.

Broder, David S. *Changing of the Guard.* New York: Penguin Books, 1980.

Brown, W. Holmes. *Rules of the House of Representatives.* Washington, D.C.: U.S. Government Printing Office, 1991.

Buchanan, Patrick. *Liberal Votes, Conservative Victories.* New York: Quadrangle, 1975.

Buchwald, Art. *The Establishment Is Alive and Well in Washington.* New York: Fawcett, 1968.

Byrd, Robert C. *Addresses on the History of the United States Senate.* Washington, D.C.: U.S. Government Printing Office, 1991.

Canan, James W. *The Superwarriors.* New York: Weybright and Talley, 1975.

Carroll, James. *Mortal Friends.* Boston: Little, Brown, 1978.

Cater, Douglass. *The Fourth Branch of Government.* New York: Vintage, 1959.

Catton, Bruce. *The American Heritage Short History of the Civil War.* New York: Dell, 1960.

Chamberlin, Hope. *A Minority of Members: Women in the U.S. Congress.* New York: Praeger, 1973.

Chelf, Carl P. *Congress in the American System.* Chicago: Nelson-Hall, 1977.

Ciardi, John. *A Browser's Dictionary.* New York: Harper & Row, 1980.

———. *Good Words to You.* New York: Harper & Row, 1987.

———. *A Second Browser's Dictionary.* New York: Harper & Row, 1983.

Clancy, Paul. *Just a Country Lawyer: A Biography of Sam Ervin, Jr.* Bloomington, Ind.: Indiana University Press, 1974.

Clancy, Paul, and Shirley Elder. *Tip: A Biography of Thomas P. O'Neill.* New York: Macmillan, 1980.

Clapp, Charles L. *The Congressman: His Work as He Sees It.* Washington, D.C.: Brookings Institution, 1963.

Clark, Joseph S. *Congress: The Sapless Branch.* New York: Harper, 1964.

Cohen, William S. *Roll Call: One Year in the U.S. Senate.* New York: Simon & Schuster, 1981.

Colby, Elbridge. *Army Talk.* Princeton, N.J.: Princeton University Press, 1943.

Cole, Sylvia and Abraham H. Lass. *The Facts on File Dictionary of 20th Century Allusions.* New York, Facts on File, 1991.

Congressional Quarterly. Congress A to Z. Washington, D.C.: Congressional Quarterly Press, 1988.

———. *Congressional Quarterly's Guide to Congress.* Washington, D.C.: Congressional Quarterly Press, 1991.

Coolidge, Louis A. *An Old-Fashioned Senator: Orville H. Platt.* New York: G. P. Putnam, 1910.

Copperud, Roy H. *American Usage and Style: The Consensus.* New York: Van Nostrand Reinhold, 1980.

Cotton, Norris. *In the Senate: Amidst the Conflict and the Turmoil.* New York: Dodd Mead, 1978.

Crowley, Ellen, ed. *Acronyms, Initialisms and Abbreviations Dictionary.* Detroit: Gale Research, various dates and editions.

Cummings, Frank. *Capitol Hill Manual.* Washington, D.C.: Bureau of National Affairs, 1976, 1984.

Darling, Charles H. *The Jargon Book.* Aurora, Ill.: Aurora Publishing Co., 1919.

Deakin, James. *The Lobbyists.* Washington, D.C., Public Affairs Press, 1966.

de Antonio, Emile, and Daniel Talbot. *Point of Order! A Documentary of the Army–McCarthy Hearings.* New York: W. W. Norton, 1964.

De Funiak, William Q. *The American–British, British–American Dictionary.* Cranbury, N.J.: A. S. Barnes, 1978.

deGrazia, Alfred. *Congress: The First Branch of Government.* New York: Anchor, 1967.

Dionne, E. J. *Why Americans Hate Politics.* New York: Simon & Schuster, 1991.

Dole, Robert. *Historical Almanac of the United States Senate.* Washington, D.C.: U.S. Government Printing Office, 1989.

Donovan, Robert J. *Conflict and Crisis, The Presidency of Harry S. Truman, 1945–1948.* New York: W. W. Norton, 1977.

———. *The Future of the Republican Party.* New York: Signet, 1964.

Doty, Robert C. "Parlez-Vous NATO?" *New York Times* (October 18, 1959).

Drew, Elizabeth. *Senator.* New York: Simon & Schuster, 1979.

———. *Washington Journal: The Events of 1973–1974.* New York: Random House, 1974.

Drury, Allen. *A Senate Journal: 1943–1945.* New York: McGraw-Hill, 1963.

Eskridge, William N., Jr., and Philip P. Frickey. *Cases and Materials on Legislation.* St. Paul, Minn.: West Publishing Co., 1988.

Evans, Bergen. *Comfortable Words.* New York: Random House, 1962.

Fiorine, Morris P. *Congress: Keystone of the Washington Establishment.* New Haven: Yale University Press, 1977.

Flexner, Stuart Berg. *I Hear America Talking.* New York: Van Nostrand, 1976.

Friedman, Philip R. *Washington Humor.* New York: Citadel Press, 1964.

Funk, Wilfred. *Word Origins and Their Romantic Stories.* New York: Funk and Wagnalls, 1978.

Furgurson, Ernest B. *Hard Right: The Rise of Jesse Helms.* New York: W. W. Norton & Co., 1986.

Gingras, Angele de T. *The Best in Congressional Humor.* Washington, D.C.: Acropolis, 1973.

Goldman, Eric F. *The Crucial Decade—and After: America, 1945–1960.* New York: Vintage, 1960.

Goldwater, Barry M., and Jack Casserly. *Goldwater.* New York: St. Martin's Press, 1988.

Goodman, Walter. *The Committee.* New York: Farrar, Straus, and Giroux, 1968.

Grabowski, Sue. *A Congressional Intern Handbook.* Washington, D.C., Congressional Management Foundation, 1986.

Green, Mark, and Michael Waldman. *Who Runs Congress?* New York: Dell, 1984.

Greider, William. *Who Will Tell the People: The Betrayal of American Democracy.* New York: Simon & Schuster, 1992.

Hadley, Arthur T. *Do I Make Myself Perfectly Clear.* New York: Henry Holt, 1956.

Hardeman, D. B., and Donald C. Bacon. *Rayburn: A Biography.* Austin, Tex.: Texas Monthly Press, 1987.

Harrington, Michael. *The Long-Distance Runner.* New York: Henry Holt, 1988.

Harris, Joseph C. *Congressional Control of Administration.* New York: Anchor, 1964.

Harris, Kenneth. *David Owen.* London: Weidenfeld & Nicolson, 1987.

Harris, Leon A. *The Fine Art of Political Wit.* New York: Crown, 1964.

Hayakawa, S. I. *Language in Thought and Action.* New York: Harcourt Brace, 1941.

Hendrickson, Robert. *The Facts on File Encyclopedia of Word and Phrase Origins.* New York: Facts on File, 1987.

Hogan, Bill, and Mike Hill. *Will the Gentleman Yield?: The Congressional Record Humor Book.* San Francisco: Ten Speed Press/Tilden Books, 1990.

Homer, Joel. *Jargon.* New York: Times Books, 1979.

Howar, Barbara. *Laughing All the Way.* New York: Fawcett, 1973.

Huitt, Ralph K., and Robert L. Peabody. *Congress: Two Decades of Analysis.* New York: Harper & Row, 1969.

Hunsberger, I. Moyer. *The Quintessential Dictionary.* New York: Hart Publishing, 1978.

Hurst, Louis, as told to Frances Spatz Leighton. *The Sweetest Little Club in the World.* Englewood Cliffs, N.J.: Prentice-Hall, 1980.

Hutson, James H. *To Make All Laws, The Congress of the United States, 1789–1989.* Washington, D.C.: Library of Congress, 1989.

Jacobson, Gary C. *Money in Congressional Elections.* New Haven: Yale University Press, 1980.

Josephy, Alvin M. *On The Hill: A History of the American Congress.* New York: Simon & Schuster, 1979.

Kilian, Michael, and Arnold Sawislak. *Who Runs Washington?* New York: St. Martin's Press, 1982.

Kirby, James C., Jr. *Congress and the Public Trust.* New York: Atheneum, 1970.

Koch, Edward I. *Politics.* New York: Simon & Schuster, 1985.

Ladd, Everett Carll, Jr. *Where Have All the Voters Gone?* New York: W. W. Norton, 1978.

Lewis, Finlay. *Mondale.* New York: Perennial, 1984.

Link, Arthur S. *American Epoch.* New York: Knopf, 1955.

Loomis, Burdett. *The New American Politician.* New York: Basic Books, 1988.

Lubell, Samuel. *The Future of American Politics.* New York: Doubleday, 1956.

McCarthy, Eugene J. *Dictionary of American Politics.* New York: Penguin, 1962.

McPherson, James M. *Battle Cry of Freedom.* New York: Oxford University Press, 1988.

MacNeil, Neil. *Forge of Democracy: The House of Representatives.* New York: David McKay, 1963.

Mathews, Mitford M. *Americanisms.* Chicago: University of Chicago Press, 1966.

Matthews, C. M. *Words, Words, Words.* New York: Scribner's, 1979.

Matthews, Christopher. *Hardball.* New York: Summit Books, 1988.

Matthews, Donald R. *U.S. Senators and Their World.* New York: Vintage, 1960.

Mawson, C. O. Sylvester. *The Dictionary Companion.* Garden City, N.Y.: Halcyon House, 1932.

Mencken, H. L. *The American Language.* New York: Knopf, 1937.

———. *Supplement One: The American Language.* New York: Knopf, 1945.

Mendelsohn, Oscar A. *The Earnest Drinker.* New York: Macmillan, 1950.

Merriam-Webster. *6,000 Words: A Supplement to Webster's Third New International Dictionary.* Springfield, Mass.: G. & C. Merriam Co., 1976.

———. *Webster's Word History.* Springfield, Mass.: G. & C. Merriam Co., 1989.

Michaels, Leonard, and Christopher Ricks. *The State of the Language.* Berkeley, Calif.: University of California Press, 1980.

Miller, James A. *Running in Place: Inside the Senate.* New York: Simon & Schuster, 1986.

Miller, William "Fishbait," as told to Frances Spatz Leighton. *Fishbait.* New York: Warner, 1977.

Morgan, Paul, and Sue Scott. *The D.C. Dialect.* New York: The Washington Mews Press, 1975.

Morris, William, and Mary Morris. *Morris Dictionary of Word and Phrase Origins,* Vols. I–III. New York: Harper & Row, various dates.

O'Brien, Lawrence F. *No Final Victories.* New York: Ballantine, 1974.

O'Neill, Tip, with William Novak. *Man of the House.* New York: St. Martin's Press, 1987.

Ornstein, Norman, Thomas Mann, and Michael Malbin. *Vital Statistics on Congress.* Washington, D.C.: Congressional Quarterly Press, 1991.

Paine, Albert Bigelow. *Thomas Nast: His Period and His Pictures.* New York: Macmillan, 1904.

Parker, Robert, with Richard Rashke. *Capitol Hill in Black and White.* New York: Jove, 1986.

Partridge, Eric. *A Dictionary of Slang and Unconventional English.: Two Volumes in One.* New York: Macmillan, 1961.

———. *A Dictionary of the Underworld.* New York: Bonanza, 1961.

———. *The Gentle Art of Lexicography.* New York: Macmillan, 1963.

Patman, Wright. *Our American Government and How It Works.* New York: Bantam, 1948, 1968.

Peabody, Robert L. *Leadership in Congress.* Boston: Little, Brown, 1976.

Pearson, Drew, and Jack Anderson. *The Case Against Congress.* New York: Pocket Books, 1968.

Pei, Mario. *Language of the Specialists.* New York: Funk & Wagnalls, 1966.

———. *The Many Hues of English.* New York: Knopf, 1967.

———. *Words in Sheep's Clothing.* New York: Hawthorne, 1969.

Pei, Mario, and Frank Gaynor. *Dictionary of Linguistics.* New York: Philosophical Library, 1954.

Pepper, Claude Denson, with Hays Gorey. *Pepper.* New York: Harcourt, Brace, Jovanovich, 1987.

Phillips, Kevin P. *Post-Conservative America.* New York: Random House, 1982.

Plano, Jack C. *The American Political Dictionary.* New York: Holt, Rinehart and Winston, 1982.

Polsby, Nelson W. *Congress and the Presidency.* Englewood Cliffs, N.J.: Prentice-Hall, 1964.

Potter, Charles E. *Days of Shame.* New York: Signet, 1965.

Pringle, Henry F. *Theodore Roosevelt: A Biography.* New York: Harvest, 1956.

Pullen, Dale. *The U.S. Congress Handbook.* McLean, Va.: U.S. Congress Handbook, 1991.

Rapoport, Daniel. *Inside the House.* Chicago: Follett, 1975.

Reader's Digest: *Success with Words.* Pleasantville, N.Y., 1983.

The Reader's Digest Treasury of Humor. Pleasantville, N.Y.: The Reader's Digest Association, 1975.

Redman, Eric. *The Dance of Legislation.* New York: Simon & Schuster, 1973.

Reedy, George E. *The U.S. Senate.* New York: Crown, 1986.

Rees, Nigel. *Why Do We Say?* London: Blandford Press, 1987.

Regan, Donald T. *For the Record.* New York: St. Martin's Press, 1988.

Remini, Robert V. *Henry Clay, Statesman for the Union.* New York: W. W. Norton, 1991.

——. *Respectfully Quoted: A Dictionary of Quotations from the Library of Congress.* Washington, D.C.: Congressional Quarterly Press, 1992.

Riddick, Floyd M. *Oral History Interviews.* Washington, D.C.: Senate Historical Office, 1979.

Ripley, Randall B. *Congress: Process and Policy.* New York: W. W. Norton, 1978.

Rocke, Russell. *The Grandiloquent Dictionary.* Englewood Cliffs, N.J.: Prentice-Hall, 1972.

Romney, Ronna, and Beppie Harrison. *Momentum: Women in American Politics Now.* New York: Crown, 1987.

Rovere, Richard H. *Senator Joe McCarthy.* Cleveland: Meridian Books, 1959.

Sabato, Larry. *Feeding Frenzy: How Attack Journalism Has Transformed American Politics.* New York: The Free Press, 1991.

Safire, William. *Coming to Terms.* New York: Doubleday, 1991.

——. *I Stand Corrected: More on Language.* New York: Times Books, 1984.

——. *The New Language of Politics.* New York: Random House, 1968.

——. *On Language.* New York: Times Books, 1984.

——. *Safire's Political Dictionary.* New York: Random House, 1978.

——. *Take My Word for It.* New York: Times Books, 1986.

——. *What's the Good Word.* New York: Times Books, 1982.

Schapsmeier, Edward L., and Frederick H. Schapsmeir. *Dirksen of Illinois: Senatorial Statesman.* Urbana: University of Illinois Press, 1965.

Schaun, George, and Virginia Schaun. *Words and Phrases of Early America.* Annapolis, Md.: Greenbury Publishing, 1963.

Schlesinger, Arthur M., Jr. *The Imperial Presidency.* Boston: Houghton Mifflin, 1973.

Schudson, Michael. *Watergate in American Memory.* New York: Basic Books, 1992.

Schur, Norman W. *British Self-Taught: With Comments in American.* New York: Macmillan, 1973.

Seldes, George, editor. *The Great Quotations.* New York: Pocket Books, 1967.

Shadegg, Stephen C. *How to Win an Election.* Arlington, Va., Crestwood, 1964.

Shaffer, Samuel. *On and Off the Floor.* New York: Newsweek Books, 1980.

Shafritz, Jay M. *The Dorsey Dictionary of American Government and Politics.* Chicago: The Dorsey Press, 1988.

——. *Words on War.* New York: Prentice-Hall, 1990.

Shipley, Joseph T. *Dictionary of Early English.* New York: Philosophical Library, 1955.

——. *Playing With Words.* Englewood Cliffs, N.J.: Prentice-Hall, 1960.

——. *Word Play.* New York: Hawthorne, 1972.

Smith, A. Robert, and Eric Sevareid. *Washington: Magnificent Capital.* Garden City, N.Y.: Doubleday and Company, Inc., 1965.

Smith, C. Alphonso. *New Words Self-Defined.* Garden City, N.Y.: Doubleday, 1920.

Smith, Edward Conrad, and Arnold John Zurcher. *A Dictionary of American Politics.* New York: Barnes and Noble, 1944.

Smith, Frank E. *Congressman from Mississippi*. New York: Pantheon Books, 1964.

Smith, Hedrick. *The Power Game*. New York: Ballantine, 1988.

Sorensen, Theodore C. *Kennedy*. New York: Harper & Row, 1965.

Stockman, David A. *The Triumph of Politics*. New York: Avon, 1987.

Stone, Irving. *They Also Ran*. New York: Signet, 1966.

Taylor, A. Marjorie. *The Language of World War II*. New York: Wilson, 1944.

Thomas, Norman C., and Karl A. Lamb. *Congress: Politics and Practice*. New York: Random House, 1964.

Truman, David B. *The Congress and America's Future*. Englewood Cliffs, N.J.: Prentice-Hall, 1973.

Tyron, Henry H. *Fearsome Critters*. Cornwall, N.Y.: Idlewild Press, 1939.

Udall, Morris K. *Too Funny to Be President*. New York: Henry Holt, 1988.

U.S. Army. *Dictionary of United States Army Terms*. Washington, D.C.: Department of the Army, 1975.

U.S. Congress. Committee on Rules and Administration. *Standing Rules of the Senate*. Washington, D.C.: U.S. Government Printing Office, 1990.

———. Committee on Standards of Official Conduct. *House Ethics Manual*. Washington, D.C.: U.S. Government Printing Office, 1992.

U.S. Department of Labor. *Dictionary of Occupational Titles*. Washington, D.C.: Department of Labor, various dates and editions.

U.S. Nuclear Regulatory Commission. *A Handbook of Acronyms and Initialisms*. Washington, D.C.: Nuclear Regulatory Commission, 1979.

Van Wagner, Ernest L. *New York Detective*. New York: Dodd, Mead, 1938.

Versand, Kenneth. *Polyglot's Lexicon: 1943–1966*. New York: Links Books, 1973.

Weaver, Warren, Jr. *Both Your Houses: The Truth About Congress*. New York: Praeger, 1972.

Weiner, Tim. *Blank Check, The Pentagon's Black Budget*. New York: Warner Books, 1990.

Wentworth, Harold. *American Dialect Dictionary*. New York: Crowell, 1944.

Wentworth, Harold, Flexner Wentworth, and Stuart Berg. *Dictionary of American Slang*. New York: Crowell, 1960.

Weseen, Maurice H. *Dictionary of American Slang*. New York: Crowell, 1938.

White, Wilbur W. *White's Political Dictionary*. Cleveland: World Publishing, 1947.

White, William S. *Citadel: The Story of the U.S. Senate*. New York: Harper, 1957.

———. *Home Place*. Boston: Houghton Mifflin, 1965.

Wiley, Alexander. *Laughing with Congress*. New York: Crown Publishers, 1947.

Winter-Berger, Robert. *The Washington Pay-Off*. New York: Dell, 1972.

Wolfinger, Raymond E. *Readings on Congress*. Englewood Cliffs, N.J.: Prentice-Hall, 1971.

Wright, Joseph. *English Dialect Dictionary*. Oxford, England: Oxford University Press, 1923.

Young, Roland. *The American Congress*. New York: Harper, 1958.